Picture Research

Leonardo

Sean Cubitt, Editor-in-Chief

Synthetics: Aspects of Art and Technology in Australia, 1956–1975, Stephen Jones, 2011

Hybrid Cultures: Japanese Media Arts in Dialogue with the West, Yvonne Spielmann, 2012

Walking and Mapping: Artists as Cartographers, Karen O'Rourke, 2013

The Fourth Dimension and Non-Euclidean Geometry in Modern Art, revised edition, Linda Dalrymple Henderson, 2013

Illusions in Motion: Media Archaeology of the Moving Panorama and Related Spectacles, Erkki Huhtamo, 2013

Relive: Media Art Histories, edited by Sean Cubitt and Paul Thomas, 2013

Re-collection: Art, New Media, and Social Memory, Richard Rinehart and Jon Ippolito, 2014

Biopolitical Screens: Image, Power, and the Neoliberal Brain, Pasi Väliaho, 2014

The Practice of Light: A Genealogy of Visual Technologies from Prints to Pixels, Sean Cubitt, 2014

The Tone of Our Times: Sound, Sense, Economy, and Ecology, Frances Dyson, 2014

The Experience Machine: Stan VanDerBeek's Movie-Drome and Expanded Cinema, Gloria Sutton, 2014

Hanan al-Cinema: Affections for the Moving Image, Laura U. Marks, 2015

Writing and Unwriting (Media) Art History: Erkki Kurenniemi in 2048, edited by Joasia Krysa and Jussi Parikka, 2015

Control: Digitality as Cultural Logic, Seb Franklin, 2015

New Tendencies: Art at the Threshold of the Information Revolution (1961–1978), Armin Medosch, 2016

Screen Ecologies: Art, Media, and the Environment in the Asia-Pacific Region, Larissa Hjorth, Sarah Pink, Kristen Sharp, and Linda Williams, 2016

Pirate Philosophy: For a Digital Posthumanities, Gary Hall, 2016

Social Media Archeology and Poetics, edited by Judy Malloy, 2016

Practicable: From Participation to Interaction in Contemporary Art, edited by Samuel Bianchini and Erik Verhagen, 2016

Machine Art in the Twentieth Century, Andreas Broeckmann, 2016

Here/There: Telepresence, Touch, and Art at the Interface, Kris Paulsen, 2017

Voicetracks: Attuning to Voice in Media and the Arts, Norie Neumark, 2017

Ecstatic Worlds: Media, Utopias, Ecologies, Janine Marchessault, 2017

Interface as Utopia: The Media Art and Activism of Fred Forest, Michael F. Leruth, 2017

Making Sense: Cognition, Computing, Art, and Embodiment, Simon Penny, 2017

Weather as Medium: Toward a Meteorological Art, Janine Randerson, 2018

Laboratory Lifestyles: The Construction of Scientific Fictions, edited by Sandra Kaji-O'Grady, Chris L. Smith, and Russell Hughes, 2018

Invisible Colors: The Arts of the Atomic Age, Gabrielle Decamous, 2018

Virtual Menageries: Animals as Mediators in Network Cultures, Jody Berland, 2019

From Fingers to Digits: An Artificial Aesthetic, Ernest Edmonds and Margaret A. Boden, 2019

MATERIAL WITNESS: Media, Forensics, Evidence, Susan Schuppli, 2020

Tactics of Interfacing: Encoding Affect in Art and Technology, Ksenia Fedorova, 2020

Giving Bodies Back to Data: Image Makers, Bricolage, and Reinvention in Magnetic Resonance Technology, Silvia Casini, 2021

A Biography of the Pixel, Alvy Ray Smith, 2021

Living Books: Experiments in the Posthumanities, Janneke Adema, 2021

Art in the Age of Learning Machines, Sofian Audry, 2021

Design in Motion: Film Experiments at the Bauhaus, Laura Frahm, 2022

Northern Sparks: Innovation, Technology Policy, and the Arts in Canada from Expo 67 to the Internet Age, Michael Century, 2022

Christa Sommerer and Laurent Mignonneau: The Artwork as a Living System 1991–2022, edited by Karin Ohlenschläger, Peter Weibel, and Alfred Weidinger, 2023

Computational Formalism: Art History and Machine Learning, Amanda Wasielewski, 2023

Picture Research: The Work of Intermediation from Pre-Photography to Post-Digitization, Nina Lager Vestberg, 2023

See http://mitpress.mit.edu for a complete list of titles in this series.

Picture Research

The Work of Intermediation from Pre-Photography to Post-Digitization

Nina Lager Vestberg

The MIT Press
Cambridge, Massachusetts
London, England

The MIT Press would like to thank the anonymous peer reviewers who provided comments on drafts of this book. The generous work of academic experts is essential for establishing the authority and quality of our publications. We acknowledge with gratitude the contributions of these otherwise uncredited readers.

This book was set in ITC Stone Serif Std and Trajan Pro by New Best-set Typesetters Ltd. Printed and bound in the United States of America.

Library of Congress Cataloging-in-Publication Data

Names: Vestberg, Nina Lager, author.
Title: Picture research : the work of intermediation from pre-photography to post-digitization / Nina Lager Vestberg.
Description: Cambridge, Massachusetts : The MIT Press, [2023] | Series: Leonardo | Includes bibliographical references and index.
Identifiers: LCCN 2022036842 (print) | LCCN 2022036843 (ebook) | ISBN 9780262045315 (paperback) | ISBN 9780262362221 (epub) | ISBN 9780262375023 (pdf)
Subjects: LCSH: Pictures—Research. | Cataloging of pictures.
Classification: LCC N4000 .V47 2023 (print) | LCC N4000 (ebook) | DDC 025.3/471—dc23/eng/20221019
LC record available at https://lccn.loc.gov/2022036842
LC ebook record available at https://lccn.loc.gov/2022036843

10 9 8 7 6 5 4 3 2 1

For Tore & Snorre

Contents

Series Foreword

Leonardo/The International Society for the Arts, Sciences and Technology fosters transformation at the nexus of art, science, and technology because complex problems require creative solutions. The Leonardo Book Series shares these aims of artistic and scientific experimentation, and publishes books to define problems and discover solutions, to critique old knowledge and create the new.

In the early twentieth century, the arts and sciences seemed to interact instinctively. Modern art and modern poetry were automatically associated with relativity and quantum physics, as if the two were expressions of a single Zeitgeist. At the end of the Second World War, once again it seemed perfectly clear that avant-garde artists, architects, and social planners would join cyberneticists and information theorists to address the problems of the new world order and to create new ways of depicting and understanding its complexity through shared experiences of elegance and experiment. Throughout the twentieth century, the modern constantly mixed art and science.

In the twenty-first century, though, we are no longer modern but contemporary, and now the wedge between art and science that C. P. Snow saw emerging in the 1950s has turned into a culture war. Governments prefer science to arts education, yet stand accused of ignoring or manipulating science. The arts struggle to justify themselves in terms of economic or communicative efficiency that devalues their highest aspirations. And yet never before have artists, scientists, and technologists worked together so closely to create individual and collective works of cultural power and intellectual grace. Leonardo looks beyond predicting dangers and challenges, beyond even planning for the unpredictable. The series publishes books that are both timely and of enduring value—books that address the perils of our time, while also exploring new forms of beauty and understanding.

Seán Cubitt, Editor-in-Chief, Leonardo Book Series

Roger F. Malina, Executive Editor, Leonardo

Preface

In the late 1990s I started out as an intern in a small specialized picture library in London. All the photographs in our collection were shot on film and stored as duplicate transparencies in filing cabinets. Two land-line telephones rang at regular intervals as clients called to place searches, which were carried out by staff rifling through hanging files in cabinets, bending over lightboxes with loupes to examine transparencies, hand-writing paper delivery notes in triplicate carbon copies, and parceling up bundles of file sheets in special envelopes marked "Please do not bend." My working day was mainly spent on my feet, and would invariably end with a dash to the local post office to get the day's search results off to clients in time for next-day delivery. A few days a week I would spend a couple of hours in front of the single office computer, inputting what we would now call "metadata" about pictures newly submitted by photographers into the computer catalog. By early 2000 I had moved on to a full-time picture research position at a national UK newspaper, and now I was the one calling up picture librarians with a list of keywords and concepts to be illustrated, and waiting impatiently for parcels of potentially relevant pictures to arrive by post or courier bike.

Within a year or two, this procedure had been considerably speeded up and automated by the widespread adoption of email and searchable websites. And by the time I did my last freelance shift on a newspaper picture desk in 2007, I could not remember the last time I saw, much less handled, a sheet of transparencies in a stiff envelope. I would now spend my entire working day sitting in front of my designated computer—one of the six or seven that made up the physical manifestation of the picture desk in the newsroom—watching photographic images from all over the world tumble into the image browser of my virtual desktop at an average rate of 6,000 per day. Most of my work entailed inputting search terms into this browser and various online image banks accessed through regular internet browsers, then digitally marking, saving, or downloading selected pictures for use, and "queuing" or uploading them onto the picture management system that was shared across the newsroom. Formerly essential tools such as loupe and lightbox were now sitting as rarely consulted relics alongside the huge, hooded screens on the image processing desk ("the scanners"), their functions having been virtualized as zooming and saving options in the picture management software. And along with many of the analog tasks and tools, a number of human operators (known to me as colleagues) were also being phased out of the picture-industrial workplace. The very profession of the picture researcher was at this point facing what business gurus like to call disruption: challenges to its core operational model from automated technology, on the one hand, and from differently skilled operatives of that technology, on the other.

Prompted by a sense that picture research as I knew it was fast disappearing and that it would be important to make some sort of record of the working practices before, under, and "after" digitization, I designed a small-scale oral history project of interviews with experienced picture researchers and editors, which the J. Paul Getty Foundation generously agreed to fund through a nonresidential postdoctoral fellowship in 2007–2008. This project was the seed from which the plant of the present book grew. In the considerable number of years that have gone by since then, many metaphorical gardeners have contributed to its development and fruition, and it will be my pleasure to acknowledge them over the next few pages.

My first and foremost thanks go to those who taught me most of what I know about research: Tag Gronberg and Patrizia Di Bello, who guided me through postgraduate study and doctoral research; Jason Shenai and Niall O'Leary, who introduced me to the delights of picture librarianship; Guy Lane, who was the nicest boss any new recruit to a London newspaper picture desk could have; and the picture desk team at *The Independent* between 2002 and 2007, whose collective struggles with recalcitrant computers and dodgy keywording directly inspired me to make a research object out of digitized research.

Insights into the past, present, and future of the picture business were generously shared, at different times and in different places, by Barry Cerasoli, Marie-Louise Collard, Rick Colls, Kevin Coombs, Delphine Desveaux, Luigi Di Dio, Nathalie Doury, Denis Fruit, Tom Gillmor, Adam Goff, Cédric Gressent, Julia Hanson, Jérôme Lacharmoise, Karen Leach, Judith Mason, Sarah McDonald, Harald Østgaard-Lund, Susi Paz, Albert Raymond, Violaine Sand, Guro Tangvald, and Caroline Theakstone. Library, archives, and museum staff who have been especially helpful in answering questions about digitization in addition to providing research materials include Tom Gillmor and Luci Gosling at Mary Evans Picture Library; Natalie Hayton and Katharine Short at DeMontfort University Special Collections; Arne Langleite and Tone Rasch at the Norwegian Museum of Science and Technology; Nils Kristian Eikeland at the University Library Special Collections, Trondheim; and Grete Irene Solvold at the University Museum in Trondheim.

Over the years, the development of this book has benefited from two terms of research leave, one granted by the Faculty of Humanities under former dean Kathrine Skretting, and one by the Equality Officer at NTNU, as well as one year of research leave funded by the Research Council of Norway as part of the project "Digitization and Diversity" (NFR 247602, 2015–2020). I am grateful to the whole project team for the opportunity to think and talk through the concept and consequences of digitization in their company, and in particular to Anne Ogundipe, who as my PhD student probably taught me more than I taught her in the course of writing her dissertation. At NTNU, three successive heads of department—Anne Marit Myrstad, Jon Raundalen, and Tore Kirkholt—have shown support through understanding and flexibility.

I wish to thank Estelle Blaschke, Costanza Caraffa, Anna Dahlgren, Elizabeth Edwards, Eirik Frisvold Hanssen, Michelle Henning, Hanne Holm-Johnsen, Geraldine Johnson, Diana Kamin, Martha Langford, Martin Lister, Shannon Mattern, Gil Pasternak, Krzysztof Pijarski, Annebella Pollen, Jennifer Tucker, Doireann Wallace, Amanda Wasielewski, Liz Wells, and Kelley Wilder for showing their interest and support as the ideas in this book have developed, either through invitations to speak at seminars and conferences or by sharing their own ideas and research on related matters.

Acknowledgment is further due to the editors and reviewers of the following publications, where I developed early ideas about two of the case studies discussed in this book: "Archival Value: On Photography, Materiality and Indexicality," *Photographies* 1, no. 1 (2008); "From the Filing Cabinet to the Internet: Digitising Photographic Libraries," in *Fotografie als Instrument und Medium der Kunstgeschichte*, ed. Costanza Caraffa (Berlin: Deutscher Kunstverlag, 2009); and "Index/Finger: Medium and Materiality in the Archives," in *The Archive as Project/Archiwum jako projekt*, ed. Krzysztof Pijarski (Warszawa: Fundacjia Archeologia Fotografii, 2011).

Pierre Auboiron, Stina Barchan, Lucy Davis, Sherry Dobbin, Francesca Fenn, Andy Kenward, Allan Ross and Christopher Wobschall, Eleanor Fraser Stansbie, Sally Waterman, Johanna von der Waydbrink, Marta Weiss, and Kendall Smaling Wood were all friends, colleagues, and lifesavers in the UK during a dramatic year of ill health that nearly put paid to both me and my research career. I thank NHS heroes Dr. Vijay Hajela and Dr. Helen Lachmann, as well as the staff at University Hospital Lewisham, for giving me back a life worth living, and St. Olav's University Hospital, Trondheim, for helping me go on living it.

"Of all the ways of acquiring books, writing them oneself is regarded as the most praiseworthy method," wrote Walter Benjamin in his essay "Unpacking My Library."[1] Without ever having read Benjamin, as far as I know, my father instilled this attitude in me from early age, and effectively fostered me as a writer from childhood. Sadly he did not live long enough to see anything I wrote published in book form. But Benjamin's statement is also an occasion to note that, while this whole book has been written by me, I hardly did it by myself. The work of other writers and scholars has illuminated my path to writing it, and these are acknowledged in citations throughout the book. The emotional and professional support of a host of friends and colleagues have helped me stay on the path, and among these special recognition is due to Anna Dahlgren, Anne Karine Kleveland, Julia Leyda, Matilde Nardelli, and Margrethe C. Stang. Jane Jones, Kali Handelman, and the Elevate 2020 group helped me discover a new way of living with writing; the intermediary skills of Summer McDonald at Ideas on Fire helped me pinpoint the argument I was really making all along; and Laura Portwood-Stacer has been online agony aunt extraordinaire. Many thanks are also due to those who, with immense tolerance and patience, have helped bring the book into print: Virginia Crossman, Sean Cubitt, Gabriela Bueno Gibbs, Doug Sery, Noah Springer, and not least the anonymous reviewers for the MIT Press, whose incisive and supportive comments helped to make the whole thing much better. Paula Clarke Bain's splendid index has added further value to the finished book.

I thank my mother, Britt Lager Vestberg, for everything that mothers should always be thanked for, as well as for knowing not to ask how the writing's coming along. And finally, my greatest debt of gratitude is to Tore Brembu and Snorre Lager Brembu, who have both come into my life during the writing of this book and thus have never known me not to be working on it. There is no way this book can balance out all the time I have missed spending with you because of it, but I dedicate it to you anyway, and promise that you will have my full attention now.

Introduction

Picture research is essentially the work of looking for pictures. Whenever you search online for a photo, GIF, or meme to post on social media, you're doing picture research. In most cases, a quick web search is likely to satisfy your needs, whether you are looking for an illustration to include in a presentation or publishing project, or simply curious to see what a particular thing or person looks like. If you need to archive the relevant picture for future use, downloading the file will take a matter of seconds. As a user of contemporary visual media, you will be accustomed to the instant accessibility and automated archiving of all kinds of pictures. Even if you do recall a time before the internet, you may still find it hard to imagine how pictures were stored and searched for without the use of cloud services and search engines.

What search tools were needed when pictures were filed away in archives and libraries? Whose labor, skill, and judgment ensured that the printed pages of books, magazines, and newspapers were regularly filled with fresh and engaging illustrations? And what kind of work is required to make historical media available in digitized formats for contemporary online audiences? This book reveals the work of intermediation that takes place between producers and consumers of pictures by showing how it has historically been performed by specialist intermediaries ranging from engravers and publishers via librarians and archivists to editors, researchers, and digitizers. Engaging the concept of "picture research" on multiple levels, this chronological account defamiliarizes the everyday experience of instantly accessible online picture sources by shedding light on search tools and procedures that now appear strange and exotic, but which were once as mundane and culturally invisible as the websites and search engines we take for granted today.

In its most straightforward interpretation, the term *picture research* (or "photo research") is a standard combination of two nouns that denote a specific kind of work, mainly performed within the fields of publishing and advertising. It entails finding, retrieving, and administrating the costs of reproducing visual illustrations for use in print, broadcast, or online media outlets. Historians of photography have tended to ignore this field of archive-related photographic work and its specialized corps of professionals, even as they (we) have mythologized the site of the photographic archive. One intention behind the title of this book is therefore to signal its focus on the human skill, physical effort, and tacit knowledge that characterized work in pre-digital libraries and archives, over and above the infrastructure of the institutions themselves or the materiality of the objects preserved in them (although I will have things to say about those, too). The title also alludes to the book as an invitation to visualize, imagine, illustrate, or represent, in other words, to "picture" research. This ambiguity is inspired by the title of another book, *Picture Theory* (1994) in which W. J. T. Mitchell sought "*to picture theory* as a practical activity in the formation of representations."[1] In a similar sense, this book aims to picture research of visual materials, whether carried out for scholarly, commercial, or private purposes, as a practical activity involving specific mediating technologies, professionals, institutions, and practices.

Picture research emerged as a profession in the twentieth century thanks to the expanded market for mass-reproducible illustration that was enabled by photography. The historical practice of picture research is therefore intimately bound up with the history of photography as a technology of mass reproduction in a way that historians of photography have tended to overlook. When digital technologies of image capture and transmission began to replace photographic ones in the early twenty-first century, it deeply affected the work of picture research. In the same way that photography remains present across the wealth of digital media that shape our daily lives now, however, the legacies of picture research persist in the vast collections of digitized photographs, books, and other historical documents consulted online by millions every day. Once we recognize this, it becomes clear that the work of collecting, archiving, and researching, which shored up the pictorial economy of the twentieth century, also belongs to a deeper media history of digitization. In this respect, *Picture Research* can be read in conjunction with Sean Cubitt's *The Practice of Light: A Genealogy of Visual Technologies from Prints to Pixels*, which accounts in detail for the myriad of practical ways in which visual media have come "to work the way they do."[2] Where Cubitt presents "a history of materials and practices" involved in "making things with and about light," I offer a history of people and practices involved in helping photographs—pictures made with light—do their work of being looked at.

Twentieth-century practices of accumulating cultural assets by means of photography, and the historical conditions under which those practices developed, are not simply a matter of interest to historians of photography and visual culture. Archives, libraries, and museums of every kind are constantly seeking to meet ever-increasing expectations of direct access to digitized cultural objects by researchers, funding authorities, and the general public. In order for the digitized versions of collections to do justice to the documents, records, and artifacts they represent, it is imperative for those designing and doing the work of digitization to understand how those objects were initially acquired, collected, classified, and disseminated. Reading this book will help anyone involved in digitizing visual cultural artifacts to make sense of the cultural biographies that cling to photographic reproductions, whether they have circulated primarily as commodities or archival documents. Knowing how analog picture libraries and picture research worked will also be useful to researchers who find themselves working mainly with digitized historical sources consulted through online repositories, as it will add further layers of interpretation to these sources.

Palpable Pictures and Immaterial Images

The objects, events, and representations discussed in this book all fall within the horizon of what I call the *pictorial economy*. I use this term to encompass the totality of picture-makers, pictures, and picturing techniques available at any given time, including the reproduction technologies, distribution networks, and cultural practices by means of which pictures are brought to the attention of viewers. The definition is inspired by Lisa Gitelman's notion of a "scriptural economy," a term she has borrowed from Michel de Certeau to describe "the totality of writers, writings, and writing techniques that began to expand so precipitously in the nineteenth century."[3] The concept also bears more than a passing resemblance to Stephen Bann's notion of a "visual economy," which designates "the sum total of all the means of visual reproduction available" at a given time, including "the available means of publication and dissemination."[4] Deborah Poole has offered another conception of a visual economy, modeled on political economy, to describe an "organization" of the visual that "bears some—not necessarily direct—relationship to the political and class structure of society as well as to the production and exchange of the material goods or commodities that form the life blood of modernity."[5] This aligns with my idea of a pictorial economy in its emphasis on the social as well as material conditions that enable images to circulate.

In spite of these precedents, I prefer to speak of a pictorial rather than a visual economy. This is because I find the term *visual* too limited (restricted to the sense of sight) and at the same time too extensive (encompassing everything there is to be seen) to be productive in the specific context of this book, which is about ways of handling pictures more than it is about ways of looking at them. For similar reasons, I choose the term *economy* because it carries distinctive connotations to markets and commodities that are not as immediately generated by the word *culture*.[6] That said, the concept of a pictorial economy makes sense within the wider context of a visual culture only because the establishment of the former depends on the existence of the later. In short, a pictorial economy stands in relation to visual culture much in the way that a retail economy stands in relation to material culture.

Photography cuts across both pictorial economy and visual culture. For as long as it has been a technology for the production and reproduction of visual information, photography has produced a multitude of commodity forms—from family portraits and tourist views to pornographic scenes and scientific records—that have been traded across a variety of private and professional markets. Both as a technology for the manufacture of commodities and as a "bureaucratic medium" of registration, administration, and surveillance, photography's primary mode of production has been that of inscription.[7] "The camera has always been part of a larger assemblage, like a computer wired to its peripherals," as photo historian John Tagg has observed.[8] The "inefficient chemical information-storage system" provided by pre-digital camera and film was but one cog a "machinery of capture" that required "the storage and retrieval system of the filing cabinet" in order to be complete.[9]

The photographs to be encountered in this book are for the most part products of this machinery: they are pictures produced as copies, records, or documents of *other* pictures, with the primary objective of being kept on file. Just as literary works are "statistically exceptional" instances that make up "a narrow segment of the historical printing and publishing history," as Matthew G. Kirschenbaum has noted, photographs produced for display on gallery walls or in magazines and newspapers form a negligible percentage of historical and contemporary photographic practices.[10]

"Writing was a tool of data processing well before it was a storage device for speech, let alone law or literature," John Durham Peters has observed.[11] Photography—"light writing" in Greek—has likewise been a tool of data capture and record management to an even greater extent than it has been a medium for self-expression. At least this has been the case until the pictorialization of instant communication across digital social media in recent years. The proliferation of text messaging, email, and social network sites may have led Peters to view "digital media" as "machines that convert everyone into writers," yet the photographic affordances of smartphone-based social media applications can just as surely be said to turn everyone into photographers.[12] As any number of messages are assembled from assorted emojis, GIFs, and visual memes retrieved from the inexhaustible sources of imagery that are readily available on the web, however, we might as well say that digital media are machines that turn everyone into picture researchers.

I deliberately use the word *picture* throughout this book, even in contexts—like online searches—when contemporary parlance might have warranted the word *image*.[13] My usage largely follows Mitchell's pragmatic distinction based, as he puts it, on the "vernacular" expression that "you can hang a picture, but you can't hang an image."[14] Pictures are, on this definition, the material forms in which images manifest themselves, even when these material forms are not necessarily hangable in the way that an oil painting is. A JPEG file, for instance, cannot be hung on a wall; for that you would need to transfer its image content to another substrate, like an inkjet paper print. It is nevertheless a picture because the file format is a way of representing information that conjures up an image. And even in its seemingly immaterial form as data, the JPEG relies on hardware for its existence, just as a mental picture relies on a human brain for its manifestation.

In my slightly modified version of Mitchell's distinction, images are like information and pictures are like data, in the most basic definition of the latter term as the forms through which information may be apprehended.[15] Put another way, images are, like information, always open to interpretation, and their meanings can never be finally settled. The format or material manifestation of pictures, or data, however, can be determined and agreed upon. To give an example, two people may never agree on what is going on in Édouard Manet's *Bar at the Folies-Bergère* (1882), but they can both verify that it is an oil painting on canvas measuring roughly one by one and a third meters. Similarly, in a digitized surrogate version of the artwork viewed online it may be determined that the *image* of the painting appears in the *picture* format of a JPEG, although it is still possible to disagree about the extent to which this digitized picture accurately represents all the visual information contained in the original painting format.

The image/picture distinction is the foundational principle of the entire pictorial economy, which is kept going by the constant circulation of images through an equally constant iteration of pictures. In the course of the twentieth century, this circulation took on actual economic significance through the establishment of an entire field of cultural production, known as the picture industry, which is dedicated to its commercial exploitation. As I employ the term, the picture industry properly emerged about a century after the 1839 unveiling of the daguerreotype, which was the first viable photographic picture-making technology to be patented.[16] By the 1930s, the opto-chemical principles of inscription by light had been applied across a range of technologies to engender not just a medium for the quick and easy production of new pictures—photography in its conventional sense—but also a range of technologies for the mass-scale reproduction of existing ones. Photomechanical printing methods enabled the industrial-scale manufacturing of commodities such as illustrated newspapers, magazines, and books, which in turn required access to a steady stream of pictorial content. The task of producing and procuring this content became the business of the picture industry.

The pictorial economy, as we recall, includes all kinds of pictures and picture-makers, as well as all the tools and practices both for making pictures and for sharing them. The picture industry, by contrast, is limited to the agents and apparatuses involved in the mass production and mass dissemination of what I call pictorial commodities. These are commodities that either derive or enhance their use value from visual imagery. They may take the form of the aforementioned newspapers, magazines, and books, but they are also encountered and consumed as websites, film and television documentaries, advertisements, corporate reports, public information material, or retail packaging. The picture industry capitalizes on the image/picture distinction by capturing immaterial images and materializing them in picture formats that can be incorporated in such commodities. Stock photography accounts for a large part of this business, but the picture industry extends beyond that field to include virtually any actor that has an economic stake in the commercial exchange of pictures, as distinct from the innumerable noncommercial exchanges that also take place within the overall pictorial economy.

Until the late 1990s, when design historians began charting the historical emergence of stock photography, the "pictures for rent" that are the stock-in-trade of the picture industry had languished under the threshold of interest among scholars of visual culture.[17] Although media and cultural studies had long traditions for studying and critiquing the visual content of advertisements, for instance, research in these fields tended to ignore the mechanisms by which many of the pictures featured in them came to be there. Like the "rented-out" pictures themselves, the picture industry as a system of cultural production was hiding in plain sight. Around the turn of the century, this changed. Books like Paul Frosh's *The Image Factory* and Matthias Bruhn's *Bildwirtschaft* brought serious attention to stock photography as a form of commodity capitalism producing the visual consumables of contemporary culture.[18]

This coincided with an increasing interest in the cultural legacies of photographic archives, which to some extent overlapped with a turn to the materiality of photographs as objects, often conceived in opposition to the aesthetics of photographs as images. Archives and photographs were of course the two cornerstones of stock photography, and in the early 2000s they were both being destabilized by digitization—therefore the picture industry was, too. In hindsight it seems obvious that all of these fields of scholarly investigation were at some fundamental level responding to the perceived effects of digitization on their respective objects of research, be they photographs, archives, or stock photography. If nothing else, the quiddity of photographs and archival documents, which had thus far been taken for granted or failed to register as such, hove into view when confronted with or subsumed by their digitized versions.

In the pre-digital era, photographic prints and slides shared the same "transparency" in the sense that one tended to look past their material manifestations in order to see what was represented in them.[19] Prints and slides, hanging files, index cards, and filing cabinets were all "environmental" media, in Marshall McLuhan's sense of the term, in that they constituted the experiential horizon within which our dealings with photographs and archives took place.[20] For most people, including workers in the picture industry, there was no more need to reflect on silver halides, paper stock, or drawers being the building blocks of a photographic archive than there is for native speakers of any language to reflect on the grammatical structure of their sentences. "But in the case of environments created by new technologies," claimed McLuhan, "while they are quite invisible in themselves, they do make visible the old environments."[21] Like a native speaker realizing the particularities of sentence structure in their own language when learning to speak a new one, we are made aware of the old and comfortable environments when we are confronted with new ones. It is in keeping with this logic that the material infrastructures of photography first became recognizable as such when digitization seemingly began to disintegrate them.

An illustrative example is from the opening paragraph of Joanna Sassoon's frequently referenced text on "photographic materiality in the age of digital reproduction," published in 2004: "Digital images are produced without the intermediaries of film, paper or chemicals," it began, before going on to suggest that, due to their "direct conversion of light into a digital format to create a stable image, 'photographs' that only exist in the digital form can be seen in one context as a truer version of photography (writing with light) than those that require the creation of a physical intermediary to view the image in a material form."[22] In practice, the digital capture of photographic images is just as reliant on intermediaries as chemical photography, only these intermediaries are not silver halide emulsions but light-sensitive CCD chips and their programmed reaction to exposure.[23] Compared to the time-consuming darkroom processing of photographic film and paper prints, digital photo processing is so fast, automatized, and invisible inside the "black box" of the camera computer that its very instantaneousness makes the resulting image seem transparently immediate.[24] The digital technologies that make up the "new environment" are in this respect doubly invisible because manufacturers consistently hide their proprietary processing technologies from view, either by creating impenetrable layers of physical protection around devices or by enlisting patent law protection over algorithms.

The combined effects of digital technologies being both new and predominantly black-boxed go some way to explain why the digitization of photographs was often described as a process of dematerialization in these early years of the century. Frosh argued that "digital technologies, by dematerializing and reconfiguring the photograph before our very eyes . . . disenchant photography just as photography disenchanted the visible world."[25] Much of the writing that in these years attended to the materiality of photographic objects worked against this tendency, implicitly seeking to re-enchant photography by re-materializing the photograph as "a three-dimensional thing, not only a two-dimensional image."[26] In their introduction to an influential essay collection that in many ways epitomized the material turn within photography studies, Elizabeth Edwards and Janice Hart considered that "in the digital age . . . the materiality of many images evaporates into a series of electronic pulses."[27] In the same volume, Sassoon wrote of digitization as a "translation from the material to the digital image," while Joan M. Schwartz considered it a hallmark of "this age of electronic images and digital reproduction" that "the photograph is often circulated and viewed as a dematerialized, decontextualized image."[28] My own contribution to this debate, slightly later in the decade, proposed that digitization extracted "the use value of the image from the paper print and transferred it to the immaterial format in which the image will henceforth be stored and exchanged."[29]

Photo-materialist writing of this kind typically pitched a brief and unspecified concept of an "immaterial" digital image against the glorious materiality of exemplary historical photographs, ideally bearing the marks of having been circulated as souvenirs, commodities, or scientific documents, or incorporated into other items of material culture, such as albums or lockets. The exemplars were frequently drawn from museum collections or institutional archives, and even when the main objective of the study may have been to determine and interpret the "cultural biography" of the thing itself, this often uncovered details about the networks through which the object had traveled.[30] An explicit objective of this strand of research was moreover to supplement and expand the traditional purview of photographic history. Having been cast in the mold of art history, this had so far "fallen short," as Geoffrey Batchen put it, of "ordinary, commercial photographic practices."[31]

The object-oriented writers on photographic materiality and the system-oriented critics of stock photography in many ways seemed to have wildly diverging approaches and objectives. Yet their interests converged around photography's role in the production, distribution, and consumption of "ordinary" pictures that are designed to be incorporated into other objects, whether frames and lockets or feature articles and advertisements. They also shared an impatience with dominant disciplinary paradigms, both within cultural studies and photo history, that privileged the analysis of "image content" seen in virtual isolation from material support, and interpreted without due regard for the means and systems of production, as well as circulation and consumption.[32] It is unimportant whether either of these bodies of work were knowingly or unknowingly prompted by the absorption of photography into the invisible environment of digitization. The effect remains that by bestowing scholarly attention on the transient and overlooked cultural forms of photography, these writers ensured the consecration of these forms as durable objects of research, worthy of serious attention. The seed to the present book was sown precisely at the intersection of these two discourses, where I found something missing, namely, the human factor represented by archivists, librarians, and picture researchers working at the interface between such ordinary photographs and their publics.

This gap in the literature has been gradually filling in over the past decade. Studies by Estelle Blaschke and Diana Kamin have documented the lasting legacies of several early twentieth-century photographic picture collections, as well as some of the influential librarians and archivists who put them together.[33] A recent archival study of the famous Magnum Photos collective by Nadya Bair has directed attention away from legendary photographers and onto the crucial roles of picture editors, agents, publishers, and other auxiliary professions in developing the postwar market for photojournalism, while Zeynep Devrim Gürsel has explored the impact of digitization on current-day "image brokers" in news organizations working to bring contemporary photojournalism and wire agency pictures to global audiences.[34] All of these studies draw attention to the picture industry's reliance on what Peters calls "brokers and intermediaries," whose "medium-specific tactical skills," honed across picture collections in both public and private organizations, were instrumental to the efficient circulation of photographic commodities in the rapidly expanding pictorial economy of the twentieth century.[35]

Intermediaries are, broadly speaking, actors who "make markets work."[36] In economics, any agent that facilitates transactions between producers and consumers is defined as an intermediary. Sociologists and cultural studies scholars have developed the term "cultural intermediaries" to describe those professions operating "at the intersection of culture and economy, [where] they perform critical operations in the production and promotion of consumption, constructing legitimacy and adding value through the qualification of goods."[37] This concept is helpful in describing the roles fulfilled by picture librarians, researchers, and archivists in the picture industry because it implies, correctly, that any trade in pictures relies on the circulation of cultural as well as economic capital.[38]

Ideas of Intermediation

The work that intermediaries do is what I call "the work of intermediation" in this book. Throughout the chapters that follow I use it as an analytical anchor that signifies the productive contribution of the go-between in the space between pictures and their audiences. While I generally attribute this work to a human agent, such as a librarian or researcher, it is nevertheless a process that also involves nonhuman tools and technologies. Earlier, we saw the concept of physical intermediaries invoked to describe the functions of emulsion film, photographic paper, and chemical processing agents in the production and circulation of pre-digital photographs. The digital capture and display of images is equally reliant on the hardware and software of computational processing, as already noted.

Literary critic Katherine Hayles has adopted the term *intermediation*—seemingly without regard for its specific meaning in economics—to theorize the "dynamics of human-computer interaction."[39] In this understanding, the prefix *inter-* does not indicate a third-party go-between, mediating between two actors, but rather a dynamic relational process in which two or more agents of mediation (human or nonhuman) are to-ing and fro-ing among themselves. Intermediation is a way of accounting for the intricate "feedback loops [that] connect humans and machines, old technologies and new . . . , analog processes and digital fragmentations" that, according to Hayles, resist the "linear causality" that characterizes much thinking about so-called new media.[40] Citing the influential writings of Friedrich Kittler and Lev Manovich as examples of a "tendency to regard the computer as the ultimate solvent that is dissolving all other media into itself," Hayles proposes intermediation as an alternative framework for understanding the ongoing "interactions" between digital and pre-digital media.[41] In the chronologically ordered chapters that follow this introduction, I mobilize both the economic and the media-theoretical conceptions of intermediation at different moments.

It is ironic that Hayles should have chosen the term *intermediation* to designate an analytical framework developed for the study of digital artifacts. For if digitization has been expected to deliver one thing, it is not intermediation (in the economist's or sociologist's sense of the term) but rather disintermediation. In economics, this is what happens when intermediaries are bypassed in some way, so that consumers or users can get direct access to the goods held or produced by suppliers.[42] Frequently glossed as "cutting out the middleman," the concept of disintermediation has also been intermittently deployed in media studies.[43]

Communication theorist Elihu Katz traced the phenomenon back to the Protestant Reformation, when the printing of Bibles in vernacular languages enabled people to "reach God directly . . . rather than through the intermediacy of the priest."[44] Katz sketched out two paths that disintermediation can take: either the sender addresses an audience directly, in order to exert influence over the traditional intermediary, or the sender tries to dispense with the function of the intermediary altogether, but in fact ends up merely replacing it with another mediating agent.

Politics provides illustrations of both these variants. In the twentieth century, democratic leaders and dictators alike would address the public directly over radio in connection with important events. In the twenty-first century, meanwhile, presidents and prime ministers are routinely bypassing edited media outlets and using social media networks to communicate with core supporters as well as to put pressure on the traditional intermediaries of government, whether bureaucrats, elected representatives, or members of the judiciary. The prescient historical overview that Katz first outlined in 1988 is a useful reminder that media have—paradoxically—been deployed as agents of disintermediation long before the existence of digital communication networks. It is nevertheless clear that internet-based platforms for communication and commerce have made disintermediation a business model in its own right.

Disintermediation by digitization is virtual in a double sense, first, because it takes place on digital platforms, and second, because it is for that very reason not actual disintermediation but rather "reintermediation."[45] The travel industry is a textbook example of this process. Travel agencies were rapidly going out of business from around 2000; their knowledgeable staff were bypassed as airlines, hotels, and tourist authorities started offering travelers direct online access to travel advice and booking systems. At the same time, third-party platforms providing aggregated access to the booking systems of airlines and hotels were establishing themselves as the new, indispensable intermediaries between the public and its next holiday. Online booking platforms may have disintermediated travel agents in their incarnation as people possessing certain kinds of professional knowledge and experience, but only to automate the services rendered by those agents as algorithmic search engines in online databases.[46] Thus the travel industry of the 2000s illustrates the stubborn dynamics of intermediation, in which cutting out a "middleman" almost inevitably gives rise to new, if slightly different intermediaries. The story of the travel industry around the turn of the century is remarkably similar to that of the picture industry in the same period, as chapter 5 will show. In both cases, the technology that first acted as an agent of disintermediation turned out to be an agent of reintermediation.

The technical process of creating digital surrogates for existing documents, records, and artifacts relies on optical instruments such as cameras and scanners that derive from photographic technologies. Photographs furthermore make up a considerable bulk of the documents, records, and artifacts that have so far been digitized. This relationship between photography and digitization is played out in chapter 6, which considers two examples of how photographs come to be digitized. These illustrate the feedback loop between analog and digital media, identified above by Hayles, where two technological systems interact with and intermediate each other. While there is little doubt that digitization has disintermediated photography as a technology of capture and accumulation throughout the picture industry, my suggestion in chapter 6 is that we also think about it the other way around, recognizing how photography has intermediated digitization. Like "the mother's body is forming the fetus," as Hayles puts it, "the fetus is also re-forming the mother's body."[47] And as photographic technologies, documents, archives, and libraries have given shape to digitization, so digitization has reconfigured—recoded, if you like—the aesthetic form as well as the informational content of those same technologies, documents, archives, and libraries.

The work of intermediation manifests itself in a variety of ways, and may be studied through a range of research objects. The case studies analyzed in this book are pictures and printed texts that I have chosen for their ability both to illustrate and to embody the material practices involved in this work. They include a visual joke circulated by means of lithography in the 1830s, the back of a photographic print from the 1950s, an outdated handbook from the 1970s, a television drama from the 1990s, a printed brochure from 2004, and a photographic transparency of unknown date, digitized in 2013. I consider these media artifacts as carriers of meaning, of course, but equally as what media theorist Wolfgang Ernst calls "archive[s] of cultural engineering," documenting the material histories of their own making.[48] In this respect my approach has affinities with the field of media archaeology; however, it is probably better designated as a form of media antiquarianism. The main difference, as Ernst himself has explained, is that while the true archaeologist "goes so far as to exclude any human presence from the representation of the material past . . . the antiquary must always intervene by singling out an object and telling its story."[49] If there is one thing that the stories I have to tell in this book have in common, it is that the objects I have singled out to write about speak of a human presence.

MACHINERIES OF INTERMEDIATION

Photography and digitization are both terms that were initially coined to describe specific technical processes and ended up designating cultural phenomena. It can be hard to agree on definitions of these terms when trying to pin them down as objects of research and analysis, and possibly even harder when adopting them as markers of historical time. Defining the period covered by this book as running from pre-photography to post-digitization, I have effectively designated photography and digitization as events, which they are not, of course, in a regular sense. The purpose is rather to indicate how the work of intermediating between pictures and their publics has been shaped by cultural and technological practices carried over from before the emergence and eventual dominance of photography as a medium of mass visual reproduction, and how photography in its turn persists beyond its ostensible disintermediation by digitization.

The double-aspect conception of television as both technology and cultural form developed by Raymond Williams can provide one model for understanding "photography" as a set of entangled relations between hardware and infrastructure, on the one hand, and practices that make use of them, on the other.[50] At the level of technology, photography combines earlier inventions such as the camera obscura and light-sensitive emulsions in order to produce mechanical inscriptions of visual information. At the level of cultural form it both reproduces older, existing forms like portraits or landscape views and allows for the emergence of new forms like the snapshot and the mug shot.[51] While the concepts of technology and cultural form may be adequate to describe what photography is, however, they do not quite convey how it has been put to work in the modern pictorial economy. Tagg's previously cited concept of photography as a machinery of capture comes closer to describing it. Yet in order to account for the various ways in which photography enabled not just a new mechanized making of pictures but an unprecedented industrial-scale sharing of them, we also need to acknowledge photography's embeddedness in machineries of accumulation, extraction, and transmission, which in turn serve the purposes of intermediation.

The examples analyzed in this book offer glimpses of these machineries at work, the functions that photographic technologies and cultural forms fulfill within them, and the ways in which they interlock with other components of each machinery. Once apprehended by photographic capture, the accumulation of pictorial records and documents requires practices of collecting, archiving, copying, and storing that are the traditional remit of intermediaries like archivists, picture librarians, curators, and connoisseurs. This machinery permeates all the chapters of this book, but it is especially palpable in chapters 2–4, which explore photographs, texts, and moving images representing picture librarians at work.

The creation of value through and from such accumulations of photographs is made possible by methods of extraction that range from collection owners charging fees for the reproduction of their photographs to researchers mining photographic archives for visual historical documents. Epitomized in the concept of intellectual property that forms the central topic of chapter 1, mechanisms of extraction also include practices of (re) search and retrieval in analog picture libraries (chapters 2–4), appraisal and collection of historical or discarded pictures for future exploitation (chapter 3), and selective digitization of analog holdings for commercial or public distribution (chapters 4 and 5).

Finally, I call the machineries of transmission those organizational as well as infrastructural channels through which pictures are distributed, disseminated, published, networked, shown, seen, and otherwise shared across both time and space. In chapter 1, they come into view as the print shop windows, scrapbooks, and albums in which nineteenth-century lithographs and photographs were most frequently encountered, but also as a CD-ROM from the 1990s, filled with illegitimately scanned reproductions of artworks. In chapters 2 and 3 transmission channels are exemplified by printed periodicals for a seemingly ever-growing mass market, as well as by the various means of surface and airborne communication that were involved in getting pictures from suppliers to clients and back again. And as chapters 4–6 tumble into the contemporary era, virtually all avenues of transmission have been reintermediated, along with those of capture, accumulation, and extraction, in the machinery of digitization.

Just like television and photography, digitization can be described as a constellation of technologies and cultural forms, in the sense that it combines existing technologies of computing and visualization, incorporates and modifies established cultural forms (from news and advertising to personal letters and self-portraits), and facilitates new cultural forms like websites and multiplayer online games. Unlike television and photography, however, the term *digitization* clearly designates a process rather than a medium. In that respect, digitization is more like globalization or industrialization, in that it describes at once a number of practical, technical, and material processes, and a set of abstracted cultural, social, and political processes. At the very basic dictionary-level definition, digitization is a process of making something digital that was not digital before. This description may apply to something small and specific, such as the digital capture of an image contained in an "analog" photographic paper print. It may equally apply to something as large and unwieldy as the technology-led transformation of an entire society, such as "the digitization of America."[52]

Some writers have argued for a distinction to be made between "digitization" as a term denoting the technical process of making digital and "digitalization" as a term describing the cultural adoption of digital technologies.[53] I do not find this distinction useful enough to adopt, and will use the term *digitization* to cover both aspects. One rationale for this choice is that the examples of digital resources discussed in this book are not "electronic documents" originally captured or produced on networked digital devices but rather surrogates of historical, analog, visual materials that have been produced by means of a digitization process.[54] Another reason is that it is precisely the connotations of a technical and material procedure of acquisition, reproduction, and exploitation that lend digitization its power as a concept through which to apprehend broader processes in culture and society since the late twentieth century. Digitization works in this respect as a collective term for the relentless processes of capture, accumulation, extraction, and transmission of information that have come to dominate everyday life.

Sheltered behind its primary meaning as a material process of making digital, the concept of digitization is able to do a lot of ideological work. Under the modified rubric of "mass digitization," generally applied to large-scale undertakings to make whole collections of cultural objects available online, it has "attained the status of a cultural and moral imperative and obligation," as Nanna Bonde Thylstrup has observed.[55] Corporate organizations like Google and public cultural memory institutions like libraries, archives, and museums have all adopted a variety of strategies (often in collaboration with each other) in order to "get digitization done." Yet the question of why or whether it is necessary or desirable to digitize at all is rarely raised outside critical scholarship.

The public rhetoric of mass digitization as a task that simply needs doing is exemplified by two statements emanating from two national memory institutions in Norway and Canada. First, the former National Librarian of Norway articulated the following circular argument, on the occasion of the official opening of the National Library's digitization factory in 2012: "As more and more [material] becomes digital, it is important to digitize that which is not digital to ensure that it will not be forgotten."[56] And second, a promotional video posted the same year on the Library and Archives Canada website stated that "the future is digital. Converting as many of our assets as possible into digital form means they have the best chance of standing the ultimate test . . . the test of time. When you convert documents, films, paintings, photographs, music into digital form, they are no longer the prisoner of their original format."[57]

These two statements illustrate that, like all imperatives and obligations, the digitization imperative appears both ahistorical and apolitical—just doing what needs to be done—when it is of course a phenomenon tied to a particular historical moment and a particular kind of politics. This is effectively a politics of intermediation, in the economic sense of the word. Seeking to control transactions between suppliers (e.g., libraries, archives, museums) and users (e.g., readers, researchers, visitors), it operates at macro, meso, and micro levels, across global, national, and local contexts, as well as in public, charitable, and corporate organizations. The political aspects of digitization manifest themselves in this book through an intellectual property dispute over digitized reproductions of artworks examined in chapter 1, the digital platformization of the picture industry, which looms on the horizon in chapter 4 and becomes a lived reality in chapter 5, and the precarious labor involved in large-scale digitization projects, which comes to light in the sixth and final chapter.

FROM PRE-PHOTOGRAPHY TO POST-DIGITIZATION

The work of intermediation takes many forms in this book, as it proceeds in chronological order from the pre-photographic world of printmaking, via the photographically enabled work of picture librarianship and picture research, to the laborious procedures of digitizing photographs for online distribution. Part I, "Before Digitization," covers the best part of two centuries in the course of three chapters, while in part II, "Under Digitization," the same number detail developments that span little more than thirty years. Each of the six chapters that follow is centered on a concept, object, institution, or practice that somehow represents or crystallizes the particular period in which it is set.

In chapter 1, the concept is copyright, a legal institution without which there would be no picture industry. This chapter explains the legal conditions for mechanical reproduction and mass distribution of pictures before photography entered the market, discussing the intermediary functions of drafters, printers, and photographers as well as their roles as economic agents in a pictorial market economy.[58] Juxtaposing the moment just before photography was invented in the 1830s with the moment just as digitization was rearing its head in the 1990s, chapter 1 explores how the law regulated relationships between those who created original pictures and those who brought reproductions of those pictures to a mass audience, as well as the legacy bestowed by the business practices of pre-photographic intermediaries such as engravers and printers on a photographic picture industry confronting digital disintermediation.

The library is the key concept of chapter 2, designating the central production unit of the postwar picture industry. Set mainly in the 1950s, this chapter finds the picture industry proper coming into its own, as mature photographic technologies of both image capture and document reproduction contribute to an acceleration in the market for illustrated periodicals. Focusing on a photograph of the picture-industrial production line, it reads this representation in tandem with a set of guidelines on efficient picture librarianship that was published around the same time, to show how pictures were accumulated and processed for reproduction across the expanding range of illustrated print commodities, and what tools and systems existed for classifying, preserving, and searching through pictures stored in paper and emulsion formats. Considering who performed this work of intermediation, and what kind of skills and knowledge they needed to carry it out, this chapter further reveals the picture library as a gendered workplace, which nevertheless offered white-collar women a rare environment in which to forge a career in the early postwar period.

Chapter 3 focuses on the central theme of research, the work of intermediation that brought the contents of libraries to the attention of viewers. This chapter exposes the many stages of intermediation involved in procuring and producing pictorial commodities during the period in the mid-1970s when a truly global market for stock photography emerged. Its protagonists are Hilary and Mary Evans, who together founded the eponymous Mary Evans Picture Library in London and edited the *Picture Researcher's Handbook* across eight editions from 1975 until 2006. Through a close reading of the first edition of this handbook, this chapter reveals how its recommended standards of good research practice reflected the affinities between researchers and collectors as cultural intermediaries with an ability to transform the significance of an object by the power of their knowledgeable attention.

Part II of the book opens with an exploration of intermediation as a performance of search and re-search in a library setting. Chapter 4 sees the arrival of digital technologies to disrupt established practices of picture librarianship and picture research in the 1990s. It shows that everyday experiences of digitization occurred more in the realm of discourse than of lived reality until the end of that decade by analyzing a television drama set in a picture library that showcases the picture librarian as a highly skilled cultural intermediary. Reading this fictional representation alongside contemporaneous research by information scientists seeking to automate the work of intermediation performed by picture librarians, this chapter explores the expectations that picture professionals harbored about the capabilities of digital technologies to enhance the work of capturing, accumulating, extracting, and transmitting pictures to a public, as well as the affordances offered by picture libraries, which in return could serve the purposes of digitization.

Disintermediation characterizes chapter 5, which picks up when the efforts of information scientists to reconfigure picture research as a problem for computing had come to fruition in the early 2000s. Focusing on the digital disintermediation of traditional picture libraries and the reintermediation of picture research through platformization, exemplified by Getty Images, the chapter shows how digitization solved specific problems inherent to the work of accumulating, extracting, and transmitting pictures, and that the particular solutions it offered had consequences both for the business models of picture libraries and for the work of picture research. Giving voice to practicing picture researchers interviewed during the period, it also demonstrates how individuals experienced the disintermediated search offered by online platforms as empowering in comparison to having their search terms interpreted by human intermediaries in the form of picture librarians.

Finally, chapter 6 illustrates the concept of reintermediation in the 2010s through visual evidence of the labor of digitization itself—the practical processes of rendering of photographic originals into digital surrogates—that enables the disintermediation represented by searchable online repositories. In this chapter, Hayles's notion of intermediation as mutual feedback comes particularly to the fore as I explore the dynamic relations between photographic and digital reproduction technologies first in a series of documentary digital photographs showing digitization activities, and then by tracing the digitization history of one individual photographic slide. This chapter also develops the concept of post-digitization to denote a pattern of behavior that assumes everything worth seeing or reading will already have been digitized.

Across its six chapters, this book traces a history of the modern pictorial economy through the work of intermediation that has been successively enabled by pre-photographic, photographic, and digital machineries of capture, accumulation, extraction, and transmission. In doing so it makes visible and explicit the invisible labor that has built and still sustains the visual commodity culture that has characterized everyday life in the global north for the best part of a century. Intermediation is like infrastructure in the sense that as long as it's working, we don't notice it. Lifting the lid on the machineries of intermediation to show their working, this book shows why and how it matters.

I

Before Digitization

1

Rights and Reproducibility

When photographic technologies emerged in the late 1830s they were put to work within a pictorial economy that provided employment for a wide range of producers and purveyors engaged in the mass production and mass distribution of pictures as commodities. Rather than immediately revolutionize the production and consumption of pictures upon its invention, photography entered into a preexisting "economy of sharing" that had developed across Europe during the eighteenth century.[1] The opening-up of princely and private collections of art to the public was in line with Enlightenment ideas of civil improvement—it was increasingly considered an act of public spirit, rather than mere benevolence, to allow others to "contemplate" and "converse with" works that had hitherto been preserved for their owners' pleasure.[2]

This extension of visual access to works of art resulted in the emergence of what Pascal Griener has called a "republic of the eye," in which democratized access to art enabled images to float free of their material instantiations in physical pieces of private or public property, and circulate through the "immaterial gallery" of commonly held visual ideas.[3] There was money to be made from lifting such immaterial images out of the visual commons and fixing them in the physical form of new pictures. Thanks to developments in industrial printing technologies, these could be mass-produced and thus made affordable to segments of the public that had never before been in a position to buy a piece of art. In its early decades, photography was but one of several competing and complementary technologies of reproduction that sought a share in this expanding market for pictorial commodities.

Although they varied greatly at the level of technical execution, all of these procedures involved at least two intermediary operations. First, a printable copy must be made from the original image, usually by an engraver who incised the visual motif onto a printing plate. This plate was then submitted to a printing shop, where dedicated operatives applied ink and pulled a certain number of copies from it. In addition to the engraver and the printer came a third intermediary, the publisher, who made the resulting prints available to members of the public, either in the form of individual items for purchase or as part of other printed commodities such as illustrated books or periodicals. This division of labor among artists, engravers, printers, and publishers had been legally recognized in the United Kingdom since the eighteenth century, through two successive laws collectively referred to as the Engravers' Acts.[4] As early instantiations of copyright legislation, these acts accorded printable pictures the status of intellectual property and institutionalized reproducibility as the most valuable affordance of a visual commodity.

Photography in itself did nothing to dispense with any of the intermediary functions involved in printmaking. Photographic images that were to be reproduced in books or periodicals had, like drawings or paintings, to undergo the same procedure of transferal via the engraver's hands onto the printing plate. It was only toward the end of the nineteenth century that components of the photographer's machinery of capture, including optical projection techniques and light-sensitive chemical emulsions, were successfully incorporated into the printer's machinery of transmission. This happened through the development of so-called halftone processes, which facilitated the industrial-scale manufacture and circulation of photographic illustration that, in turn, constituted the material conditions in which the twentieth-century picture industry could emerge and grow.[5] In this chapter I locate the origins of this industry in the intertwined histories of printmaking and photography. Rather than rehearse a technological narrative of optics, chemistry, and machinery, however, my account will highlight the legal provisions that were instrumental in establishing the work of intermediation as a legitimate source of revenue and income in an industrialized pictorial economy.

Setting up part I of the book, which deals with the period before digitization, this opening installment threads a through line from the pre-photographic world of popular printmaking in the 1830s to the post-photographic scenario heralded by a nascent form of digital picture distribution in the 1990s. The next two chapters expand on other aspects of the pre-digital picture library business, as chapter 2 considers classification and retrieval systems in the 1950s, and chapter 3 explores the work of collecting pictures for the purpose of commercial exploitation in the 1960s and 1970s, as well as the work of searching for them, in a world without the World Wide Web. All three chapters in part I focus on practices of capture, accumulation, extraction, and transmission before the advent of digital technologies. In writing them I have nevertheless also decided to include reflections on how their respective research objects have been found, viewed, or studied through the online resources that characterize post-digitized scholarship. The story begins, however, with neither a website nor a photograph, but with a lithograph, a printed pictorial commodity whose individual biography well-nigh embodies the history of intermediation in the picture business from pre-photography to post-digitization.

Before Photography

The "desire to photograph" that Geoffrey Batchen identified among the "proto-photographers" of the late eighteenth and early nineteenth centuries was not just a scientific desire for machine-assisted accuracy.[6] It was equally a response to a growing cultural appetite for pictures. This is humorously illustrated in *The Connoisseur* (figure 1.1), a hand-colored lithographic print produced by G. E. Madeley from a drawing by G. Spratt and published by Charles Tilt in London in 1830. It depicts a human figure holding a lorgnette, or magnifying glass, who is dressed from head to toe in pictures of every imaginable genre, from vignetted miniature portraits, via floral compositions and antique busts, to animal portraits, historical portraits, landscapes, seascapes, and even what looks like a hunting trophy. The figure's outfit made up of pictures is roughly readable as a dress of some sort, and in combination with what is visible of the hair style this makes it likely that we are looking at a woman. This connoisseur of pictures is depicted in the print as entirely submerged by her objects of interest, yet at the same time a walking display of them. Rather

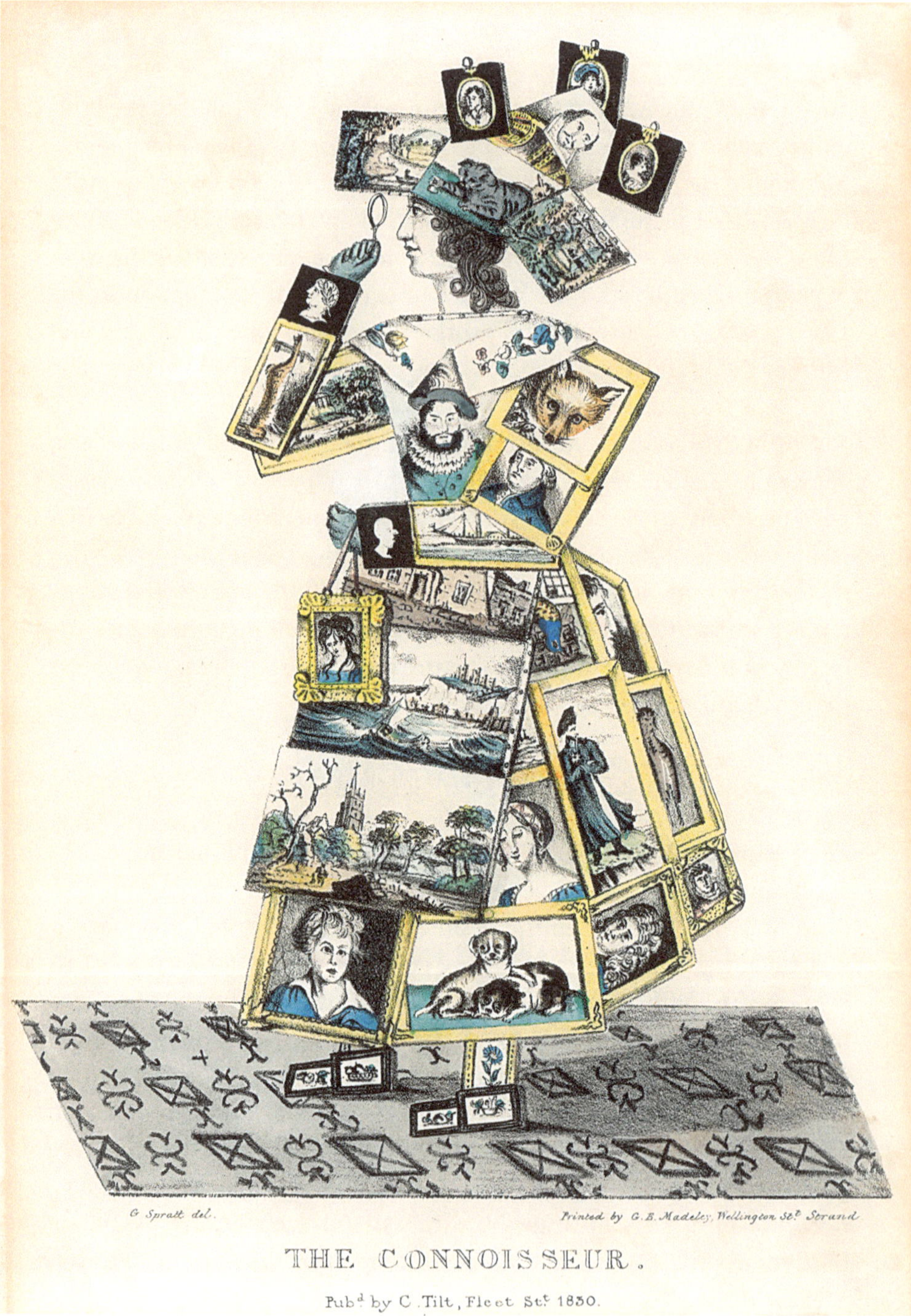

FIGURE 1.1

The Connoisseur. Lithograph by G. E. Spratt, printed by R. Madeley, published by C. Tilt. 1830. © Mary Evans Picture Library.

than keeping this hoard of imagery for her own pleasure, *The Connoisseur* shares her pictures with the world around.

As a picture that contains other pictures within its own frame, this lithograph belongs to the category of "metapictures," conceptualized by W. J. T. Mitchell as pictures that are easy to think with, because they seem to theorize their own condition from within.[7] This particular lithograph pictures itself as the product of a visual culture in which image reproductions circulated more widely, more rapidly, and for a greater variety of purposes than ever before. In this chapter, *The Connoisseur* figures both as a product of the pre-photographic printmaking industry and as a "device" that helps us "reflect on the nature of pictures" as commodities produced, collected, monetized, and circulated within historically specific pictorial economies both before and after the invention of photography.[8]

Published as part of a series called "Trades," it was distributed through the print shop of Charles Tilt in London's Fleet Street as one of several so-called composite caricatures, including figures like "The Entomologist" (a man made up of insects) and "The Conchologist" (a woman made up of shells). Judging from the representation of its frontage in another comic print of the period, the page for the month of March in George Cruikshank's *Comic Almanack* for 1835 (figure 1.2), Tilt's shop was situated on a rounded corner with large display windows on either side of the main entrance. Around 1830 these provided Londoners with "the best place to see each week's new graphic production," according to historian James A. Secord.[9] From Cruikshank's rendition it seems that every pane of glass in each of the shop windows displayed a different print, suggesting that upward of thirty pictures might be on display at the same time.

In the 1820s–1830s personal albums and scrapbooks fulfilled the functions that we would today associate with social media.[10] These books and albums would incorporate mass-produced pictures alongside private drawings and writings, not unlike social media users today who appropriate and combine private snapshots and comments with images from all kinds of other sources to display on their profiles. Secord emphasizes how the composite caricatures that proliferated in late Georgian visual culture fed into a particular trend in English humor during this period, which manifested itself in a taste for "puns, puzzles, and visual conundrums,"

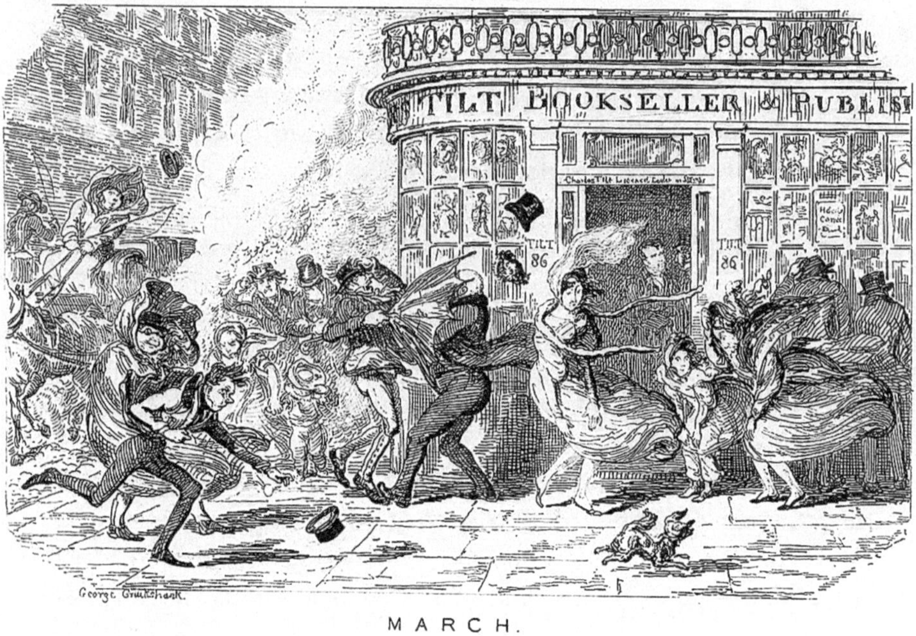

FIGURE 1.2
Illustration for the month of March 1835, from *George Cruikshank's Steel Etchings to the Comic Almanacks: 1835–1853*, printed c. 1880, published by Pickering & Chatto. Reproduction: Agefotostock/Alamy.

and a predilection for the "droll."[11] Popular prints and scraps—the ready-made cut-out images from which the scrapbook takes its name—were often used as raw materials for new visual compositions and composites in the personal album culture of the early nineteenth century. Prints like *The Connoisseur*, which in the original measures roughly the same as an A5 piece of paper, were produced in easily portable sizes precisely to facilitate their circulation. Indeed, Secord reports that the series to which it belongs was explicitly advertised by Spratt and Madeley as "adapted for the Scrap-Book, &c."[12] The embeddedness of such prints in nineteenth-century album and scrapbooking practices is demonstrated, as Secord points out, by the fact that surviving specimens nearly always bear the hallmarks of having at some point been trimmed and glued onto other sheets of paper, if they are not preserved still attached to pages of scrapbooks that have been systematically "disaggregated" by dealers for sale as individual collectibles.[13] Despite the connotations of elitism inherent in its original title, in other words, *The Connoisseur* was itself very much a mass market commodity produced for maximum circulation within the pictorial economy of its day.

The figure represented in *The Connoisseur* is clearly gendered as female, and this is significant on at least two levels. For one, the making of albums and scrapbooks was a typical activity for ladies of a certain class, and often with an intellectual ambition. Scrapbooks allowed women to display scientific as well as artistic interests and skills within an informal format that was socially acceptable in ways that ostentatious displays of learning by women were not, for most of the nineteenth century. As Patrizia Di Bello writes about an album compiled by the wife of a prominent doctor and educational reformer in London between 1825 and 1847: "Anna Birkbeck's album constructs her participation in a world of culture that still involves her in a public sphere of scientific, political, educational and artistic endeavors; but her participation is constructed as being based on individual encounters and personal exchanges."[14] In this way, married women might deploy their personal albums as social tools in the expansion of cultural and intellectual networks through which their husbands' careers might prosper. Viewed in this context, the figure of *The Connoisseur* could be said to represent the typical audience for which small-format, popular prints were produced: women who constructed their social appearance through collected and assembled pictures. On another level, however, the figure could also be read as an allusion to the role of women in the very production processes of hand-colored lithographic prints. Secord cites evidence suggesting that George Spratt, the drafter behind this print and the others in the same series, in fact worked in companionship with his wife, and possibly also his daughter, in order to produce the designs that were printed by Madeley and sold by Tilt.[15] While it is not known in which specific capacities Mrs. Spratt was involved in the production of these particular designs, it is likely that she had a hand, as it were, in the delicate work of coloring that finished off each individual print.

Before 1840 there did not exist a viable technology for color printing, and so each item would have to be colored by hand. This was precisely the sort of work with which women would be entrusted: it required a delicate touch and attention to detail, it could be performed in the home—and it was badly paid. A contemporaneous example from Sweden is illustrative here. An unmarried gentlewoman named Josabeth Sjöberg (1812–1882) supplemented a small inheritance in nineteenth-century Stockholm by giving music lessons and hand coloring popular prints. In the 1840s she would receive 4½ skilling per sheet, an amount that would be roughly the equivalent of SEK33 or USD3.80 in today's currency.[16] In a historical overview of the lithographic trade in nineteenth-century Philadelphia, meanwhile, Erika Piola and Jennifer Ambrose note that, as late as 1856, one of the major lithographic houses in the city employed between 100 and 150 colorists and that "girls as young as ten to twelve years of age" might perform this work "for minimal wages."[17] Against this background, *The Connoisseur* can be said to epitomize the feminine labor that was expended on both sides of the commercial transaction that brought prints of this kind into circulation in nineteenth-century popular visual culture.

The "invisibility" of the work of women who were manual intermediaries between an explicitly male author or producer and an implicitly male reader or spectator is a recurrent feature in what Michelle Henning calls "the development of modern media."[18] As chapter 2 will make clear, picture libraries in the twentieth century would come to rely on a predominantly female workforce to perform the repetitive yet exacting labor of cataloging, indexing, filing, searching, and dispatching stockpiled photographs for advertisers and publishers to use in their manufacture of new pictorial commodities. Like the painstaking hand-coloring of prints, this work was insufficiently acknowledged and remunerated. And yet, also like hand-coloring, picture library work offered a form of employment where the secretarial or assembly-line character of the manual tasks was leavened by a certain room for creative maneuver. The lithograph possibly cocreated by the Spratts, showing a woman rendered nearly invisible by the sheer volume of pictures she is making visible to others, can in this respect also function as a metapicture of working relations in the photographic picture industry that, in the 1830s, was still a century into the future.

The Author as Reproducer

If the visual content of *The Connoisseur* may be interpreted as both a material trace and iconographic representation of women's involvement with popular lithographic production in the nineteenth century, the three names printed underneath the picture clearly identify three men as the legal progenitors of the print. In the bottom left-hand corner of *The Connoisseur,* the words "G. Spratt del." proclaim the identity of the drafter or *delineator* of the image, while a longer sentence in the bottom right-hand corner states that it has been "Printed by G. E. Madeley, Wellington St.t. Strand." Finally, centered on the page just below the title of the print are the details of where and when it has been made available to the public: "Pub.d by C. Tilt, Fleet St.t. 1830." These textual devices explicitly acknowledge the three different trades that have been involved in producing the picture-commodity, and by the same token three named persons stake their individual claims to a share of property in it. Teasing out what this peritext tells us about the legal framework and business conventions that underpinned the popular print industry in the first half of the nineteenth century will be useful for understanding how existing practices in the printing business carried over into the photographic businesses that would soon begin to trade in the same market.

The presence of the three names and the specification of their functions is partly explained by the expectations of its contemporary audiences. In the nineteenth century, "it mattered to consumers," as Tom Gretton has noted, "how printed pictures had been made; their production history, including the amount of skilled work that had gone to make them, affected how consumers regarded them."[19] As importantly, it also mattered to the law how printed pictures were made. The significance of incorporating all this "production history" into the single sheet of paper carrying the printed image is apparent only if one is familiar with the demands set by the late eighteenth-century Engravers' Act, which was still the relevant piece of intellectual property legislation in force in the United Kingdom at the time this print was produced. The 1777 Engravers' Copyright Act (17 Geo. III, c. 57) was the final version of a piece of legislation first enacted in 1735, which regulated trade in visual images up until the introduction of the Fine Arts Copyright Act in 1862 (25 &

26 Vict., c. 68).[20] The full title of the original 1735 Act (8 Geo. II, c. 13) had stated its purpose in the following terms: "An Act for the encouragement of the arts of designing, engraving, and etching historical and other prints, by vesting the properties thereof in the inventors and engravers, during the time therein mentioned." As legal scholar Ronan Deazley has commented, this was the first UK law to grant copyright in "something other than literary works," and it was equally the first time legislators "acknowledged that the value of a given work lay in an artist's particular representation of a subject," and not merely in its physical manifestation as a printed object.[21] Mark Rose makes the same point in an article that further highlights the fact that the painter and engraver William Hogarth was among the petitioners for the bill and "the principal beneficiary of the act."[22] The "time" referred to in the title of the original act was a period of fourteen years from first publication; this was extended in 1766 to twenty-eight years (7 Geo. III, c. 38), at the same time as the designation of the works protected was reworded to cover engravings of previously existing drawings, models, pictures, or sculptures.[23] In 1777 additional provisions were made to ensure "that any engraver who copied an existing print must have the express consent of the proprietor" and to increase the level of damages that the rights-holders might sue for in case of infringement.[24] In all three iterations of the Engravers' Act, however, the principle held firm that pictures—mainly understood as paintings or drawings—in themselves were not protected by copyright, but "merely the *design* of the picture *when coupled with engraving*."[25] As Deazley emphasizes, in his account of the discussions that eventually led to the approval of the Fine Arts Copyright Act in 1862, anyone who wanted to claim exclusive reproduction rights to an image must first have it engraved and the resulting engraving published, in order to achieve protection. It was only after 1862 that "the moment of publication" was removed from any consideration of the copyright term and replaced with the artist's lifetime, plus thirty years.[26]

With this legal framework in mind, we may turn back to the names inscribed on *The Connoisseur*, and other prints in the same series, and read them as a tripartite copyright notice: a design, or image, invented by Spratt had been printed (in legal terms engraved) by Madeley, and finally published by Tilt, specifically in the year 1830, from which the term of copyright was calculated. Including this information on the printing plates themselves, so that they were automatically included in each copy, was the obvious technical solution to the problem of how to keep track of a large number of circulating copies, even if it was no guarantee, given the purchasers' predilection for trimming and tailoring prints before including them in individual and often highly original scrapbook "mash-ups." Specifying each contributor's role in the making of the print was another technical solution to the problem of acknowledging how indispensable the making of original (as in previously uncopied) artworks was to the process of mass-produced reproductions, within a copyright regime that did not yet recognize "originality" as a value in itself.[27] It points to the more or less institutionalized conventions for due recognition and remuneration that existed among mutually dependent or appreciative communities of practice—such as painters or drafters and engravers or publishers—long before such recognition was enshrined in law.[28] If this harmonious account seems overly optimistic about business relationships in the early nineteenth-century print trade, it is also possible to read the three names as a cautious enumeration of the individuals fulfilling what Michel Foucault famously called the "author-function."[29] Although his classic essay restricts itself to "books or texts with authors," Foucault provides an important reminder that texts "were assigned real authors, other than mythical or important religious figures, only when the author became subject to punishment."[30] A key function of the author in the early modern print trade was, in other words, to take the blame (and the punishment) should a printer produce something to which the sovereign took exception.[31] The practice of including the names of designers or drafters on printing plates may therefore have been in the interest of printers and publishers, who thus implicitly distanced themselves from responsibility for any incendiary or offensive content.

We cannot know the individual motivations that Spratt, Madeley, and Tilt had for their particular collaboration. Yet the series of prints for which they assumed joint authorship still exemplifies how the 1777 Engravers' Act enabled a balance to be struck, for practical business reasons, between the immaterial rights of the inventor or designer of an image and the proprietorial rights of the producer of the material picture in which it was instantiated. The careful inscription of the three authors on the plate of *The Connoisseur* can in this context be understood also as a symptom of the destabilizing impact of lithography on established hierarchies of pictorial reproduction. A lithograph "has the great merit that no intermediary process has to come between the original and the print," according to the *Picture Researcher's Handbook*, and "a good lithograph is easily mistaken for a drawn original."[32] This quality was at odds with the value placed on "mediation" over "origination" both in law and among contemporary connoisseurs in the nineteenth century.[33] Lithographs simply did not convey in any visible form the skill and labor of the printer as distinct from that of the designer or *delineator*, and this characteristic accounted for "its under-achievement as a high-status reproductive technology," as Gretton has it.[34] Because lithography "completely did away with any need for the translator-middle-man engraver with his inevitable systematized grammar and syntax of linear webbing," according to Estelle Jussim, the technique "offered the autographic artist the ability to create a print that would be practically identical with his original."[35]

The apparent disintermediation effected by lithography did not mean that illustrators started pulling their own prints directly from the stone or zinc on which they had inscribed their designs. They continued to rely on collaboration with printmakers in possession of all the relevant machinery and chemistry, with the important difference that this contribution was no longer discernible in the visual expression of the resulting print. As much as Spratt needed documented acknowledgment of his input as illustrator, Madeley needed recognition as a printer or, in legal terms, "engraver." In a study of the graphic arts through the framework of 1960s information theory, Jussim considered that "lithography had provided the release from an interference on the part of the engraver," where the idea of interference referred to a perceptible informational "noise" introduced into an artist's visual "message" by the printmaker's work of translating the "codes" of drawing into those of graphic reproduction.[36] Once this step of the printing process was removed, all the merits of a printed picture could be attributed to the original artwork alone. Conversely, it meant that artists could not rely on engravers to improve on their designs: what you drew was what you got.[37]

With this technical knowledge in mind, the motif drawn in the specific lithograph known as *The Connoisseur* can be decoded as a figure hidden behind pictures. It can be read as an allegory of the lithographic process itself, where the printer is obscured by the very qualities that make the printer's products desirable to consumers. The only hint of a human operator is the face peeking out among the pictures, a visual corollary of the name and address supplied on the print that announces the picture to be product of a printing press and not purely the skilled hand. What *The Connoisseur* figures in its capacity as a lithograph, on this reading, is the transparency of transmission that Jay David Bolter and Richard Grusin call "immediacy": the illusion that a mediated experience is unmediated.[38] Spectators looking at *The Connoisseur* would look *through* the print, and see only the hand-drawn picture reproduced in it.[39]

From Mechanization to Digitization

Transparent transmission was also the goal of photography in the version developed by William Henry Fox Talbot (1800–1877), who is credited with inventing the "paper-based negative-positive system" that established the principles for photography as a technology of mass reproduction.[40] Talbot's system proposed "the elimination of the artist as the primary codifier of information," as Jussim put it, by substituting a medium "which bypassed the artist and the engraver, relying upon Nature itself for codifying the message to be transmitted."[41] Indeed, material transparency was integral to the negative-positive process dubbed the calotype that Talbot patented, because its capacity for reproducing multiple copies depended on the exposure of light through the paper on which the first negative had been fixed, in order for a positive image to appear on a second sheet of paper. Ironically, however, "the texture of the paper was visible," and the calotype thereby reintroduced such discernible traces of the reproduction process in the final picture as had been erased in the earlier process of lithography.[42] Talbot's chief interest nevertheless lay in mechanizing the production of pictures, not necessarily in removing all signs of the production process itself.[43]

The canonical narrative, which is based on his own writings, presents the English inventor of photography as motivated in his experiments by his own lack of accomplishment as a drafter.[44] Accordingly, when Talbot invented a mechanism that would allow anyone to "draw" accurately from life, regardless of natural ability or educated skill, he both resolved a personal issue (as it might be termed in current-day parlance) and enabled others to overcome similar limitations. From this perspective Talbot's invention did not necessarily entail a deskilling of established producers, because the "pencil of nature" was meant to disintermediate drawing by clumsy hands, not skilled ones. At the same time, frequently used metaphors of early photographic picture-making, including "sun pictures," "pictures painted by light," and the previously noted "pencil of nature," were clearly articulations of a discourse intent on what Steve Edwards has called "the displacement of human agency from the scene of production."[45]

In the early years of photography, it was the technological apparatus itself that was subject to legal protection and dispute. The daguerreotype process developed by Louis-Jacques Mandé Daguerre (1787–1851), in collaboration with Joseph-Nicéphore (1765–1833) and Isidore Niépce (1795–1868), is widely considered to have become the first mass-market photographic technology because the French state effectively made its patent "open access" in return for the payment of a lifetime pension to its inventors. Daguerre nevertheless took out a separate patent on his invention in England, where Talbot—his canonical rival as the titular inventor of photography—also took care to patent his various attempts at establishing a reliable way to capture and preserve his "photogenic" drawings, "and rigorously prosecuted those who infringed on his legal rights."[46]

While it may have been the first stable photographic technology to be widely adopted, the daguerreotype was nevertheless a unique and non-multipliable object, in the form of a direct positive image preserved on a reflective and nontransparent metal surface. It was only as various negative-positive processes started dominating the market in photographic technologies from the mid-nineteenth century that mass reproduction became a more prominent characteristic of photography.[47] Once the lines of mass photographic reproduction were firmly established, around 1870, disputes of photographic ownership shifted from patented technologies of production to copyright of the visual contents of their products.

Most historical accounts of the relationship between photography and copyright focus on the earliest court decisions and forms of legislation that did grant protection to photographs, or on the ways in which photographers devised what we would now call "workarounds" in order to take advantage of copyright legislation that did not explicitly protect them. Well-known examples from the historiography of photography include Eugène Atget, who in early twentieth-century Paris claimed to be the "author-publisher" of his own photographs, and Napoleon Sarony, who in late nineteenth-century New York successfully claimed authorship of a portrait of the writer Oscar Wilde, on the basis of "his own original mental conception" being expressed in the elaborate staging and posing of the sitter.[48] Scholarship on photography as intellectual property has tended to focus either on debates about the recognition of photographers as artists (or rather, authors) or on legal disputes among inventors, patentees, and practitioners over the technological apparatus of photographic picture-making.[49] These issues are of fundamental importance for understanding photography's role in the histories of both art and law, and equally relevant to historical accounts of photography as an area of business.[50] Yet they do not quite account for the complexity of rights systems that have enabled "intermediaries and rights representatives," as Estelle Blaschke puts it, "[to place] themselves squarely between the production and distribution of images."[51]

Looking back to the eighteenth-century Engravers' Acts nuances the standard narratives about photography as intellectual property that focus on technological patents or recognition of artistic authorship by illuminating the deeper structures of the pictorial economy in which the new technology had to carve out its niche. The basic principle of these early copyright laws was that a new and monetizable right arose in the moment that a picture was copied or its image content transferred into another medium. It is the same notion that underpins the business models of picture libraries and other content providers to this day, even when they are ostensibly looking after the moral rights of creators. When the pictorial economy was under industrialization in the eighteenth century, an obvious justification for recognizing the makers of copies above the creators of originals was that the intermediary who made a mechanically reproducible copy (whether or not this was the same legal subject or historical person as the maker of the original) added a value to the previously existing picture that was not initially there. In contemporary parlance we might specify this value as a set of affordances, such as mobility, reproducibility, distributability, or even preservability.

With the advent of photography, those affordances no longer needed to be added after the event of picture production because they had become embedded in the picture-making technology itself. As photography eventually took over from earlier reproductive technologies, such as lithography, it added its own intrinsic affordances to previously existing images. These have in turn been internalized in current-day digital reproduction technologies, which add their own inherent capabilities of instantaneous transmission and *networkability* to the aggregated values of the various modes and methods of copying that went before. When the mechanical reproduction techniques of photography were first being challenged by digitization, however, these capabilities were not immediately recognized as valuable.

The emergence of photography in the 1830s had caused anxiety among drafters and engravers until they found ways to work with the new technologies rather than against them. Similarly, when digital reproduction techniques began challenging photography's reproductive hegemony in the 1990s they were first met with suspicion by a number of actors who would ultimately harness them to the benefit rather than detriment of their businesses. Once again, the issues at stake were less concerned with the moral rights of artists as authors of original pictures than with exploitation rights arising from the skilled production of reproducible copies. The next part of this chapter fast-forwards to a moment in the late 1990s when a picture library sued a computer software company over the digital appropriation of its photographic reproductions, asserting its ownership of the photographs on the basis of legal principles that could be traced back to the eighteenth-century Engravers' Acts.

After Photography

Graphic reproductions of well-known works of art had been a staple commodity in the pre-photographic print market, and the visual documentation of artworks was one of the obvious applications of the photographic medium that even its early detractors conceded.[52] In the photographic picture industry that came into its own from the 1930s onward, the photographic capture of preexisting or previously published images, which were either in the public domain or considered "orphaned works," was a viable way to create new pieces of commercially exploitable intellectual property.[53] It could be a profitable business to mine old books, periodicals, and print shops for illustrations by unknown or long-dead artists, and record them in easily reproducible photographic formats, as will be exemplified in chapter 2 by the Bettmann Archive and in chapter 3 by the Mary Evans Picture Library. There were also profits to be made from photographic reproductions of works by famous artists, typically held in public museums or private collections, which were regularly in demand by both the publishing and advertising industries.

In 1972, the Bridgeman Art Library (hereafter Bridgeman) had been founded in London to serve precisely this constituency of clients with high-quality reproductions, executed by skilled professional photographers, at a time when permissions to photograph in public museums, let alone private art collections, were often severely restricted. Cofounder Harriet Bridgeman gave a brief account of the picture library's business model in a handbook on picture librarianship published in the early 1980s.[54] Here she described its function as that of "a central 'bank'" in which was deposited "a large selection of art material from a very diverse number of sources," including "art galleries, museums, and other public collections, dealers, and private owners from all over the world."[55] The photographic reproductions provided by Bridgeman responded primarily to the demand by art publishers for "a high degree of technical excellence and faithful adherence to the original," and for that reason most of its stock was held in large-format transparencies of "a minimum size of 4 × 5 inches," which were moreover preserved "in Kodachrome boxes" residing "in fireproof cabinets for insurance purposes."[56] In addition, the library served a number of art-book publishers that were keen to generate further income from originally commissioned reproductions by making them available for reuse by others. By the late 1990s, Bridgeman had been furnishing high-end art publishers worldwide, for the best part of thirty years, with the sort of technically excellent photographs that were crucial to the production of anything from lavish coffee-table books on Impressionist painting to scholarly monographs on Renaissance sculpture. The measure of their excellence as photographs was, to a great extent, their material transparency: readers of a book illustrated by Bridgeman would look at the photographs and see only the artworks reproduced in them.

And yet in 1998 the picture library sued a desktop publishing company for infringing its copyright in a selection of these reproductions that were not meant to be noticed, in a case brought before the Southern District Court of New York.[57] The defendant was the Corel Corporation, a software company, which as developers of the graphics package CorelDRAW was one of the pioneers in desktop publishing software during the late 1980s. In the 1990s, Corel had acquired digital copies of artwork reproductions originating in the Bridgeman files and included these in CD-ROMs of so-called clip art distributed to its customers. As the original artworks had long since fallen into the public domain, Bridgeman sued for breach of copyright in the reproductions as such, claiming that their photographers' skilled efforts in rendering the originals as faithfully and comprehensively as possible had generated new intellectual property rights inherent in the *photographs* of the artworks.

This argument rested on the same principle that underpinned the previously discussed Engravers' Acts, namely, that the person who makes a reproducible copy of a picture owns the right to reproduce that copy. Its application by Bridgeman in this case demonstrated the longevity of a legal logic that was developed to account for pre-photographic printing practices but persisted long after the laws that enshrined it had been replaced by legislation tailored to accommodate more recent technologies. The persistence of this principle in UK legal opinion was testified by Geoffrey Crabb in another chapter of the same handbook on picture librarianship in which Harriet Bridgeman had outlined the business model of her art library. The two key principles outlined Crabb's disquisition on "copyright in artistic works" were explicitly referenced by Bridgeman in her own contribution to the volume, and they help to contextualize her company's swift and confident reaction to Corel's appropriation.[58]

The first was that "if a copyright painting is photographed there will, in the finished photograph, be two copyrights, one in the photograph itself and another in the painting," and the second, that "[t]o copy a photograph of a painting, where the painting is out of copyright, will require permission only in respect of the photograph."[59] At the time of its publication in 1981 Crabb's interpretation of copyright was grounded in the

UK Copyright Act 1956, and the same principle was carried forward in its replacement, the Copyright, Designs and Patent Act 1988, which granted photographs protection on the same level as works of art. This principle had not only been observed by Bridgeman since its foundation in the 1970s, but the intermediary work of administrating the "two copyrights" on behalf of both rights-holders to artworks and to their reproductions was the cornerstone of its very business model.

Under US law in 1998, however, Judge Kaplan of the Southern District Court ruled that since the photographs were "substantially exact reproductions of public domain works, albeit in a different medium," this did not amount to a sufficient quotient of originality to award status as a work of authorship.[60] Although this judgment was passed in a US district court, and as such carried no precedence outside its immediate jurisdiction, the *Bridgeman v. Corel* verdict reverberated in the United Kingdom in both the legal profession and the picture industry. Intellectual property specialists suspected that a different verdict would have resulted had the case been tried in a British court, due to the lower threshold for "originality" that had thus far been set by UK judges.[61] Nevertheless, as Simon Stokes has reported, the judgment caused the UK Museums Copyright Group to seek further legal clarifications from copyright lawyers and spurred debate among legal scholars in the United Kingdom.[62] Indeed, as late as 2007 the case was not closed, as far as Bridgeman was concerned. In May that year it joined forces with the British Association of Picture Libraries and Agencies (BAPLA) to stage a mock "retrial" of the case in the context of a one-day conference hosted by a University of London law school.[63] At this event the informal verdict went unsurprisingly in Bridgeman's favor, although not without weighty arguments having been provided against it.

In 2007, just as in 1998, the discussion revolved around the question of "slavish copying" versus "skill, labour, and judgement" in the making of photographs from paintings. As we have already seen, Bridgeman's lawsuit was grounded in a long-held principle in UK law, dating from the eighteenth-century Engravers' Acts, that copying a work from one medium into another medium gives rise to a new original. In other words, once the works of art had been reproduced in photographs, it was the photographs, not the paintings they depicted, that constituted the "works" the copyright of which had been infringed, in this case, by Corel. By the same logic, albeit at the risk of admitting its own wrongdoing, Corel might have claimed new copyright in the digitized versions of photographic reproductions, citing the "sweat of the brow" principle with reference to the skill and judgment involved in scanning and file processing. This, of course, it did not do, instead relying on the presiding judge to rule that the skill required to produce good photographic reproductions of paintings was not sufficient to distinguish a Bridgeman photograph from a "slavish copy," for which no copyright protection should be granted.[64]

The characteristics of the new medium into which the photographic reproductions were copied did not receive much attention, neither in 1998 nor in 2007. In view of the limited processing capabilities of regular personal computers in 1998, this may be understandable. At the time, the potential for the digitized versions of Bridgeman's images to be distributed was largely confined to CD-ROMs, which meant that the files needed to be accessed and downloaded via their physical storage medium rather than browsed over the internet. In this respect, Corel's unauthorized appropriation of material was more akin to photocopying chapters from a book, or making 35-mm duplicate transparencies, than to the wholesale file-sharing that is current practice on the World Wide Web.

Within a few years of the final verdict in *Bridgeman v. Corel* in 1999, however, the exponential expansion of computer processing power had enabled the development of streaming and file-sharing technologies that effectively rendered the notion of individual copies redundant. Just five years or so later, the grounds of a similar dispute would no longer have been a limited number of compact discs distributed to selected homes and offices, but the virtually (rather than simply theoretically) infinite copying and sharing of image files over the internet. From this perspective, the *Bridgeman v. Corel* case exposes at least two points of both material and conceptual importance. One is that the transformation from emulsion-based transparency to networked digital image file marks the point at which control over photographs as pieces of property became detached from their accumulation as items in physical and permanent storage. Instead, it became a question of controlling their movements, in the state of "permanent transfer" that equals storage in digital archives,[65] and of keeping them "updated" to ensure their continued accessibility across digital platforms.[66] The second point is that the labor, skill, and judgment expended by pre-digital picture libraries in establishing large collections of reproduction-quality photographs in standardized, easily transmissible formats also produced readymade data sets for extraction and exploitation as online content—at least by those who had the technological apparatus required.

Again, the timing is important. In the late 1990s, as we will see in chapter 4, the picture industry had not quite grasped the enormity of the change that was coming, and purveyors of quality imagery like Bridgeman were still wedded to the format of the transparency. By the early 2000s, however, the dynamics of the industry had changed dramatically in favor of digital search and delivery (on which there will be more to say in chapter 5). If Corel had waited just another couple of years to show an interest in Bridgeman's images, chances are that instead of being taken to court it might have been offered a licensing agreement to digitize the whole collection.

Placing Pictures on the Internet

This alternative approach was in fact taken by Corbis, another North American business venture that in the mid- to late 1990s was engaged in turning photographic reproductions of artworks into "the capital of information technology."[67] While the Corel Corporation had appropriated the photographic reproductions created by Bridgeman for its own purposes without asking, the US-based Corbis Images had been set up to partner directly with museums and art collections under licensing agreements that gave it rights to digitize artworks and distribute digital reproductions of them.[68] Originally conceived by Microsoft's Bill Gates under the name Interactive Home Systems (IHS), the idea behind the enterprise was for people to be able to curate their own exhibitions of digitized pictures—representing originals ranging from Old Master paintings to documentary or stock photographs—on screens displayed in their private homes.[69]

Unlike Corel, Corbis had first tried to claim "a separate copyright protection" in the digital files created from content owned by other rights-holders, on the basis that "the digital reproduction of an artwork or photograph could be considered as fundamentally distinct from the original."[70] This attempt at securing a separate copyright in digital surrogates failed, perhaps for the same reasons that Bridgeman was unable to assert its copyright in photographic reproductions under US law. In retrospect, Gates's initial business model of an interactive display system for the home may be recognized as a sort of streaming service for still images, and thus a precursor to the subscription-based platforms for music and moving images that eventually came to dominate home entertainment in the 2010s. Yet this concept, which would later prove highly successful for other media, never properly came to fruition for Corbis. Combined with the difficulties of coming to acceptable terms with museums as well as their photographers, this failure led the company to change its strategy from making digitized versions of public artworks to gathering existing collections and archives of photographs under its own umbrella.[71]

This meant abandoning the (then) innovative concept of a digital home delivery service for pictures and adopting instead a digital hybrid of two well-established business models of commodity capitalism: the department store, on the one hand, and the picture library, on the other. Announcing itself, fully trademarked, as "*The* Place for Pictures on the Internet," Corbis created an online platform that was to resemble "a department store or a shopping mall" for private customers.[72] Any member of the public with access to the internet and a suitable web browser was here invited to consume digitized imagery in various ways, ranging from purchasing prints and posters or downloading free screensavers to perusing online exhibitions or emailing digital postcards (figure 1.3). Designers, picture researchers, and other "creative professionals" could take a different route from the same online landing page, and enter a virtual picture library made up of more than one million digitized picture files that had been created from the collection of twenty million photographs that Corbis had acquired by the late 1990s. In retrospect, the promotion of Corbis as a one-stop shop in the 1990s prefigured at least two affordances of the web that would be fully realized in the course of the 2000s. The first of these was "the consumption imperative," which Google would eventually put at the heart of all its web-based functionalities.[73] The second was the ability of pictures to keep computer users

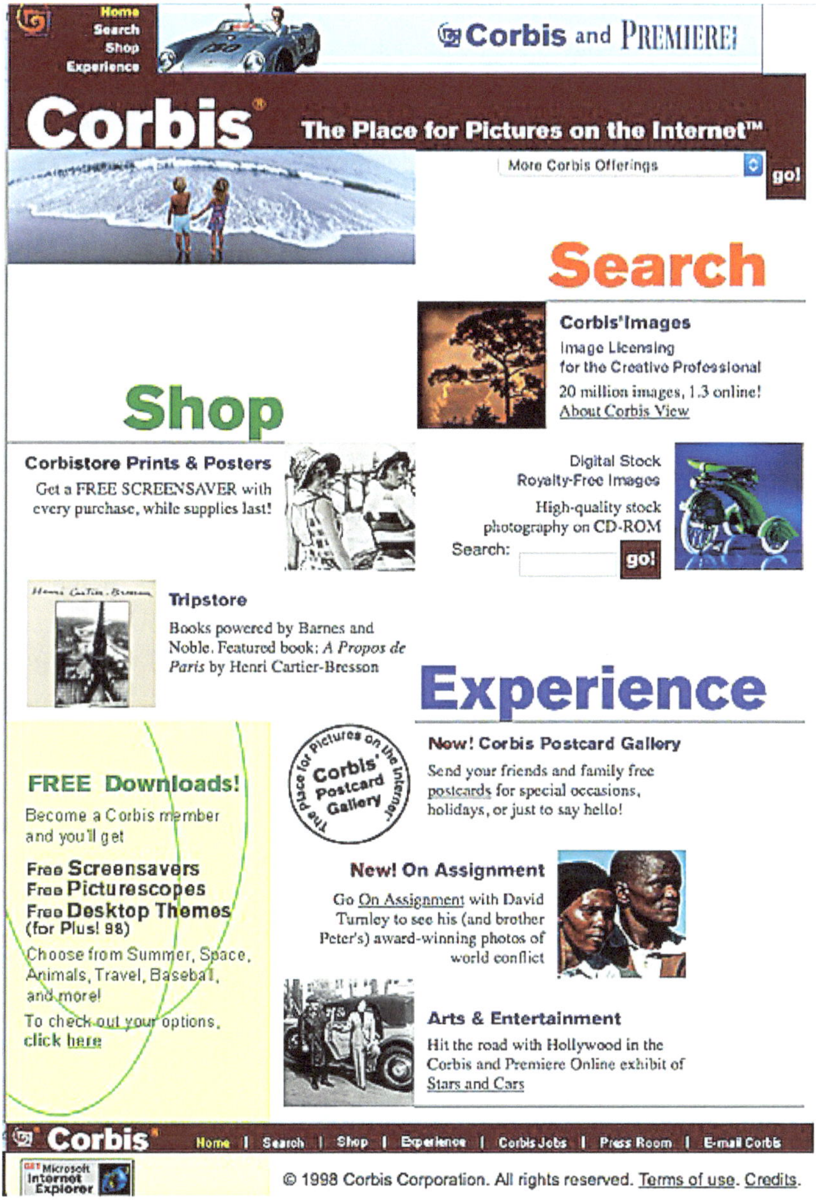

FIGURE 1.3
"The Place for Pictures." Corbis website, July 9, 1998 (screenshot February 28, 2022). The Wayback Machine, https://web.archive.org/web/19980709163614/http://www.corbis.com/.

almost permanently engaged online, thus generating an inexhaustible flow of data traffic that could be monetized far more efficiently than the reproduction rights of any number of digitized library pictures.

For its part, Corel's appropriation of photographic content also exposed home computer users to the valuable affordance of picturability. Once the graphical user interface (GUI) had become a standard feature of personal computers, both users and producers were minded to make more out of its capacities for picturing.[74] In the early years of personal computing, many activities were simply designed as "ways to keep technology busy," as Sherry Turkle has memorably put it.[75] Corel's distribution of low-resolution clip art along with its software can be seen in this light as keeping the graphics card busy, mainly in order to enhance the appeal of personal computing in general, and of Corel's graphics software in particular. Similarly, the CD-ROM format in which the digitized art reproductions were distributed may have been a short-lived format in itself, yet the multimedia experience it presented was "prefigurative" of the web to come, as photo theorists Andrew Dewdney and Frank Boyd predicted back in 1995.[76] By shipping its software together with a readymade digital picture library from which users could help themselves when designing virtual pages, Corel previewed the "infrastructural" role that pictures would soon come to fulfill on the World Wide Web.[77] Bridgeman's lawsuit exposed, even if it did not thematize, the ease with which digitized archival pictures could be dislodged from their original locations or contexts and incorporated into new collections or archives, which could circulate indiscriminately across digital networks.

In this final aspect, Corel's actions were symptomatic of a new economy of sharing, which was emerging both alongside and within the World Wide Web, where the affordances of personal computing (copying and pasting) were mapped onto the hacker ethics of early internet users.[78] This digital sharing economy sought to bypass the very notion of intellectual property under the popularized slogan that "information wants to be free," which is probably less of an ontological statement about information than it is a rationalization of habits formed by a generation of lifelong internet users conceptualizing "all information as potentially a gift."[79] According to this logic, attractively articulated by McKenzie Wark, the "reproducibility" of "the digital" operates in such a way as to make it "neither theft nor property, unless the artifice of the law makes it so."[80] Yet this concept of freely gifted digital reproducibility, when applied to digitized versions of analog "information," fails to recognize the work of intermediation (archiving, preserving, scanning, captioning, file processing) that is required not only for the process of digitization itself to take place, but in order to ensure the information is available to be digitized in the first place.[81] This work of intermediation, which includes conserving, communicating, and commercializing historical pictures like *The Connoisseur*, shows its workings in the digital surrogates and online interfaces that constitute the commodities and marketplaces of the twenty-first-century pictorial economy.

The Digital Afterlife of a Lithograph

So far I have considered *The Connoisseur* as a representative piece of pre-photographic printed ephemera: a mass-produced commodity made for circulation in the fast-moving pictorial economy of early nineteenth-century London. I have unpacked the significance of the print as a representative of the lithographic process, suggesting that it also works as an allegory of this particular form of printmaking, which effaces virtually all visible trace of the printmaker in the picture itself. The historical context of its material production also provided the background for my reading of the print as a piece of intellectual property, the authorship and thus extractive potential of which was carefully divided among the three men named on the print itself. This was in keeping both with the legal provisions of the Engravers' Acts that were in force at the time of its publication in 1830 and with the workarounds that mutually dependent communities of practice had devised to maximize their benefits from this legislation.

In accordance with the terms of the 1777 Engravers' Act (17 Geo. III, c. 57), *The Connoisseur* fell into the public domain when its protected term of twenty-eight years' copyright ended in 1858. At that point, this most carefully authored picture found itself free to be captured or appropriated by whomever, for whatever purpose. It is impossible to know now the extent to which the print was first distributed, and even less how it might have been disseminated after its copyright term ran out, but what we do know is that several copies survived into the twentieth century and beyond. I have been able to identify four such extant items, all of which have at some point been digitized and circulated online. One copy is held in the John Johnson Collection of printed ephemera at the Bodleian Library in Oxford; a second is to be found at the Minneapolis Institute of Art (MIA); a third belongs to a private collector at an undisclosed location; and a fourth resides in the archives of the Mary Evans Picture Library in London. Each of these extant copies of *The Connoisseur* and their corresponding digitized surrogates reside in, and thus exemplify, different kinds of repositories that afford different levels of access to the picture. The work of intermediation therefore reveals itself in different ways across the respective interfaces that grant access to these digitized objects.

The Oxford copy forms part of an academic research collection within a major university library. A small digitized version of it is displayed on the home page of the digital library guide to the John Johnson Collection (figure 1.4), which is aimed at students and researchers at the University of Oxford. In order to access a high-resolution file, however, it is necessary to have institutional privileges or a subscription to the ProQuest database in which it is stored. Both of these interfaces underline the status of the library as a custodian of historical documents that are being guarded and preserved for the purposes of study and research.

The digitized surrogate of the MIA print, by contrast, is freely available as a high-res file on the museum's own website, where it can be studied in close detail using digital tools for zooming and scrolling (figure 1.5).[82] This online collection display further includes a wide range of catalog information about the item, such as medium, size, and provenance, which would be important to students and scholars who might use the website for research purposes. Interactive features in these displays of metadata invite further exploration of the collection database, while clickable icons for downloading, printing, and sharing are conducive to appropriation and creative engagement with the digitized object. Just like the original print had been adapted to the scrapbook, a key social and creative medium of its own time, this digital surrogate has in other words been adapted both for contemporary social media and for online research practices.

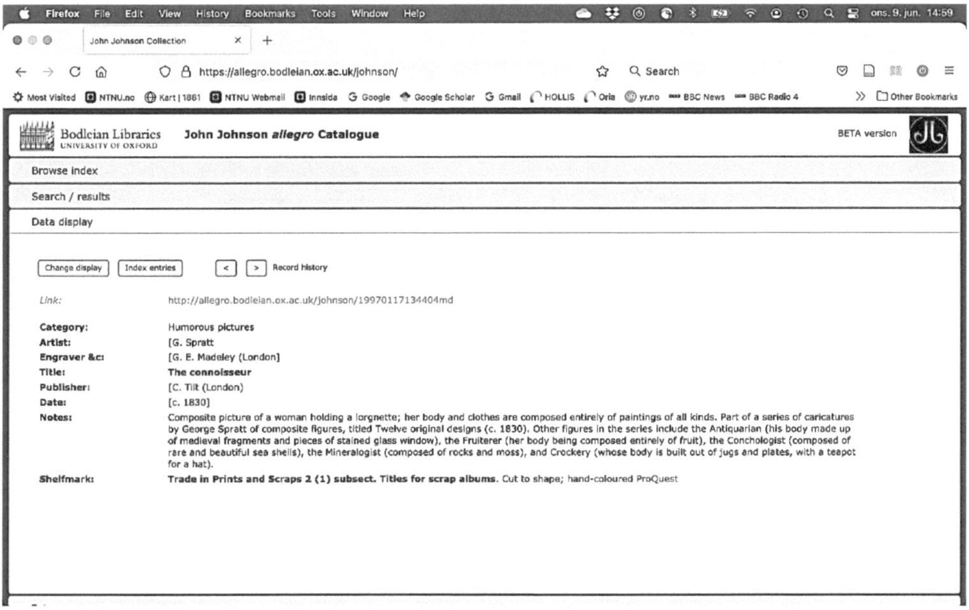

FIGURE 1.4
The Connoisseur catalog view (screenshot June 9, 2021). John Johnson Collection, https://allegro.bodleian.ox.ac.uk/johnson/19970117134404md.

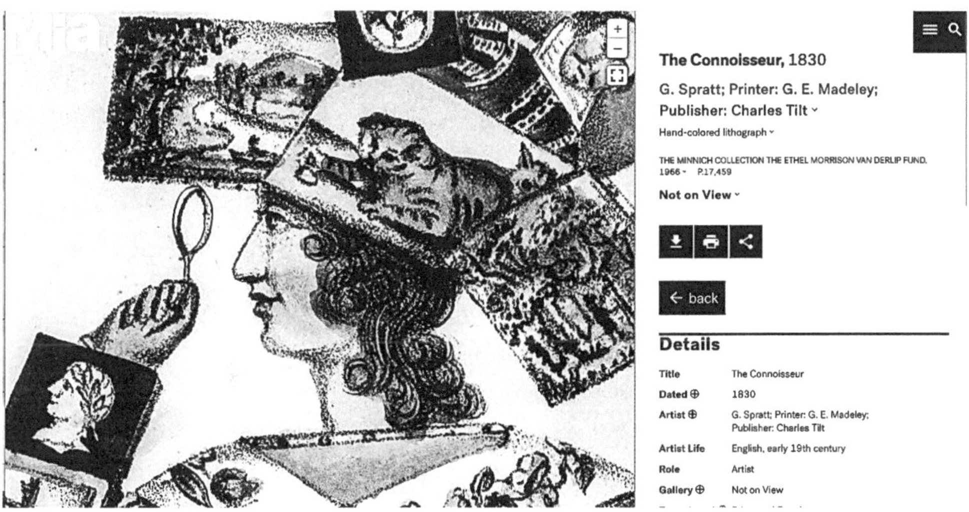

FIGURE 1.5
The Connoisseur detail view (screenshot June 27, 2021). Minneapolis Institute of Art, https://collections.artsmia.org/art/77469/the-connoisseur-g-spratt.

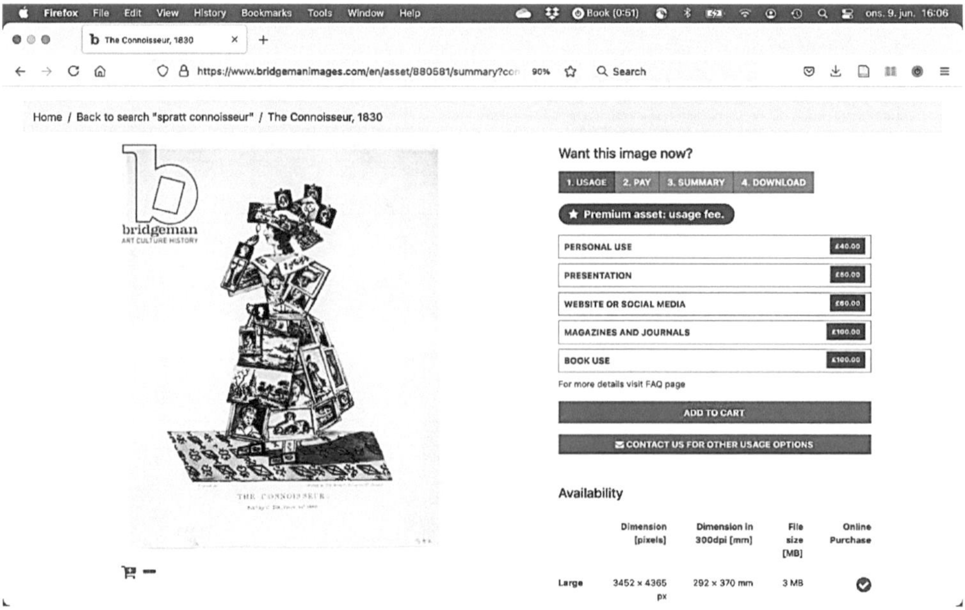

FIGURE 1.6
The Connoisseur search result view (screenshot June 9, 2021). Bridgeman Images, https://www.bridgemanimages.com/en/search?filter_text=spratt%20connoisseur%20&filter_group=all&filter_region=NOR&sort=most_popular.

The comprehensive online presentation of *The Connoisseur* underscores the status of the original print as a museum object, while at the same time opening up for engaging personally and creatively with its digital surrogate in a manner that harks back to its origins in nineteenth-century popular visual culture. It also signals the publicly funded art institution's double mission to serve both the general public and the scholarly community on a not-for-profit basis. Producing and maintaining a large online collection with high-resolution illustrations and frequently updated catalog information nevertheless requires the work of many professionals—web designers, programmers, curators, scanning operators, computer maintenance workers—whose labor is not free.

This may go some way to explain why the same digital surrogate, alongside those of more than 4,000 other items in the MIA collection, is offered for licensed reproduction through Bridgeman Images (figure 1.6). This platform, which is the fully digitized and most recent incarnation of our old acquaintance, the Bridgeman Art Library, locates *The Connoisseur* in an online environment that is very different from the museum website, even though both are platforms for searching and viewing artworks. Here, the picture appears in low resolution and with a Bridgeman watermark, billed as a "premium asset," and is accompanied by a price list as well as a list of available file sizes.[83] Compared to the affordances of the MIA website, which to some extent reconstruct by digital means the opportunities for personal appropriation and play with paper that were enjoyed by the lithograph's users and audiences in the 1830s, the Bridgeman platform reinserts *The Connoisseur* into a digital version of its earliest context of reception: the marketplace for pictures.

The same goes, to some extent, for a third and privately held copy of the print, which was put up for auction at Bonhams during the summer of 2020, but returned unsold to its owner when it failed to fetch the desired price.[84] And it is certainly the case for the fourth and final copy, which is held by the Mary Evans Picture Library (MEPL) in London. The picture library licenses reproduction rights to *The Connoisseur*, just like Bridgeman Images. It has also stamped its ownership on the picture in an unusual way, presenting and promoting it under the alternative and wholly anachronistic title of "Picture Library Girl." Since the 1970s, the figure covered in pictures has functioned as a totemic image for MEPL and its mainly female staff of picture librarians, and it appeared prominently in a piece of self-promotion by the picture library that I will examine in closer detail in chapter 3. For now, suffice to say that MEPL's appropriation of *The Connoisseur* demonstrates how historical pictures, once strictly circumscribed by the intellectual property laws of their own day, eventually form part of a visual commons from which anyone can help themself, extracting new kinds of value through new acts of capture, accumulation, and transmission.

Conclusion

The eighteenth-century Engravers' Acts had forged a profitable link between rights and reproducibility when they enshrined the value of an original design or image as a function of its inscription in a reproducible medium. This recognized and formalized the mutually beneficial bond between artists and the intermediaries who enabled their works to reach an audience. In the first half of the nineteenth century, photography dispensed with the skill of drawing as a prerequisite for the creation of original images, compressing the operations of capture and reproduction into one and the same medium. In this respect the new technology destabilized the relationship between originals and their reproductions, or between authors and reproducers. Although photography to some extent disintermediated the function of the illustrator, it by no means dispensed with the intermediary services of either printer or publisher. Photography did enable the production and reproduction of pictures and text on an unprecedented scale in the course of the nineteenth century, but not through one unified version of the medium. Rather, one set of photographic technologies enabled a rapid expansion of picture-making, through the development of cameras, emulsions, support formats, and retail systems, while another set of photomechanical technologies enabled an increased output of printed commodity forms, incorporating illustrations that may or may not have been produced by means of photographic capture. In short, by the end of the nineteenth century, photography had made it easier to make pictures, and photomechanical printing had made it easier to disseminate pictures together with text. At this point, a niche in the pictorial economy opened up for a new kind of intermediary to facilitate transactions between producers of pictures, on the one hand, and reproducers of pictures, on the other. Enter the picture library.

2

How Picture Libraries Worked

Picture libraries both were and were not like other libraries. First proposed by Oliver Wendell Holmes in 1859 as a public picture distribution service on the model of lending libraries, the term *picture library* may conjure up the idea of a public or at least nonprofit institution.[1] Yet in the twentieth century it first and foremost came to denote a commercial business.[2] Inspired by the ambulatory infrastructure of circulating libraries, rather than architectural edifices for the storing and reading of books, picture libraries were both products of and agents in a rapidly expanding pictorial economy.[3] From the late 1940s to the mid-1970s this was fueled by accelerated demand for illustrated "commodity forms," ranging from daily newspapers and weekly and monthly magazines to illustrated books and television programs.[4] In these decades, developments in infrastructures, technologies, and markets for photographs took place at several levels simultaneously.

At a macro level, manifestations could be identified in the shape of an expanding market for illustrations, created by the steadily growing advertising and publishing industries. This development was in its turn tied to the widespread adoption of halftone screen printing, as well as the expansion of reliable airmail services and telecommunications systems facilitating access to picture sources from across the globe. At the micro level, which is the focus of this chapter, individual picture libraries and press agencies strove to catalog, index, and cross-reference their holdings in ways that would help researchers locate the most relevant pictures in their files in the shortest time possible. In the middle, there emerged a meso level of interfaces between micro-level and macro-level actors, through the foundation of specialist organizations and the publication of directories and handbooks, which will be further explored in the next chapter.

In his tentative periodization of stock photography, Paul Frosh has called the long period from the invention of photography up until the 1970s as "a 'primitive' age," when "stock photography barely exists, or exists only in potential."[5] Throughout this period, the cultural functions of what was later to be labeled stock photography were supplied, in his words, by "an inchoate mass of small agencies serving a diverse range of sectors and purposes," with no conception of themselves as a specific sector of business as such.[6] Around the mid-twentieth century, however, and especially from the 1950s onward, there was a discernible tendency toward consolidation, whereby smaller agencies and collections were incorporated into larger libraries or meta-collections. The same period saw a professional discourse about practices of accumulation, extraction, and transmission developing among custodians of both public and commercial picture collections. In this chapter, two documents produced and distributed in different media exemplify how this discourse found expression in the UK picture business around 1950.[7] The first example is an article from 1950, aimed at a readership of librarians and documentation specialists, which describes the classification and retrieval system of the Hulton Picture Post Library. The second is a promotional photograph from the Keystone Press Agency, dated 1951, which includes an explanatory caption about the workings of its picture library. Analyzing these documents reveals details of not just how picture libraries functioned but also how they were designed to function, as settings in which the work of intermediation could be carried out with speed and efficiency.

This chapter focuses on the picture library as a central unit of production in the pictorial economy of the early postwar period. Exploring two different but related examples from the 1950s, it shows how picture librarians worked to accumulate collections; devise classification systems; optimize filing, search, and retrieval practices; and promote the value of their services to meet the accelerated demand for photographically mediated illustration by the press, publishing, and advertising industries. Through close readings of two texts that each describe the operations of a picture library—the Hulton Picture Post Library and the Keystone Press Agency—an idealized picture emerges of the library as an efficient machinery for the accumulation, extraction, and transmission of pictures, staffed by a skilled and educated workforce. On this basis, the chapter can be read as a contribution to a yet-to-be-written labor history of the photographic industry in the twentieth century. It could and should also be read as contributing to what Lisa Gitelman calls "a deeper history of sorts" for the important recent work carried out within critical information studies and critical data studies, which traces the historical and human factors that have shaped contemporary digital practices.[8]

Library Services as a Business

All kinds of libraries see it as their mission to accumulate and look after collections of items in order to transmit them, either to contemporary users/readers or to future generations. The twentieth-century picture library had the added—indeed, often primary—mission of extracting profit from its collections.[9] In order to do this, it must transform the pictorial contents of its files into another commodity form, which we might call intermediary or transitional: the kind of commodities that either constitute the content or augment the value of consumer commodities. Yet unlike the goods traded in regular commodities markets—natural resources like oil and gold, or agricultural products like grain or livestock—pictorial content is not used up once it has been used. "Images can be used, and reused, in a way most consumer goods cannot," as Andrew Ross has pointed out, and therefore "'consuming' a Pepsi ad is quite different from consuming a can of Pepsi."[10] Once picture libraries had established their worth as intermediaries between photographers and mass-media outlets in need of illustrative or documentary material, the "reuse value" of images emerged as perhaps their most significant revenue stream.[11] Accordingly, the pictures stocked by picture libraries were available "for rent," not for purchase, and certainly not to borrow.[12] Picture libraries were providing content as a service, in other words, decades before cloud computing popularized the concept.

The picture library business model may be summed up in one word: intermediation. In economics, an "intermediary" is broadly defined as "an economic agent that purchases from suppliers for resale to buyers or that helps buyers and sellers meet and transact."[13] This is as precise a description as any of the basic purpose of a picture library, which is to accumulate pictures and transmit them to potential viewers. According to Daniel Spulber, the work of intermediation adds value to a product by "transporting, storing, repackaging, assembling, preparing for final use, and adding information and guarantees."[14] This description of services corresponds to the full gamut of picture library tasks, from collecting, classifying, captioning, and indexing, via filing, storing, and conserving, to copying, displaying, distributing, and licensing. The value added by these intermediary acts together justified the payment extracted by picture libraries from clients, the accumulated profit from which was, in business terms, what made a picture library viable.

Although she does not enlist this concept of intermediation as developed by economics, the photo historian Estelle Blaschke has given a detailed account of the picture library as a business model that demonstrates its relevance. In her study of the Bettmann Archive, a legendary picture collection founded in the 1930s by Dr. Otto Bettmann (1903–1998), Blaschke has noted that its promotional literature emphasized the thoroughness and navigability of its classification system over the impact of its pictures.[15] This was due to Bettmann's realization, as a trained librarian, that in the commercial market for photographic reproductions the monetization of photographs was predicated on the "indexability" of the photographic image rather than its indexicality.[16] The index card catalog was "a fundamental component of the company's capital" from its inception in Berlin in 1933 and the essential factor that enabled Bettmann quickly to resume his business, and eventually realize the full potential of it, after arriving in New York as a refugee from Nazi Germany in 1935.[17]

Bettmann's catalog index was developed from the book classification systems he had learned as an art librarian and adapted to the visual character of the items in his picture collection, among other things by the inclusion of a miniature reproduction of the image—a "thumbnail"—attached to the index card.[18] In a newsletter to clients issued in 1941, as quoted by Blaschke, Bettmann extolled the efficiency of the index card system in the following terms: "It takes us exactly 60 seconds to check out files. . . . The secret of this rapid-fire service is revealed by the card index. . . . This specialized index enables us to answer specific questions and assemble pictures in a very short time."[19] For the first thirty years or so that it was in business, access to the Bettmann Archive for its clients was effectively mediated by lists of words.

In the mid-1960s, however, Bettmann "hatched rather a grandiose scheme," in his own words, and decided to "make the Archive itself the subject of a book," which would be self-published under the title *The Bettmann Portable Archive*.[20] The intention of the book was "to serve both as a pictorial encyclopedia and as a catalog of what we had to offer," enabling customers "to draw inspiration in absentia from our files."[21] As it included the classification number for each image reproduced, the *Portable Archive* also functioned much in the same way as mail-order catalogs of the same period, with the important difference that it was not freely distributed but had to be bought.[22] In the paradoxical title of the book, Blaschke recognizes "the intentions and business philosophy of the Bettmann Archive quite accurately," arguing that it captures the contradiction between the circulation of commodities and the preservation of cultural heritage that Otto Bettmann seemed to resolve with such remarkable success.[23]

Another paradoxical impression derived from Blaschke's account is Bettmann's emphasis on the speedy delivery of old pictures. As the name of the business already indicated, the Bettmann Archive did not first and foremost deal in newsworthy images, even if it did eventually acquire a news agency arm. The vast majority of Bettmann imagery was of a historical or generic kind, frequently accumulated by the photographic copying of pictures reproduced in library books, a practice that Bettmann himself described as "free[ing]" images from their enclosure in books and periodicals.[24] The Bettmann Archive in many ways pioneered this particular version of the picture library business model, which for the most part used photography to recapture and accumulate previously existing images and claim ownership in their reproductions as new pieces of intellectual property.

In view of the relative timelessness of its content, then, the repeated references to speed and efficiency in Otto Bettmann's promotional writings were likely meant to communicate something about the character of the business itself, as opposed to the commodities of which it was a purveyor. On the one hand, this could be tied to professional standards of librarianship, the profession within which Otto Bettmann was trained. On the other hand, it can be read as a recognition of the commercial standards operated by the publishing and advertising industries, to which the Bettmann Archive was catering. Blaschke's analysis of Bettmann's US-based business indicates that its success derived from his ability to enlist the first set of standards in the service of the second. The case studies I examine below similarly show how the information management systems of two UK picture libraries were publicized as defining features and key selling points of each business. Together they conjure up a picture industry in which both suppliers and buyers were increasingly "entranced by efficiency."[25]

SOAKING IN PICTURES: THE HULTON PICTURE POST LIBRARY

The first example is an article on the organization of the Hulton Picture Post Library, written by Charles Harvard Gibbs-Smith (1909–1981) and published in the *Journal of Documentation* in 1950.[26] Known in his later years as an aviation historian, Gibbs-Smith spent most of his professional life at the Victoria and Albert Museum in London, where, among other things, he curated the 1939 exhibition celebrating the centenary of the invention of photography.[27] During the Second World War he directed the Photograph Division of the UK Ministry of Information, and was thus in charge of providing visual propaganda material for both the UK government and the Allied Forces, before returning to the V&A as Keeper of Museum Extension Services after the war.

In 1947 Gibbs-Smith had been asked (he did not specify by whom) to devise a classification system for the Hulton Picture Post Library, which contained among its holdings the visual archive of the well-known UK magazine *Picture Post*. By the time his article outlining and evaluating the plans behind this picture library appeared, three years later, Gibbs-Smith claimed to have already planned several other "large photo libraries," and as a result of which "come to the conclusion that every library has to be treated individually and that no standard system can be imposed for the sake of standardization." The main criterion that any picture library must fulfill, according to Gibbs-Smith, was to "be organised for its users, not its librarians." In the case of the Hulton Picture Post Library, it not only served the various titles owned by the publishing group that ran it, but also made its contents available "for the general use of the British Press and publishers."[28]

At the time of publication, the Hulton reportedly held "over four million items" and was still expanding, with some time yet to go until it would reach the "ten million items, and possibly more" for which Gibbs-Smith had been told to prepare it. Not only was the library and its classification system intended to "cover every 'picturable' activity and topic in existence, to-day or in the past"; it also contained "pictures" in practically every medium of visual reproduction as yet invented, from "prints, engravings, and lithographs" to "photographs; post-cards; illustrations from books; and press-cuttings." The Hulton Picture Post Library was in other words a huge repository of visual and textual data, from which its users in the daily and weekly press expected to extract relevant information with almost immediate results. This "overriding" concern, that "a press library must produce the largest possible number of pictures on any given topic in the shortest possible time," meant that the principles of "much established library practice" must be sacrificed in the service of "organised expediency."[29]

In his recommendation for classification and retrieval systems to be designed with a view to the needs of end users, rather than system operators, Gibbs-Smith was an early exponent of a topic that has been repeatedly raised by writers on picture librarianship and other kinds of visual resource management.[30] And yet the fact that the classification system was being operated by human beings was a crucial factor in his design recommendations. In profound acknowledgment that it was people using their own memory as a primary working tool who would be rifling through the library's holdings day in and day out, he argued that letters were a better basis for a fast-working classificatory system than numbers: "The human eye and brain, when tired (or fresh), will obviously make far fewer errors in sorting three letters, which by their spelling and familiarity immediately suggest the subject, than in sorting on the basis of impersonal numbers."[31] The three-letter code system, which, for instance, meant that "funerals were under FUN, singing was under SIN," could, according to one former employee, also cause inadvertent merriment among staff, no doubt functioning as an additional mnemo-technic aid (see figure 2.1).[32]

Aside from technical questions of classification principles and image retrieval aids, Gibbs-Smith also made recommendations on the quality of staff: "if the best is to be had of a picture library," he claimed, the people working in it should have "a high standard of education" and access to "an extensive reference library of books." Among the twenty-four members of staff at the Hulton library in 1950, around half were educated to university level, including those in charge of the main classificatory sections and all those working as "classifiers" within each section. In addition to these graduate-level positions, the library employed "a number of 'cross-referencers' and filers," plus staff involved in darkroom processing and tasks related to the physical dispatch and receipt of material to and from clients.[33]

A metaphor that crops up repeatedly in Gibbs-Smith's account of the Hulton Picture Post Library is that of picture librarians being "soaked in their material." In other words, picture librarians should be looking *for* pictures chiefly by means of looking *at* pictures, "otherwise the immense visual experience necessary in a picture librarian is never built up." Accordingly, the textual information—metadata, if you like—about pictures must be kept in the same place as the pictures, with classificatory codes typically pasted to the back of prints, along with their captions, while "the main divisions and symbols could be easily learnt and retained in memory." Visual aids such as color-coding and large-sized letters for the main sections were further examples of archive-technical solutions that made image retrieval not only faster, for the sake of users, but also less eye-straining for the picture librarians. In direct contrast to the approach advocated by Otto Bettmann, as cited above, the visually oriented search methods advocated by Gibbs-Smith led him to recommend "against a detailed subject card-index," on the grounds that it was difficult to maintain internal consistency and "almost impossible to put right" if brought in disarray, and not least that it would take "librarians away from the picture material in which they must continually soak themselves to be of any real service to the clients."[34]

In the concluding section of the article Gibbs-Smith also identified typical challenges that any picture library would inevitably face. The

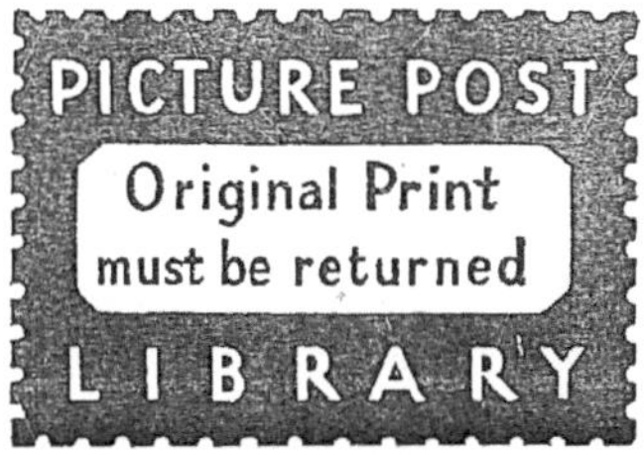

Fig. 1. Standard Owner's Label

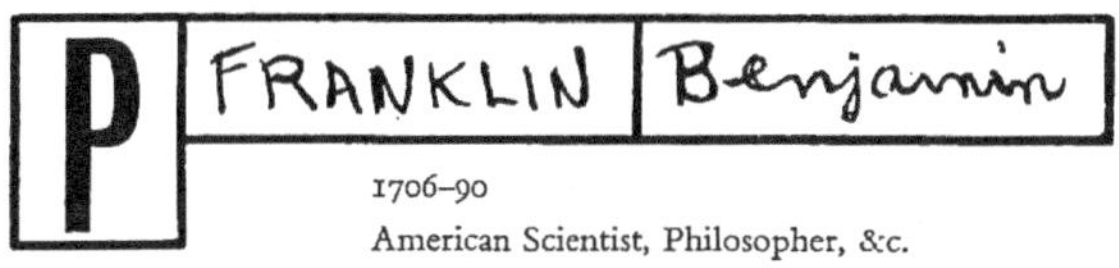

Fig. 2. Portrait Section (in Red)

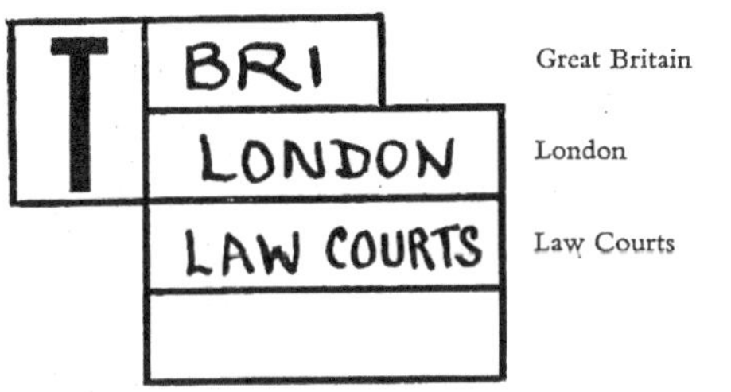

Fig. 3. Topography Section (in Green)

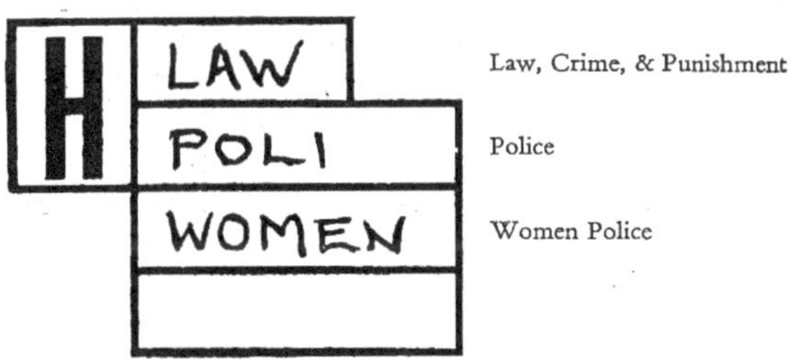

Fig. 4. Historical Section (in Blue)

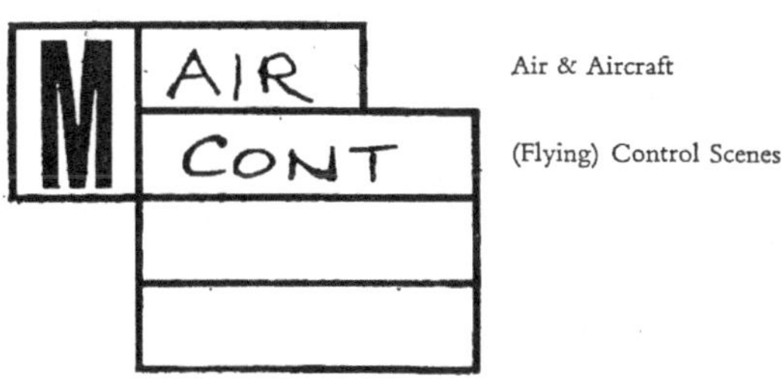

FIGURE 2.1
Facsimile of Gibbs-Smith classification system. From *Journal of Documentation* 6 (1950).

first of these was the problem of there simply existing too many pictures of potential relevance to any given subject, and the related problem of users having too vague an idea of what they are looking for, so that it required "much turning over of pictures for the idea to crystallise in the light of the available material." The second "occupational disease" was "the inadequacy and inaccuracy of the captions inherited from other days and other libraries."[35] If one were inclined to believe, then, that image overload and messy or unreliable metadata were occupational diseases of internet-based image searching in the twenty-first century, reading Gibbs-Smith convinces one that, in fact, these are hereditary conditions carried over from the pre-digital data management of picture libraries.

A useful way to conceptualize classification systems, in picture libraries and elsewhere, is to think of them as a "scripts" to be performed by picture librarians and archivists.[36] In his article about the Hulton Picture Post Library, Gibbs-Smith presented one such script, tailored to site-specific performance, we might say, within the library he had designed himself. Otto Bettmann advocated a different approach, through his presentation of the ideal index card, although, as Blaschke reports, this script was rarely performed verbatim. These systems and recommendations were devised with a similar intention to that which has motivated any number of archive manuals, with the important difference that the picture libraries designed by Gibbs-Smith and Bettmann were intended to serve rather different purposes than the archives described in the Dutch Manual and other prescriptive works on classical archival practice.[37]

For instance, the notion of "original order," which runs through most paper-based archives, decrees that archives of different origins must not be "mixed with the archives of other creators, or placed into artificial arrangements based on chronology, geography, or subject."[38] Observing this principle would not improve the functionality of a picture library devised for busy members of the press, as envisaged by Gibbs-Smith, and would frequently be of direct hindrance if the main purpose of a collection is to realize the maximum commercial potential of the maximum number of pictures, as the Bettmann Archive sought to do.[39] Nevertheless, as both the Hulton Picture Post Library in London and the Bettmann Archive in New York expanded on a regular basis by acquiring other collections in their entirety, original order would often be inadvertently respected anyway, for reasons of sheer material overload.

Since it was impractical to re-catalog huge collections of items that were already organized according to their own internal order, meta-collections like the Hulton would eventually have a number of classification systems running alongside each other. An unintended consequence of this was that library collections eventually took on the characteristics of archives, in which information might be gleaned not just *through* the documents available—say, a photograph of an office interior from the 1950s providing insight into office furniture and clerical staff hairstyles of the period—but also *about* the documents themselves, such as where the photograph came from, where it had been previously filed or published, when it had changed ownership, and, in later years, whether and when it had been digitized.[40] The next item of analysis provides a striking example of this phenomenon.

How a Picture Library Worked: Keystone Press Agency

One of the large collections that was absorbed by the Hulton Picture Post Library, complete with its own cataloging system, was the holdings of the Keystone Press Agency in London. The illustrations reproduced here as figures 2.2 and 2.3 display two sides of the same archival photographic print originating from this collection. Like *The Connoisseur* in chapter 1, this photograph captioned "Picture Library" functions as a metapicture that helps to reflect both on the settings and activities pictured within it and on the wider pictorial economy in which it has circulated, both in its paper-based print form and as a digital surrogate.

The paper print is currently held by the Hulton Archive in London, which is the historical archives division of the global visual content provider, Getty Images, and the most recent incarnation of the Hulton Picture Post Library. This forms the core of an enormous meta-collection that since the 1990s has incorporated a long succession of other historical collections. In April 2020 its total holdings were estimated at around 80 million prints and negatives, of which roughly 1 percent had been digitized and made available online.[41]

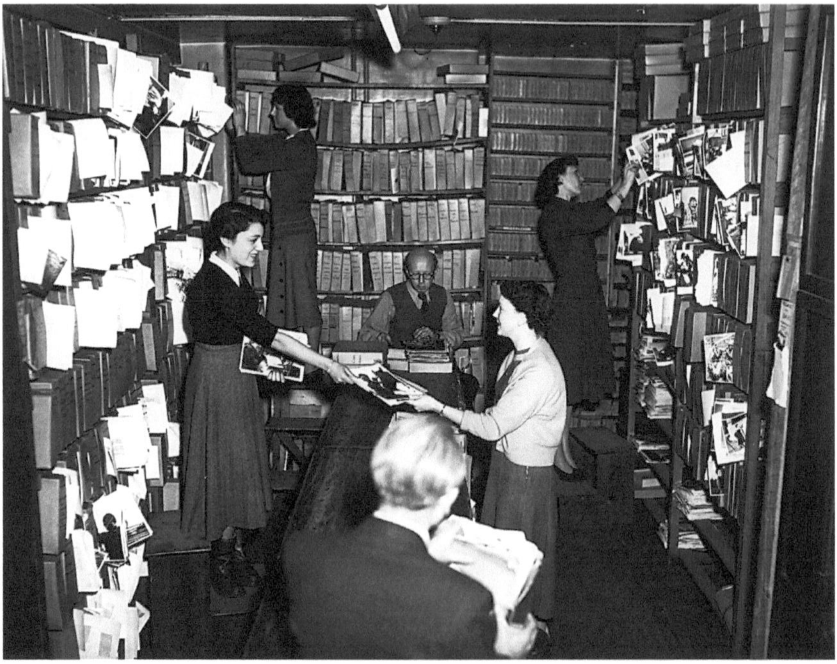

FIGURE 2.2
"Picture Library," recto. Keystone Picture Library. 1951. Photographer: Fred Ramage/ Getty Images.

09753428

KEY SUB	PROFESSIONS LIBRARIANS BOX 703	KEY FS8290-3

1951

How a Picture Library Works

Good general knowledge, an interest in current affairs and a good memory are just three of the virtues which go to make up an efficient picture library assistant. Do you want photographic documents for the illustration of your book, for illustrated magazines, for your advertising scheme or for lecture purposes. do you want show or greeting cards, or a life size photograph of the Dali Lama for display purposes, or for reference from which to draw, paint or sculpture General MacArthur. Or perhaps you are looking for a series of photographs on the domestic life of the flea for a film strip. Whatever you are looking for in pictures, it's more than possible you will find it among the 100,000 negatives and the million odd prints filed away in the picture library of **Keystone Press Agency**, one of the world's most practical picture libraries. Chief Librarian, Martin Prince, has developed a unique power for memorising the photographs in his vast stock and his assistants, by using the time saving cross-index system, are proud of their ability to produce the required picture in a short time.
Pictures are constantly pouring into Keystone library from all parts of the world perpetuating for all time historic events and the march of progress.
O.P.S: A section of the photographic library where experienced staff are busy filing stock prints in boxes under subject headings.

KEY FEATURES

HG HULTON GETTY

Copyright

PLEASE RETURN TO AND CREDIT HULTON GETTY
UNIQUE HOUSE 21-31 WOODFIELD ROAD LONDON W9 2BA
TEL 0171 266 2662 FAX 0171 266 3154

FIGURE 2.3
"Picture Library," verso. Keystone Picture Library. 1951. Facsimile from Getty Images.

Among the materials that have been digitized is the image on the emulsion-coated front, or recto, of the print (figure 2.2), which can be located in the editorial section of the Getty Images website (gettyimages.com). The black and white photograph shows people at work in a small, chaotic room stacked floor to ceiling with shelves and box files, among which numerous photographic prints are sticking out. In the online version, it carries the main caption "Picture Library" and the following, more detailed description: "November 1951: A busy scene in Keystone Press Agency picture library which stores 100,000 negatives and a large collection of prints. (Photo by Fred Ramage/Keystone Features/Getty Images)." The reverse side, or verso, of the print from which this digital surrogate was produced shows a longer, more detailed caption, as well as a number of letter codes and stamps (figure 2.3). The most eye-catching elements on this side of the print are the boxes arranged in a grid in the top left-hand corner, carrying the two three-letter codes "KEY" and "SUB" plus the keywords "Professions—Librarians—Box 703," and the stamp in the bottom right-hand corner claiming "Copyright" on behalf of "Hulton Getty." These two elements correspond to the "ownership label" and "grid stamp" specified by Gibbs-Smith as essential features of the technical classification system in a picture library (figure 2.1).[42] Between these stamps or labels appear the date 1951, as well as a longer text, under the heading "How a Picture Library Works":

> Good general knowledge, an interest in current affairs and a good memory are just three of the virtues which go to make up an efficient picture library assistant. Do you want photographic documents for the illustration of your book, for illustrated magazines, for your advertising scheme or for lecture purposes. Do you want show or greeting cards, or a life size photograph of the Dali [*sic!*] Lama for display purposes, or for reference from which to draw, paint or sculpture General MacArthur. Or perhaps you are looking for a series of photographs on the domestic life of the flea for a film strip. Whatever you are looking for in pictures, it's more than possible you will find it among the 100,000 negatives and the million odd prints filed away in the picture library of Keystone Press Agency, one of the world's most practical picture libraries. Chief Librarian, Martin Prince, has developed a unique power for memorising the photographs in his vast stock and his assistants, by using the time-saving cross-index system, are proud of their ability to produce the required picture in a short time.

> Pictures are constantly pouring into Keystone library from all parts of the world perpetuating for all time historic events and the march of progress.
>
> O.P.S. A section of the photographic library where experienced staff are busy filing stock prints in boxes under subject headings.

Together, the two sides of the print form a historical document from which can be gleaned information both about the postwar picture library business in general and about the specific picture library in, for, and about which it was produced. The immediate effect of the caption is to support a reading of the photograph as a visual record of the layout and organization of the picture library at the Keystone Press Agency, as well as of the people working in it, at the time the picture was taken in 1951. On closer reading, the long discursive caption is clearly a promotional text extolling not just the contents of Keystone's files but also the skills and abilities of its workers and the efficiency of its production line. In this capacity it provides a textual snapshot of a successful picture library in the postwar decades, which is immediately recognizable from the description provided in the article by Gibbs-Smith, discussed previously in this chapter. In addition to boasting of its knowledgeable staff, efficient retrieval system, and international networks of acquisition as well as distribution, the caption also gives a glimpse of the wide range of clients, from publishers and advertisers to merchandisers, lecturers, and artists, who made use of the agency's services and products.

Keystone Press Agency had been founded in the United States during the First World War through the merger of Keystone View Company, a Pennsylvania company that had specialized in lantern slides and stereographs since the 1890s, and Press Illustrating Service, which furnished the New York press with newsworthy photographs.[43] Its instigator was the Hungarian-born Bert Garai (1890–1973), who is probably best described as a press entrepreneur. He was never really a journalist or photographer as such, although he happily turned his hand to both writing and photography, but more of a fixer, editor, manager, and, perhaps above all, a salesperson. Having started out in 1914 translating photo captions from French and German into English for the US distribution of photographs supplied by European agencies, Garai persuaded the US owner of Keystone to let him open a press agency in London soon after the war ended in 1918, and in the course of the 1920s and 1930s he expanded the European side of the business to include offices in Berlin, Paris, and Vienna—all managed by "brothers and nephews."[44] By the late 1930s, Garai had managed to buy out his former boss and business companion in the United States and headed the international network of agencies all by himself. The photograph reproduced as figure 2.2 is credited to Fred Ramage (1900–1981), who, not coincidentally, was a staff photographer at Keystone from the 1920s to the 1960s and dubbed by Garai as "one of the best cameramen on Fleet Street."[45]

From his first job translating captions, Garai claimed quickly to have learned that "the value of something depends to a considerable extent on *what you call* it."[46] Avoiding the hard-sell tactics of his colleagues and competitors, he apparently developed a special knack for writing precisely the sort of "extended 'caption'" that, in his own words, "added weight to the photograph" in a way that material from competing agencies did not.[47] Another way of putting it might be to say that where other agencies wrote picture captions, Garai wrote newspaper-ready copy. This is a good example of how the value added by the intermediating function of a picture agency is what turns a photograph into the commodity that is an agency picture, a commodity of which the image in itself is only one component.[48]

Against this background, the extended caption on the back of the print showing picture librarians at work in the Keystone files may be read today as more like the sort of text we would classify as "advertorial," that is to say, advertising disguised to look like editorial content. Reading the text as a piece of promotional literature, it is instructive to consider which aspects of the Keystone business operation it emphasizes. For instance, there is a striking abundance of adjectives and adverbs relating to time and efficiency: the library and/or its staff (figure 2.3) are described as "efficient," "practical," and "time-saving." This seems to indicate that Keystone and its clients both valued efficiency and expediency above most other qualities. Yet the use of words such as "knowledge," "memory," "memorising," "ability," and "experienced" underscore that speed did not compromise quality and thoroughness.

It was common in the pre-digital era of news photography to distinguish between "fast" and "good" photographs, as Zeynep Devrim Gürsel

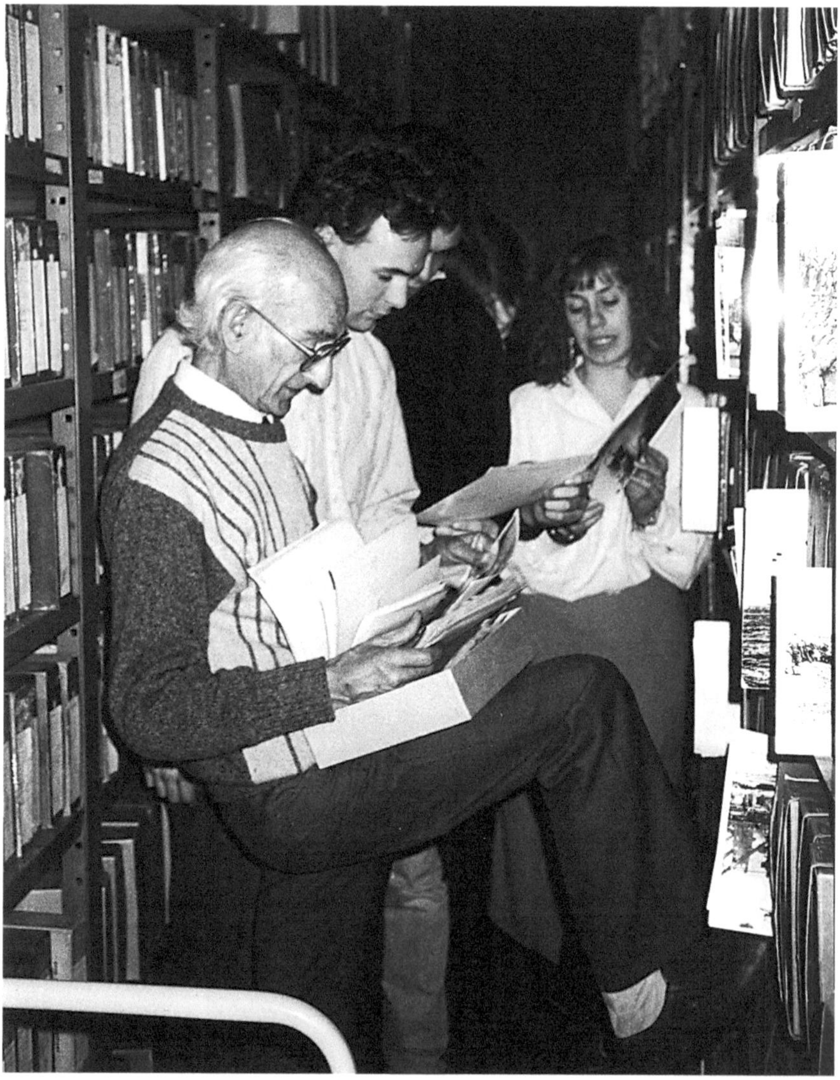

FIGURE 2.4
Researchers examining photos in the archive boxes files in the Keystone library stacks. Circa 1985. Photo by Hulton Archive/Getty Images.

has documented.[49] What the Keystone agency seems to communicate through this caption is that it provides a service that is both speedy *and* high-quality. Additionally, by mentioning how new material is "constantly pouring" in from across the globe, "perpetuating for all time historic events and the march of progress," Keystone draws specific attention to itself as a linchpin not only in a worldwide network but also in a historical chain of events. Another clear impression is that most of the qualities emphasized in the caption are the "virtues" held by the human beings working in the library, rather than the excellence of the pictures they are shown to be handling. This is entirely in keeping with Gibbs-Smith's emphasis on the human eye, brain, and memory as the key operational tools in a picture library, just as the scene in the photograph (figure 2.2) seems directly to illustrate "the constant 'soaking' of the librarians in their material," which in his view was imperative to its efficient functioning.[50]

While the scene in the picture library was clearly staged and furnished with its promotional caption in order to extol the Keystone brand, it is nevertheless difficult to imagine where a photograph such as this would have been published at the time. Even if photo agencies and illustrated magazines from the 1930s onward "knew that one way to grow their readership was to turn photographers into celebrities," as Nadya Bair has noted, they were less interested in revealing "the stages of collective thinking and decision-making" that went on in editorial offices, notwithstanding the fact that they were just as crucial to the appearance of any picture-led story in a newspaper or magazine.[51] The likelihood is therefore that the extensively captioned photograph was bundled in with one of the several daily dispatches of news photographs that photo agencies supplied to their regular clients, hand-delivered by a corps of ambulating sales staff. I have not been able to find a contemporaneous publication of the Keystone library picture, nor has it been possible to recover information about who exactly wrote its extended caption. It cannot therefore be established whether or not the caption writer was familiar with the article by Gibbs-Smith on the Hulton Picture Post Library.

In the absence of a documented connection between the two texts, their similarities can instead be understood as near-simultaneous articulations of prevalent ideas within the postwar picture business, aimed at two different kinds of audiences. Gibbs-Smith wrote for a specialist readership of librarians and information professionals, explaining the necessity of classification methods and working practices that went against the grain of librarianship as these readers knew it.[52] The caption writer at Keystone, however, addressed a client base that might not need to be told what a picture library was, but that could perhaps do with additional enlightenment on what kinds of skills, systems, and services they were paying for the benefit of using whenever they chose to give an assignment to this particular agency. Both texts could in this way be said to contribute, each in their own sphere, to increased professional awareness, if not exactly public knowledge, of how the intermediary work of picture libraries enhanced the value of their pictorial commodities.

Perhaps the most abiding impression from closely reading these two texts, however, is that efficiency and economy were not criteria that were introduced with electronic image retrieval. Indeed, it would be more accurate to say that these long-established requirements are rather what has made the picture business particularly keen to adopt new technologies promising cheaper and faster ways of retrieving and distributing its products. The article by Gibbs-Smith set out a recipe for picture libraries wishing to provide a fast, reliable, and professionally organized picture rental service, while the promotional caption from the back of the Keystone print outlined the sort of client expectations its picture library was prepared to fulfill. The next part of this chapter will consider whose work it was to follow that recipe and deliver a service that met those expectations.

Women in the Picture Trades

A striking feature of the Keystone Press Agency photograph shown in figure 2.2, which I have not yet addressed, is that it depicts four out of six picture librarians as women. Assuming, for the sake of argument, that the photograph includes everyone employed in the picture library at the time, this would mean that women accounted for two thirds of the Keystone library workforce in 1951. For his part, Gibbs-Smith does not give details about gender balance in his account of the staffing levels at the Hulton Picture Post Library. He does, however, mention "Mrs Max

Parrish, the Chief Librarian," who clearly was a female counterpart to the Keystone agency's (Mr.) Martin Prince, and in the context of describing the rationale of his color-code classification system notes in passing that it "makes initial sorting easy for the filer, so *she* can separate prints in to the main sections."[53] The choice of pronoun here seems to support Craig Robertson's observation, in his recent history of the filing cabinet, that "information as something you can have at your fingertips starts with the fingers of women."[54]

According to one of the picture researchers I interviewed for this book, who worked at the Hulton in the mid-1970s, the twenty-seven-strong staff at that time was exclusively female. The setup appeared to have been defended on the grounds of propriety, since the small storage space necessitated squeezing past each other in the files. A photograph from the same premises taken in the mid-1980s (figure 2.4) illustrates the narrow passages between the shelves, although it contradicts the impression of an all-female workplace by showing three men out of the four people depicted. By this point, however, the Hulton Picture Post Library had been acquired by the BBC, and from former employee Julia's account it seems this connection was an important attraction for those who sought work in the picture library at the time: "It was only when I got in that I realized that in fact it was a bit of a con, because we were all classified as just secretarial staff and there was no way we could apply for proper research jobs within the BBC."[55] Even before the Hulton was acquired by the BBC, then, it may have been that its same-sex recruitment policy was less due to an explicit concern about improper conduct among the files and more an unintended consequence of the librarians' lowly status as secretarial staff and a corresponding lack of career prospects.

The work of women in media has tended to be limited to the task of "processing information," whether as switchboard operators, copytakers, stenographers, or darkroom assistants, as Michelle Henning has noted.[56] Writing succinctly about the "invisibility of female labour" as a recurrent feature "in the development of modern media," Henning's examples are mainly drawn from nineteenth-century photographic industries, which appear to have replicated many of the employment patterns from the related printing trades.[57] Despite being employed "merely" to operate mechanical tools, however, women have often managed to expand

and adapt their administrative tasks into ways of creating rather than simply processing.[58] For instance, Friedrich Kittler notes that in the early twentieth century, women "found a place at university mid-way between being slaves at the typewriter and research assistants."[59] Writing about the "unseen hands" of women in the history of word processing, meanwhile, Matthew Kirschenbaum cites an example from the early days of office computing when a poet made use of boredom in her clerical job to compose a poem on her workplace computer.[60] In the publishing and advertising industries, the field of picture research has perhaps more than other auxiliary trades allowed for its practitioners to offset the secretarial routine aspects of the job with a more unpredictable and creative generation of ideas.

The photograph by Fred Ramage reproduced in figure 2.2 must be said to emphasize the paperwork part of picture librarianship, rather than its creative potential. This is especially apparent when it is viewed in the context of four other photographs taken by the same photographer on the same occasion (figure 2.5), all of which show women handling paper prints or index cards. Even if the work of filing does not lend itself to spectacular representation, however, these photographs do make visible the prominence of female labor in the pre-digital picture trades.

Women in the 1950s picture business did not rely solely on male photographers to make themselves seen. In the same year that Ramage photographed the picture librarians at Keystone, Ruth Matthews compiled and published a pioneering directory of photographers and picture agencies under the title *Who's Who in Photography*.[61] The following year, the Picture Division of the US Special Libraries Association was founded with the specific remit "to provide a channel for the exchange of pooled information" on all aspects of "documentary picture work," as well as to obtain "recognition for the professional picture specialist."[62] Its first tangible achievement was to publish *Picture Sources: An Introductory List* in 1959, under the editorship of Helen Faye, with contributions from eleven named volunteers, all of whom were women.[63]

Described on alternate pages as "a research tool for picture researchers, librarians, editors, artists, and all other professional users of pictures" and a "picture-finding tool for specialists in the field," *Picture Sources* contained contact details for 398 potential sources of illustration, implicitly

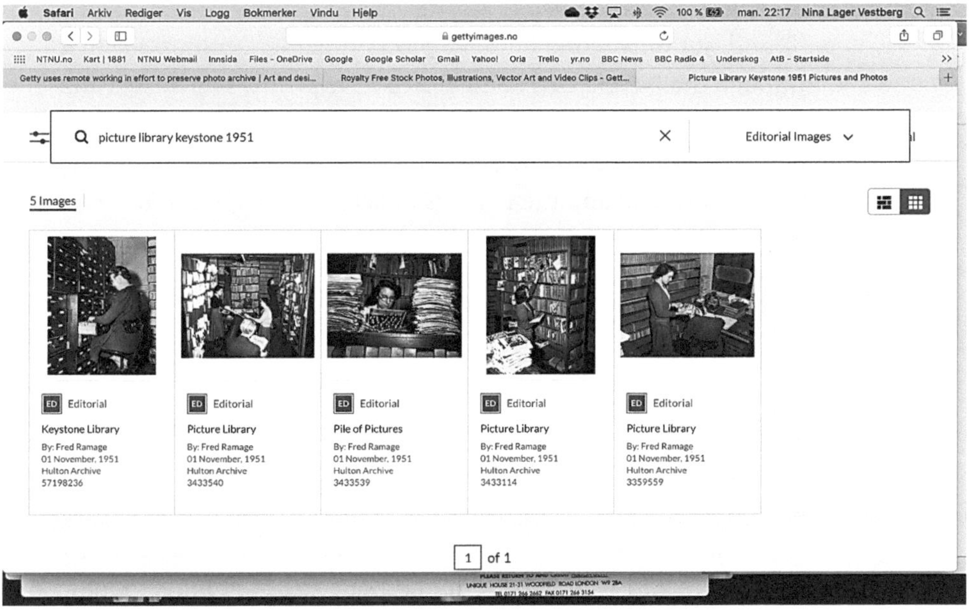

Figure 2.5

Search results for "picture library keystone 1951" (screenshot May 18, 2020). Getty Images, https://www.gettyimages.no/photos/picture-library-keystone-1951?family=editorial&assettype=image&phrase=picture%20library%20keystone%201951.

limiting its geographical remit to the United States.[64] It nevertheless included an entry for the "Hulton Picture Library" at its London address, where the chief librarian acclaimed by Gibbs-Smith as "Mrs Max Parrish" was revealed under her own name as Mrs. Mona Parrish, and from the entry immediately below it can be seen that the New York office of the Keystone Press Agency was headed by Mrs. Eva E. Jekely.[65] These make up two out of twenty-three entries in *Picture Sources* giving a name preceded by the title "Mrs." as contact person, while seven others give the title "Miss." Without being able to make an accurate count, due to the ambiguity of names and initials, it seems that virtually every one of the 100 pages in *Picture Sources* carried at least one woman's name among the contact persons listed, most of them without indication of marriage status. The textual data on gender and picture librarianship provided in *Picture Sources*, read together with the visual data represented in Ramage's metapictures for the Keystone Press Agency, support the impression that picture libraries in the early postwar decades were places in which women found not only work, but also professional recognition for that work. Although the Picture Division's aim to have picture researchers and librarians acknowledged as "specialists" can by no means be attributed to a feminist politics as such, it was the case that a good number of these specialists were women, and their efforts to achieve recognition for their profession therefore had the effect of acknowledging that fact, too.

Looking at Old Pictures

The commercial picture libraries discussed in this chapter—the Hulton Picture Post Library, the Bettmann Archive, and the Keystone Press Agency—all represent classic brand names in the history of photography for publication, which grew out of the mass market for illustrated periodicals that flourished with the widespread adoption of halftone printing in the interwar period. They each acquired huge stocks of photographic records, running into the millions of items, before at some point being taken over by or incorporated into other picture libraries. In addition to having been significant purveyors of news and illustration imagery in period under discussion in this chapter, the enormous holdings constituted by these three collections exemplify the *Nachleben* of archival photographs as data for the digitized visual content industry. There will be more to say on this topic in chapter 5, which deals with the major period of digitization in the early 2000s. In conclusion to this chapter, however, I want to come back to Ramage's photograph from the Keystone files and contextualize this particular picture within a current-day framework of circulation and reception.

As already suggested, the photographic print reproduced as figure 2.2 speaks its biography through the documentary signs of provenance, place, and function within more than one archive, as these appear on its reverse side (figure 2.3). In addition to the printed caption, the verso carries layers of metadata, from the photograph's first classification within the Keystone collection, via the number on the physical box in which it resides, to the copyright notice at the bottom (on which the address and phone and fax numbers for "Hulton Getty" are also now long out of date). The barcode sticker at the top indicates that it has been digitized and its metadata stored in an electronic catalog.[66] This view of the picture from the back illustrates how important information was carried on both sides of paper prints circulating in the pre-digital networks of press and publishing.[67]

The fact that the full text of the caption has not been transcribed as part of the photograph's metadata is, in one sense, symptomatic of how the material conditions and characteristics of photographic documents are not always understood as integral to their significance as historical sources.[68] In another sense, it points to the largely unspoken-of processes, mechanisms, and criteria by which digitization takes place. Just like Gibbs-Smith recommended bypassing the ingrained traditions of librarianship in order to enable picture librarians to process as many pictures as possible in the most time-efficient manner, the digitization processes of commercial picture collections tend to favor organized expediency over original order. Yet other historical contexts can be productively reconstituted by digitization.

As previously mentioned, looking up Ramage's Keystone photograph on the Getty Images website reveals four other photographs credited to the same photographer, taken in the same place on the same date, and featuring some of the same people (figure 2.5). Finding that it forms part of a series of similar motifs reveals the "Picture Library" photograph to have been a metapicture all along: a picture of pictures being handled in a picture library that was itself intended for circulation through a picture library. After digitization, the photograph continues to fulfill its transmissive purpose, even though neither its motif (the picture library) nor its commodity form (the print) are any longer associated with the modern virtues of speed and efficiency extolled in its caption. Rather, it is an example of how "the stock photography industry's own history is part of its capital," as Abbott Miller has observed, since the "outdated images" in its files always have the potential to "come back into fashion, imbued with camp or nostalgia."[69] When Miller wrote this in 1999, he was referring generally to old and outdated stock pictures, and not to metapictures about the historical operations of the stock photography industry itself. By the time I first came across this photograph on the Getty Images website in 2008, however, the archival practices of pre-digital picture libraries had receded sufficiently into the past to be drawing eulogies as a "lost art."[70] Once the formerly "invisible apparatus" of photographic archives—files and shelves, librarians and archivists—had become disintermediated by electronic storage media and online search interfaces, its constitutive elements reemerged as "content" for commodification in the new forms enabled by digital technologies.[71]

The black-and-white photograph of picture librarians filing paper prints had by the early 2000s become a historical document in more than one sense: it both appeared in an outmoded commodity form (the paper print) and depicted an outdated material practice (the physical filing of press photographs). For precisely those same reasons, it paradoxically had potential for remediation and redistribution in digital formats. In order for this potential to be realized, however, it must first be recaptured, or perhaps rather re-collected, from the millions of pictures among which it had been sitting for the best part of a lifetime. The retrieval and revaluation of this specific picture were due to the skilled intermediation of picture librarians in possession of the same qualities that were identified as necessary in Gibbs-Smith's article and the Keynote caption: a keen visual memory, an awareness of current trends, and sufficient immersion in the contents of their collections to know where to look for material that might resonate with contemporary issues.

Conclusion

One such contemporary concern is the cultural invisibility of what Robertson calls the "information labor" that keeps the infrastructures of capitalism working.[72] A growing body of scholarship has in recent years attested to this labor in general, and to women's role in it in particular, ranging from historical studies of office equipment and computing in the twentieth century to contemporary accounts of the "microwork" and "human intelligence tasks" that make online experiences run safely and smoothly in the twenty-first century.[73] There is also an increasing awareness that accumulated historical records reconfigured as "data" in online resources have all been collected from somewhere, and therefore carry "important traces of their own local production."[74] The picture of a picture library captured by Ramage in 1951 resonates with both these concerns because it represents a kind of intermediary labor that tends to remain below the threshold of awareness, even though, as exemplified on the back of this photograph, it leaves ample evidence of its working.

Before digitization, the work of searching, browsing, and filing that was manually performed in picture libraries and archives was ignored by the vast majority of readers, viewers, and consumers enjoying the visual commodities that were its end products. Under digitization, the mechanisms that make pictures searchable, findable, and viewable online also tend to stay out of sight for contemporary users. Engaging with historical sources that show us how and by whom visual data were being processed in the pre-digital picture industry—in short, how a picture library worked in the 1950s—may help us frame questions about how, by whom, and for what purpose it is done now (topics that will be explored in part II of this book).

Certainly, the primary purpose of commercial picture libraries in the twentieth century was to sell licenses for the reproduction of reproductions. This business model was economically enabled by legal conventions that since the eighteenth century had placed a higher value on multiplied and distributed pictures than on singular and enclosed ones. It was made practically feasible by photography, which allowed pictures to be precisely captured and conveniently stored in one and the same medium. It profited from information technologies like the filing cabinet and the card catalog to organize pictorial assets, and relied on a skilled and knowledgeable workforce to manage these assets and technologies in the service of clients. But how and why did pictures pile up in libraries in the first place? And how was it possible for anyone outside the library to find them? The next chapter focuses on the connection between collecting and research as methods of accumulation that are also methods of extraction. Jumping forward from the 1950s to the 1970s, it considers how pre-photographic pictures were exploited in new ways by photographic means, and explores the pre-digital tools and protocols that enabled picture researchers to find and retrieve pictures for further dissemination through print and broadcast media.

3

Picturing Research

We have seen how picture libraries like the Hulton Picture Post Library and the Keystone Press Agency worked to supply clients with pictures as efficiently as possible in the early postwar period. Picture librarians routinely processed requests by using a range of classification systems and finding aids, yet their most important search tool remained an intuitive grasp of a collection's contents gained from constant immersion in its material, as advocated by Gibbs-Smith. Picture researchers, on the other hand, who searched for illustrations across all kinds of different picture libraries, and often on behalf of a wide range of clients, were rarely able to perform their own searches on the basis of such embodied, inside knowledge.

In order to obtain the right pictures for each job, therefore, they first needed to accumulate information about various picture libraries and their contents, and then a set of tools and strategies for extracting relevant material from those sources. The *Picture Sources* directory was one such tool. First published in the United States in 1959, and revised in 1964, it provided contact details and information about collection content from several hundred sources, as discussed in the previous chapter. While such compiled lists of contacts were invaluable finding aids, at a time when the only other way to locate a picture library would have been by word of mouth or looking in the yellow pages of a phone book, they did not offer much advice on what researchers could expect or demand from sources, nor on what sources might demand or expect from researchers.

In 1975, a new publication entitled *The Picture Researcher's Handbook: An International Guide to Picture Sources—and How to Use Them* set out to change this.[1] Coauthored by picture librarians Hilary and Mary Evans and picture researcher Andra Nelki, it aimed to improve understanding between libraries and researchers by providing "the essential information that is the starting-point of every research assignment" alongside "a basic list of the most important sources with up-to-date information."[2] Where the compilers of previously published lists of sources had focused on pooling information for the benefit of practicing professionals, the authors of the *Picture Researcher's Handbook* also sought to educate and equip new recruits for a career in picture research.

A contemporary interview revealed the format of the handbook to have been inspired by a well-known travel guide. Evans and Evans claimed they had set out to create "an Egon Ronay of picture libraries," which would inform readers not just about "mechanical facts like fees and location, but also about the quality of service, of reproduction and other more subjective considerations."[3] Ronay's guides to eating and travel were famous for having "taught Britain how to eat," and in a similar way, the *Picture Researcher's Handbook* would teach picture researchers in many parts of the world how to do their job.[4] The book was published simultaneously in the United Kingdom, United States, and Australia, and it was revised and distributed in a total of eight editions between 1975 and 2006.[5] Within a few years of its publication, it had attained the status of industry-standard equipment, with legendary *Sunday Times* editor Harold Evans (no relation) proclaiming, "No picture researcher can stir without a copy of *The Picture Researcher's Handbook*."[6]

Even today, the *Picture Researcher's Handbook* is a helpful manual to the nuts and bolts of pre-digital picture research. Most of the businesses listed in its directory may be long since defunct or transformed beyond recognition, but the methods and procedures for undertaking a successful picture research project outlined in the general section still allow us to grasp "the sheer quantity of time and trouble needed to find a single, apparently simple, illustration" within a pictorial economy that ran chiefly on print media, postal services, and telephone lines.[7]

The publication of the handbook was an important milestone for Evans and Evans in 1975, yet there was another significant event in their working lives that occurred in the same year. This was the removal of their jointly managed venture, the Mary Evans Picture Library, from the basement of their private house to a designated business location. While the handbook had a demonstrable impact on the picture business in general, the main effect of the picture library move appeared limited to the freeing-up of space in Evans and Evans's family home, which had housed the collection since the 1960s. Nevertheless, as this chapter will demonstrate, the picture of research that Evans, Evans, and Nelki drew up in their handbook was consistent with a practice of research that was facilitated by the organization and new location of the Mary Evans Picture Library.

Written by authors who were themselves managers of a specialist picture library, it is safe to say that the handbook offered guidance for picture researchers on how to use picture sources as they would like to be used. This chapter shows how certain behaviors that were accentuated as good research practice in the book corresponded to the sorts of behavior that Evans and Evans encouraged from their clients. It demonstrates how their own collecting practices, which sustained the Mary Evans Picture Library as a business, can be understood as picture research by another name. And it highlights the affinities between researchers and collectors as cultural intermediaries with an ability to transform the significance of an object by the power of their knowledgeable attention.

The word *research* used simply to mean "the act of searching carefully for or pursuing a specified thing or person."[8] While it has long since taken on a host of other and more complicated meanings in science and scholarship, this original definition still gives a valid description of what picture research is. It is the careful looking for, and looking through, a specific class of things called pictures, in order to locate and gather representations of other specified things (or, indeed, persons). The reason for looking "with care" in this way "is so that what is being searched for and gathered can be increased, used, and utilized, or better, exploited," according to Marquard Smith.[9] Such research is speculative in the capitalist sense, as it accumulates stock with a view to its future value, like picture libraries gathering illustrations with the intention of renting them out. Yet research can also be speculative in a different sense, as a search for knowledge that proceeds from assumptions or hypotheses, and is carried out in accordance with a certain methodology. This is usually acknowledged as the remit of scholarly and scientific research; however, it is also the work of picture research proper: starting from a given brief and searching systematically through selected accumulations of given objects—in a word, data—in order to identify and extract those that are relevant and appropriate to the set topic.

A third aspect of research is the transmission to a wider public of its findings, understood as the results of the preceding two processes of searching and gathering. In the academic context of historical research that Smith discusses, "the purpose of research as a searching, a gathering, and a distributing" is undertaken "not only to interpret the world, in various ways, but to change it."[10] The aim of picture research has rarely been to effect revolutionary change in the world (although picture research is of course also undertaken on behalf of publications and media outlets that are motivated by such an ambition), perhaps not even to interpret it. The purpose of doing picture research is, rather, to discover specific things in the world—that is, pictures—and offer them up for interpretation and appreciation.

"Research," according to the writer Celeste Olalquiaga, "is taking stock of cultural merchandise, as well as of the personal baggage often tagged onto it, and attempting to reestablish its value anew, whether to discard and leave it behind or to bring it back into circulation."[11] The anthropological model of rubbish theory describes and explains the processes whereby value is recognized or created in things or ideas that have been discarded.[12] In this chapter I adopt its key concepts to focalize my account of collecting and research as practices of looking with care.

Collecting Pictures for a Purpose

Picture libraries like the Hulton Picture Post Library and the Keystone Press Agency collected pictures in order to serve the illustrative needs of the daily and periodical press, as previously noted. These libraries' holdings expanded on a daily basis as both published material and unpublished leftovers from assignments were deposited by staff photographers for their respective news organizations. In US press jargon, such archival repositories are commonly referred to as "morgues," a term that conjures up basements full of recently departed pictures.[13] The rationale for keeping old photographs figuratively on ice, rather than burying them in an equally metaphorical graveyard, has been that dead pictures, unlike dead bodies, may someday be resurrected.

This susceptibility of apparently defunct pictures to be resuscitated was what gave rise to the historical picture library as a business model unto itself. At the level of content, historical picture libraries offered alternatives both to the recently expired news of the press agency morgue and to the intentionally timeless "corporate vernacular" pictures propagated by advertising-oriented stock libraries.[14] At the level of form, however, they shared the same reliance on photographic technologies to perform the acts of enclosure that produce (new) pieces of property, which in turn might be traded as commodities in a market.

The Mary Evans Picture Library (MEPL) exemplifies this segment of the business. Founded by Mary Evans (1936–2010) in partnership with her husband Hilary (1929–2011), it had developed somewhat incidentally from the private collections that the two spouses had been accumulating on a hobby basis since before their marriage in 1956. These collections reflected their individual special interests: Mary's in dogs and anything dog-related, Hilary's in anything "fringy" and specifically paranormal.[15] From the 1950s Hilary had worked as a copywriter in the advertising industry, and in this capacity he made contacts that led to them both lending out items from their collections for reproduction. By the early 1960s Mary realized that they had the makings of a business under their own roof, and in 1964 the library was officially set up, with Hilary mainly in charge of captioning and cataloging, while Mary took care of the business side of things.

Rather than basing their stock on "photographic leftovers" from current news or advertising assignments, the greatest part of the picture library was made up of printed material and ephemera, ranging from scraps and postcards to lithographs, mezzotints, and woodcuts. Evans and Evans would add to these collections on a regular basis, in particular during annual holidays in France, from whence they would return with piles of prints and books picked up from flea markets, print-sellers, and *bouquinistes*. These were then mined by the collectors and their picture library staff for exploitable visual resources.

According to Hilary Evans, the common task of all picture libraries—and, by extension, of all picture librarians and researchers—was "to enable pictures to do their job."[16] In practice, that meant making them available to be seen by as many people as possible, typically through the mass media of newspapers, magazines, books, advertisements, or television. Photography was in this respect the most efficient and practicable means by which to transmit the contents of the library's files to its clients. Like the Bridgeman Art Library, discussed in chapter 1, MEPL therefore employed photography first and foremost as an efficient technology for reproducing and distributing copies of their collection items.

Yet unlike Bridgeman, who from an early stage had specialized in reproductions of canonical works of art, Evans and Evans were promoters and purveyors of "the 'ordinary' images which . . . defined the era in which they were created."[17] The originals of these pictures were rarely found in museums or fine art galleries, but rather "in books, on posters, in advertisements, or as prints."[18] In other words, what MEPL offered their contemporary producers of pictorial commodities—publishers, editors, designers, and advertisers—were the rights to reproduce pictures that had already been commodified. This trade in secondhand imagery relied in equal measures on the legal framework of copyright, outlined in chapter 1, and the business model of intermediation, as explained in chapter 2.

When Evans and Evans set up their picture library in 1964, the relevant intellectual property legislation in force was the UK Copyright Act 1956. This law afforded protection of "artistic works" for the term of fifty years from the date of publication or broadcast, or the year of the author's death, in cases where the work had not been published or broadcast in the author's lifetime. There were some differences between photographs and other artistic works. For instance, the copyright term for photographs was unequivocally tied to publication date only, and the same went for publication of "anonymous or pseudonymous" works, providing it was not possible "to ascertain the identity of the author by reasonable inquiry" (Copyright Act, 1956, c. 74). This meant, in practice, that by 1964 anybody was free to make use of almost any published material dating from before 1914, not least since anonymity and pseudonymity were widespread practices in nineteenth-century periodicals, and the concept of "reasonable inquiry" must have been very much open to interpretation.

By contrast, it was crucial to the operation of a picture library like MEPL that the photographic reproductions made of these public-domain works be classified as "works of art, subject to copyright like any other," as Hilary Evans noted, "so that though the original—an engraving from the

Illustrated London News for 1860, for example—is in the public domain, their photograph of that engraving is not."[19] When launching their business in 1964, therefore, Evans and Evans deliberately prioritized material published before 1914, which had already expired its fifty-year copyright limit, as per the Copyright Act 1956. Under the same act, they would secure their own intellectual property in the photographic reproductions for fifty years from the time they were first published—at whichever point in the future that might be.

While photography was the technical mechanism that allowed the rare and often fragile historical pictures collected by Evans and Evans to stay safely stored in their files, and at the same time be made available to users, it was the legal mechanism of copyright that enabled visual items in the public domain to be monetized as content in "original" photographic reproductions. In order for money to be made from the sale of rights to such reproductions, however, there must also be a social mechanism for (re)establishing these outdated pictures as culturally valuable.

Any stock or library picture is appraised on the use value of its visual content. This use value might be realized as illustrative value, for instance, when a picture is used as illustration in an advertisement or magazine article, or as what we might call informational value, in cases when a photograph functions primarily as reproduction of another object (such as an artwork) or documentation of an event (whether this be a war or a wedding). In the case of both illustrative stock photographs—generic images most often used to illustrate adverts and articles—and informational documentary news images, their main purpose is transmission: to be shown and seen, published and distributed, transferred and circulated. These are "travelling images" that move around, appearing and reappearing in a wide range of different contexts.[20]

Take, for instance, a photograph of a woman shielding herself from a downpour using a large umbrella. It may initially have been shot as a news photograph documenting extreme weather conditions in a specific location. When its immediate news value has disappeared, however, it may be republished as a generic depiction of bad weather or climate change, serve as a conceptual evocation of protection from exposure, or even illustrate a fashion item on umbrella styles. Depending on how often it is used, and on how much the picture reveals about the time and location at which it was taken, its use value will decrease either slowly or rapidly. Generally we can say that the vaguer the details, the longer the life of the picture. At some stage, however, the depicted content of most archived photographs will have reached a degree of outdatedness which in practice disqualifies the picture from further economic activity. At this point, the photograph has effectively become rubbish.

The idea that any object in human society may be categorized as either "transient," "durable," or "rubbish" comes from the social anthropologist Michael Thompson, who developed it in his influential book, *Rubbish Theory: The Creation and Destruction of Value*, which was first published in 1979.[21] According to this theoretical model of value, transient objects decrease in value and durable objects increase in value, whereas rubbish objects have no value at all. Thompson's prime example of a transient object was a car, the value of which instantly plummets the very moment it goes from being new to being secondhand, while an equally appropriate example might be a personal computer, which has a considerably lower resell value once it has left the shop.[22] An antique piece of furniture provided Thompson's contrasting example of a durable object. Such an artifact is still the most obvious illustration of its category, as indeed it should be in order for the model to be valid. In the decades that have passed since the book was published, however, the Queen Anne tallboy described by Thompson will have been joined by any number of objects that in 1979 were still firmly located in the transient category as newly produced or recently outdated.

The transformation from transience to durability goes via the "covert" category of rubbish. In Thompson's model this is the end station for transient objects that have lost all perceptible value. Once they have faded out of sight, objects in the rubbish category nevertheless retain the potential to redeem themselves by gaining access, not back into the precarious transient category from whence they came, but to the stable and desirable category of the durable.[23] For most pictorial objects, the end of their copyright term is normally the switch that automatically sets their transient value to zero, dropping them into the rubbish category of images in the public domain. From this position, the only hope of redemption for a picture is that it might sooner or later be reappraised as a document of historical interest, or perhaps discovered as the neglected work of an already-recognized artist or author. In the case of a printed portrait of "lesser known" figure, for instance, Hilary Evans might have taken a bet on receiving a request for it sometime in the future, simply based on the fact that "somebody considered this person important enough to warrant an engraving" at some point in the past.[24]

The process by which rubbish obtains new visibility within the field of the durable is complex, and dependent on what Thompson terms "a concatenation of individual creative leaps."[25] This creativity is less concerned with innovation than with imagination, memory, and recognition. It is what Olalquiaga calls the "indirect" creativity of collectors and researchers, who instead of producing "the kind of 'original' material associated with modern artistic creation . . . work with and through what already exists."[26] For collectors, "the acquisition of an old book is its rebirth," as Walter Benjamin noted.[27] A collector might buy an item "to which he may never have given a thought, much less a wishful look, because he found it lonely and abandoned on the market place," yet once it has been installed on the collector's shelf it may still never be looked at again.[28] The practice of collecting illustrates how the transformation from rubbish status to durability is an unpredictable process, in which whimsy and serendipity are always at play alongside appraisal and calculation. While collectors are the prime movers in such processes, their reappraisals must in turn be recognized and repeated by others in order for the initial creative leap to be of wider cultural or economic consequence.

In accounting for the social mechanisms that enable such imaginative leaps to gain wider acceptance, and for there to emerge a consensus that such-and-such object is not a useless piece of trash but a neglected treasure, one could do worse than read Thompson in tandem with another landmark publication of 1979, namely, Pierre Bourdieu's *La distinction. Critique sociale du jugement* (which did not appear in English translation until 1984).[29] Bourdieu's notion of cultural capital, a collective term for the various immaterial assets assembled through education and upbringing, is not only the key concept of *Distinction*; it can also be retrospectively applied to the anecdotes and case studies presented in *Rubbish Theory*. What Thompson calls "the frontier middle class," for instance, corresponds to what Bourdieu would term people of high cultural but low economic capital.[30]

These cultural intermediaries (another Bourdieuism) are the most likely agents of transfers from the rubbish to the durable category. They scan dumpsters and flea markets for cast-off objects in order to pronounce them vintage or retro as opposed to outdated, or buy rundown houses in unfashionable parts of town, then coax them into desirability through careful refurbishment and tasteful decoration. Those in possession of a large amount of cultural capital are, in Bourdieu's system, thought to make more informed and therefore more valid judgments about what is good or bad, whether it comes to music, literature, architecture, or any of the other arts. Competent as well as confident in making independent or alternative aesthetic assessments, the same individuals are equipped to do the work of reappraisal required to confer durability on a rubbish item.

The historical moment of the 1960s and 1970s, when Thompson and Bourdieu both developed their theories of value and taste, coincided with the period in which Evans and Evans established and grew their picture library. Obsessively "acquiring pictures" wherever they traveled, they hunted "treasures [that] were defined by content, not price," and found them, because "nobody was collecting the sort of thing that Hilary and Mary were interested in."[31] As collectors, Evans and Evans epitomize "those few eccentrics," as Thompson puts it, whose "aesthetic judgements" are among the first in "the long chain of individual creative leaps" that sooner or later will become, if not mainstream, then "sufficiently centric for a market to emerge."[32] This moment in the process of (re)creating value occurs when, as Thompson describes it, "sellers say to themselves, 'I won't throw that away, I might just be able to sell it,' and buyers offer, for a nominal sum, to take it off the owner's hands."[33]

As picture librarians, Evans and Evans operated on both sides of this transaction, hanging on to seemingly valueless items and buying stuff that nobody else was interested in because they might just be able to resell it. Of course, the crucial difference between the transactions involving antique dealers and print collectors and those involving picture librarians like Evans and Evans was that the latter were not primarily interested in augmenting the value of the items as such. Rather, they were intending to reproduce their pictorial content in photographic form and sell it as an *image* for illustration purposes.

The lithograph of *The Connoisseur*, already discussed in chapter 1, is a case in point. Once the copyright protection of the print expired in the late 1850s, it effectively became worthless as intellectual property. As a piece of ephemera it must have looked dated nearly forty years after it was first published. It may also have fallen out of circulation due to photographic albums replacing scrapbooks as the primary social networking tools in feminine Victorian society. The copy that eventually found its way into the MEPL collections, however, was creatively repurposed by caption writer Hilary Evans as the representation of a modern figure, a "picture library girl," and adopted in the picture library's self-promotion as an evocative avatar both of the business itself and of its eponymous co-owner. In addition to illustrating the cultural dynamics of value creation as outlined by Thompson's rubbish theory, this example demonstrates Hilary Evans's own faith in the productive potential of historical pictures "not simply as relics of the past, but as elements in creations of the present."[34]

One specific creation in which the MEPL copy of *The Connoisseur* found itself repurposed was a printed and folded invitation that was distributed among picture researchers, editors, designers, librarians, advertising executives, and publishers in London and beyond (figure 3.1). On the front it bore the legend "Mary Evans invites you" and inside it welcomed picture library clients and collaborators to "come and see the Mary Evans Picture Library in its elegant new home" during its "Open Week" in September 1975. This was organized in celebration of the library's previously mentioned move into a recently restored historic building, a fitting headquarters for a business primarily dealing in "Visual Documentation of the Past."[35] This piece of self-promotional ephemera, printed in green ink on white card, manifested the picture library's basic business model of taking an old picture in the public domain, reproducing it by photomechanical means, and distributing it to a new audience. It also illustrated, of course, the idea of the library's pictures being on the move. But above all, it signaled the housewarming event as an opportunity to meet the people metaphorically behind the pictures.

This message was further underscored inside the card, where all members of staff were listed alphabetically by name. Visitors were invited to

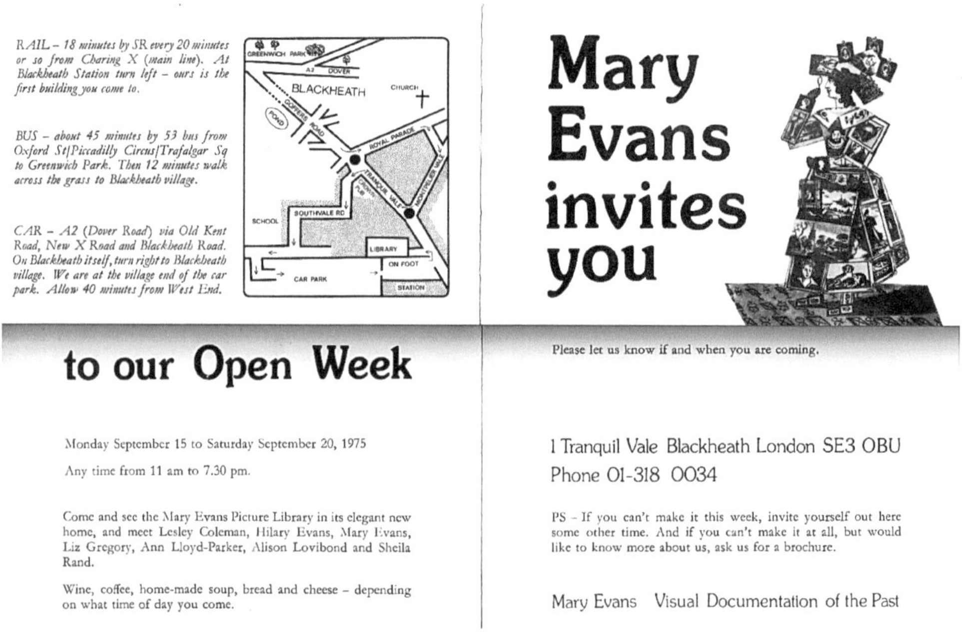

FIGURE 3.1
"Mary Evans invites you. . . ." Facsimile of invitation to Open Week at MEPL, September 1975. © Mary Evans Picture Library.

turn up at "any time from 11am to 7.30pm," and those tempted to make the journey were promised "wine, coffee, home-made soup, bread and cheese—depending on what time of day you come." This hospitality was not limited to the one open week, however, as the postscript explained: "If you can't make it this week, invite yourself out here some other time. And if you can't make it at all, but would like to know more about us, ask for a brochure." On the back of the invite there was a small map indicating the location of the picture library right next to the local train station at Blackheath, as well as detailed information about train times, bus routes, and parking facilities. Given the detailed travel instructions, as well as the promise of food and drink, this invite clearly expressed a genuine wish for clients to come and see the picture library's collections for themselves. While this preference for in-person visits was in some measure an expression of Evans and Evans's personal conviviality, it was grounded first and foremost in their personal theory of research practice, as outlined in another printed item issued from their hand in 1975: the *Picture Researcher's Handbook*.

THE JOB OF FINDING A PICTURE

Picture Researcher's Handbook: An International Guide to Picture Sources—and How to Use Them (figure 3.2, henceforth *PRH1*) drew a detailed picture of the skilled, knowledgeable, and efficient work of intermediation that was picture research in the pre-digital era.[36] Its stated aim was not just to provide contact details for collections of photographs and other visual materials in one handy volume, but also to share "practical information which can make your job easier, faster, more efficient and more economical."[37] Acknowledging that picture research was "still a relatively new and largely unknown profession," Evans, Evans, and Nelki set out to validate this work of intermediation, which "tend[ed] to be underestimated by editors, authors and other employers."[38] In an effort to remedy this lack of insight and understanding, the first edition of the handbook included a compendium of general background information, from a variety of sources, that was needed to conduct a successful search for appropriate pictures according to the technological and economic parameters of the time.

In the space of forty pages or so, this first "General" part of *PRH1* accumulated and compressed a range of skills and knowledge, otherwise distributed among art historians, photo historians, accountants, lawyers, archivists, and librarians, which it nevertheless behooved the competent picture researcher to have. This included an overview of illustration techniques from woodcuts to offset lithography and a short history of photography, as well as chapters on pay rates, copyright, collection types, and "useful books," all conveniently assembled for ease of transmission in the format of a printed codex volume. For readers who already had, or were considering how to get, a full-time job in picture research, the book offered more than tips and tricks of the trade. In fact, it outlined a fully-fledged research methodology, which detailed the recommended skills, methods, and working procedures for designing, managing, and completing a specific kind of research project.

This methodology was outlined in a five-page section headed "The Picture Researcher: The Role and the Responsibilities." Most of the section

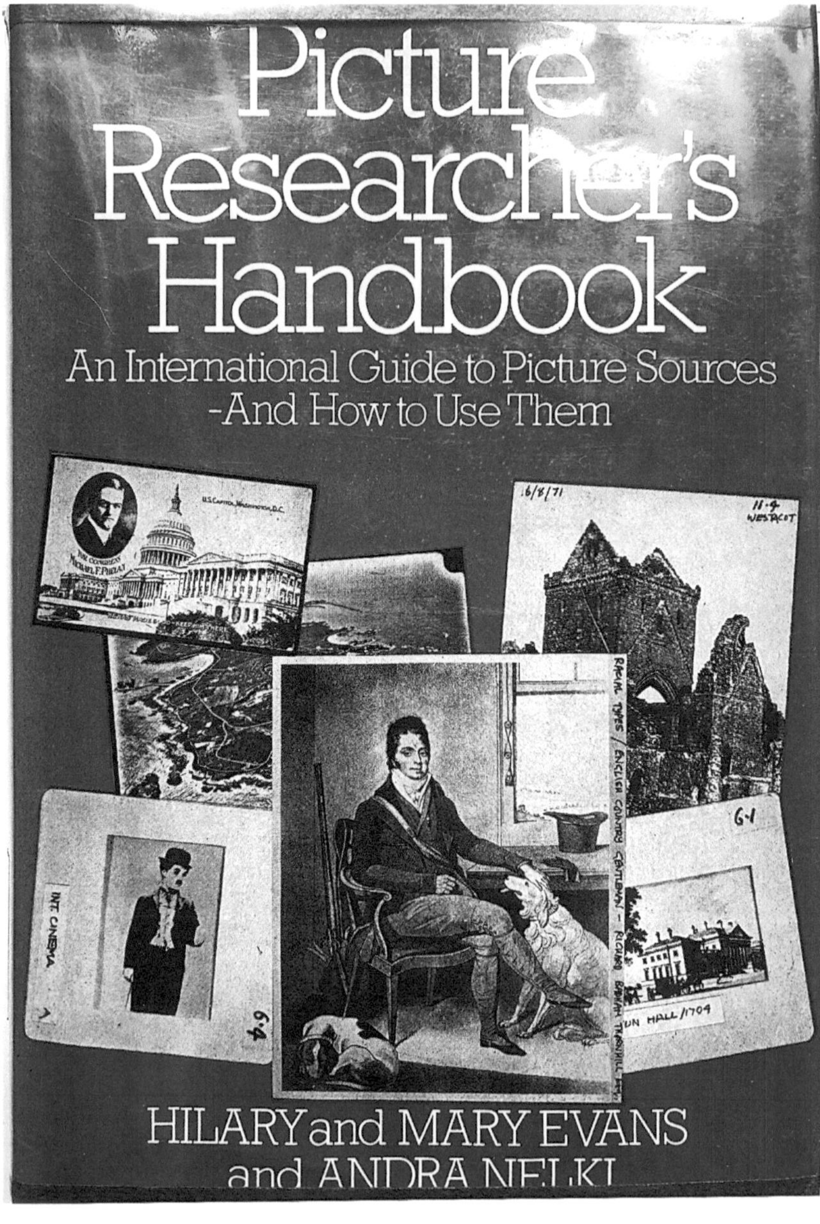

FIGURE 3.2
The Picture Researcher's Handbook. Cover of the US edition (1974).

was devoted to step-by-step descriptions of the eight separate stages of a "Picture Research Programme," which covered advice on making use of appropriate sources and technologies, preserving research material in a secure way, and making and keeping reliable records of it.[39] As professional picture researchers almost without exception worked on assignment from some kind of employer, whether as staff or freelance, it also included suggestions on how to manage relations with the employer in each phase of the assignment.

At every step there would be some tasks that were the responsibility of the employer and some that were the remit of the researcher. For instance, during the initial preparations, it was important for employers to provide as much and as detailed information about the assignment as possible—from budget and publication deadline to topic, format, and number of illustrations needed. At the second stage of primary research, "a proper understanding of the scope of the project is essential," which again meant the employer must provide as detailed a brief as possible.[40] The researcher would then be expected to work independently, reading up on the subject—ideally across several good libraries—and conducting a review of illustrated works on similar subjects to get an idea of where suitable sources might be found, before drawing up a list of all the pictures needed. This document was basically a shopping list for pictures that formed the basis for the next three stages of the process, which all pertained to the gathering-in of material.

This main research phase generally required communicating with picture libraries by letter as well as telephone, and could also involve traveling to conduct research on site. Looking after material borrowed from libraries demanded both a record-keeping system and some kind of storage equipment—ideally, a fireproof filing cabinet similar to the ones in which pictures were kept by the libraries themselves—while sturdy packaging materials were needed when returning pictures to their owners, whether this happened by post or courier.

Picture research in the 1970s still took place in a fundamentally scriptural and paper-rich environment, as the pages of *PRH1* testify. Examples range from the instruction to "apply in writing in the first instance" before making a request to the observation that one of the benefits of "commercial historical" collections over public collections was that "you can browse on your own among the picture files, instead of having to fill in a request form and wait till someone brings you the picture which you have chosen from a words-only catalogue description."[41] The last comment also throws light on the meaning of the information provided under the "availability" heading for each entry in the directory, which specified whether research was to be conducted by staff or could be carried out by researchers themselves.

The authors preferred the latter kind of source because it provided the best circumstances under which to "*get to know your sources personally*."[42] In keeping with the attitude expressed through the Open Week invite, discussed above, Evans, Evans, and Nelki highlighted MEPL as an example of a collection that welcomed researchers on site, and variations on this encouragement to visit sources were interspersed throughout the book.

While the job of the picture researcher might be conducted "perfectly satisfactorily by phone or letter," the authors explained, getting to know sources by making personal visits, meeting staff, consulting their material onsite, and learning their classification systems would "make for more efficient working in the long run," even though it might take some initial time and effort. While picture researchers on occasional visits could never get soaked in a picture library's material in the same way as its employees, dipping in to get a firsthand sense of both the contents and organization of a collection would make it easier to place concise requests later. And developing "valuable personal relationships" with staff at picture sources during personal visits could help ensure "greater co-operation and special privileges" when negotiating a particularly tricky request or tight deadline.[43]

This emphasis on the cultivation of interpersonal relationships is representative of how Evans, Evans, and Nelki repeatedly foregrounded the intermediary character of picture research as a profession. Researchers were constantly acting as go-betweens among other people involved in the production process, such as editors, designers, publishers, picture librarians, museum curators, archivists, and private collectors, and as human interfaces between objects such as pictures, books, and catalogs and classification systems, postal services, and copyright legislation. Accordingly, many of the authors' recommendations concerned the most productive ways of performing this work of intermediation.

They gave clear instructions, for instance, on how to approach and deal with sources: having first made a written application, you should "always offer to visit a source," if you were asking for more than a very few number of specific pictures, and when you had made a visit, "jot down the names of the individuals who helped you." There was also advice on how not to treat sources: "don't send your complete picture list to every source," and "don't involve them in unnecessary work." In passages such as these, Evans and Evans appeared to be speaking first and foremost from their viewpoint as owners of a picture library, rather than as jobbing picture researchers. This perspective was particularly apparent in the six-point procedure for the safe, temporary storage of pictures received from sources ("protected from damage and straightforward loss [and] theft—especially original engravings which have a real monetary value"), which must have been drawn up on the basis of at least some unfortunate experiences.[44]

The return of pictures was another topic covered in striking detail, compared to the brief attention given to the phase of actually selecting pictures for publication, and may have reflected more of an ideal scenario than a regular one. It was no doubt beneficial for picture libraries to have "unwanted pictures . . . returned at the earliest possible date"[45] so they could be made available to other potential clients. For picture researchers, on the other hand, it may have been more prudent to hang on to all the collected material until the assignment was done and dusted, and there was no longer any danger of editors or designers changing their minds. In short, the handbook's suggestions for contact procedures, requests, site visits, and return practices were probably better indications of what the directors of the Mary Evans Picture Library considered "best practice" than faithful descriptions of the working practices of professional picture researchers in the 1970s.

Throughout the handbook, the authors regularly expressed their views on what constitutes good picture research, even if only implicitly. The laudable qualities of a picture researcher were recognizable from those applied to picture librarians in Gibbs-Smith's article and the Keystone caption (figure 2.3), discussed in chapter 2. Efficiency, good general knowledge, access to a good collection of reference books, extensive visual experience, good memory, and familiarity with classification systems, catalogs, and indexes were among the essential criteria highlighted by all three sources. In addition to these qualities, however, picture researchers should in the handbook authors' opinion also have a degree of creative "flair" and good communication and interpersonal skills, exemplified as knowing "how to write letters . . . to bishops or professors or noble lords" and "how to persuade busy people to help them."[46]

Other personal advantages, such as access to an extensive network of sources and a meticulous attention to detail, could in turn be harnessed by researchers in order to "discover fresh ways of illustrating hackneyed themes."[47] The word "fresh" was repeatedly used across the handbook to indicate seldom-seen pictures that sources were commended for providing and researchers are recommended to seek out. Freshness was evidently a distinguishing trait of good picture research in the same way that originality is deemed to characterize good academic research. To achieve this sought-after quality in a selection of pictures, researchers must exercise the same independent aesthetic judgment as collectors, and be prepared to make similarly eccentric decisions when searching through picture collections.

Having built their own library by accumulating pictures that had been overlooked or discarded by others, Evans and Evans also urged researchers to keep a lookout for recently outdated pictures in among otherwise contemporary material. Discussing a type of source they defined as "Commercial collections—modern general," the authors observed that such sources, "while essentially up-to-date in their material" would nevertheless often have a significant stock of pictures "created 40 or 50 years ago." This kind of newly old material was "particularly worth knowing about," because it might have "become of historic importance," even when the holders of such material were as yet unable "to recognize its value."[48] In such cases, the intervention of the cultural intermediary, in the form of a researcher reappraising an apparently useless picture as a publishable illustration, might encourage sources to realize that it was worth looking after these items in their collection, too, as there might just be a market for them after all.

The authors' advice on searching carefully in order to find the unexpected and extracting value by bringing the previously discarded back into circulation demonstrates how Evans and Evans conceived of the intermediary functions of picture research in accordance with the cultural logic described by rubbish theory. It also exemplifies the affinities between research and collecting as methods of accumulation and extraction, outlined at the start of this chapter. Collecting as the job of locating pictures to save, and research as the job of finding pictures to study or display, together enable pictures to do what Hilary Evans termed "their job" of being looked at.[49] In this respect, research and collecting are also methods of transmission.

While this may be self-evident in the case of research, which is always undertaken with a view to disseminating the results of looking-with-care, it is equally the inevitable, even if sometimes unintended, result of collecting. "[I]nheritance is the soundest way of acquiring a collection," wrote Walter Benjamin toward the end of his essay on the unpacking of his library, "and the most distinguished trait of a collection will always be its transmissibility."[50] Some seventy years later, Wolfgang Ernst expressed the same idea in more general terms, that "storage is a transfer across a temporal distance."[51] Through their collecting practices, Evans and Evans built up a store of pictures that were both disseminated to contemporary audiences through the intermediary technology of photographic reproduction and transmitted to subsequent generations by means of archival preservation. Through their handbook of picture research, the collectors and picture librarians shared their methodology of looking and finding with more than one generation of colleagues and collaborators.

So far, I have been reading the *PRH1* for what it explicitly tells us about picture research in the 1970s, or at least about how Evans and Evans conceived of the profession from their own viewpoint as collectors and librarians. In the final part of this chapter, I turn my attention to what the volume implicitly tells us about picture research in the same period, now that we must necessarily read it across a significant temporal distance.

It would have been entirely possible in the mid-1970s to set oneself up as a professional picture researcher on the back of the *Picture Researcher's Handbook*, using the sections on tradecraft as a working manual and the directory of sources as a primary picture-finding tool. Several decades after it first came out, the information conveyed by the *PRH1* is of little use to someone searching for, or looking to publish, pictures in an almost exclusively online environment. What it has lost in currency, however, the handbook has gained in historical interest.

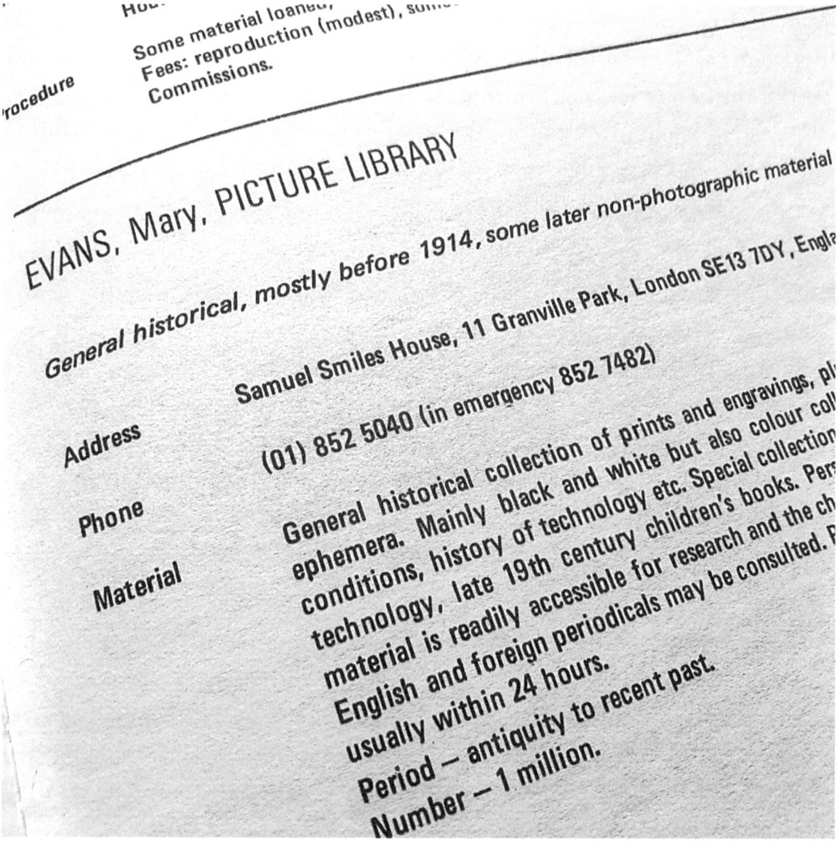
Some material loaned,
Fees: reproduction (modest),
Commissions.

EVANS, Mary, PICTURE LIBRARY

General historical, mostly before 1914, some later non-photographic material

Address Samuel Smiles House, 11 Granville Park, London SE13 7DY, Engl

Phone (01) 852 5040 (in emergency 852 7482)

Material General historical collection of prints and engravings, ph ephemera. Mainly black and white but also colour coll conditions, history of technology etc. Special collection technology, late 19th century children's books. Pers material is readily accessible for research and the ch English and foreign periodicals may be consulted. usually within 24 hours. Period – antiquity to recent past. Number – 1 million.

FIGURE 3.3
Entry for Mary Evans Picture Library in *The Picture Researcher's Handbook* (1975). Photograph by author.

The directory part, which makes up the greatest bulk of the volume, is now useless for contacting picture libraries, but provides a fascinating primary source both to the business histories and to the historical geographies of press and publishing—in the United Kingdom as well as worldwide (figure 3.3). To take one example: the entry for "Evans, Mary, Picture Library" states that its material is "General historical, mostly before 1914, some later non-photographic material." This entry supports the point I made earlier in the chapter about Evans and Evans setting up their business in 1964 to exploit the profit potential in reproductions of pictures that had exceeded their fifty-year copyright limit. Another piece of information to observe is that the Hulton Picture Post Library had changed owners by the mid-1970s, and acquired the new name of the Radio Times Hulton Picture Library. As for the Keystone Press Agency, it instructs researchers to apply to either "Monochrome or Colour Librarian," indicating not only that the agency had by this time acquired a substantial collection of color photographs (100,000 to be precise) but also that this collection clearly was stored separately from the two-million-strong monochrome collection.[52] Reading these directory entries today is like flipping through the index of a book from which all the other pages have been torn out, leaving "little more than a teasingly abstract trace" of the actual story.[53]

To the extent that real-life experience may be glimpsed from this metaphorical index, it conjures a world made up of archives and archivists, libraries and librarians, office spaces and office hours, postal addresses and telephone numbers, paper prints, transparencies, and photostats. The geographical range of sources included in the directory, and the multilingual instructions for its use, indicate that picture research in the 1970s was an international field of operation.

The directory testifies, above all, to the reliance of picture libraries and their clients on worldwide postal services and telephone systems for the communication and exchange of orders and items. The actual "Indexes" section, meanwhile, which made up the third and final part of the volume, points most clearly to the paper-based environment of books and card catalogs within and by means of which picture researchers for most of the twentieth century worked and searched. Over thirteen pages, this section featured four different indexes: "Subjects discussed in Part One," "Geographical," "Specialist Subjects," and "Alphabetical List of Sources." Leafing through it now gives a stark reminder of—alternatively a startling insight into—the painstaking character of picture research before search engines.

Finally, the picture of picture research that emerges from the book is one that teems with human actors. Phoning and writing to picture librarians and curators (and bishops and lords), meeting editors and authors, going on visits, getting to know people in useful places, persuading busy people to help—everywhere, intermediation occurs as interlocution. All of this talking and writing must necessarily also have taken time, the sort of time that existed in the 1970s, in the sense that all aspects of the work unfolded "on the scale of the precise systems of communication, transmission, and archiving that were in place" at that time.[54] Those days and those times are gone, but the book itself remains in circulation, in our time, in the not-quite-covert circuits of online secondhand booksellers.

In the world of book publishing, handbooks are the most transient of commodities, moving rapidly from "new and updated" to old and obsolete, and sinking fast into Thompson's invisible rubbish category from which they are unlikely to be recovered. Collectors and researchers have a mutual interest in this kind of "dead stock"—transient commodities that, in Olalquiaga's phrase, "missed [their] allotted loop" in the marketplace and are therefore "destined to the secondary circuits of recycle or resale."[55] It would of course be far from accurate to say that *The Picture Researcher's Handbook* missed its go on the book-market merry-go-round, since its reiteration in seven subsequent editions confirms that it was a viable commodity for several decades. Yet each time a new edition was published, any unsold copies of the incumbent one would have been remaindered and many reference copies would have been deaccessioned as their replacements hit the shelves.

This self-induced cycle of obsolescence is the integral paradox of all successful commercial ventures that rely on the epithet "new and improved" as their selling point. The same phenomenon has nevertheless been beneficial to my own research on the history of this particular handbook. Having been able to procure secondhand copies of various editions for a pittance via online booksellers, I have in the course of the research process become a collector myself. "Even though public collections may be less objectionable socially and more useful academically than private collections, the objects get their due only in the latter," claims Benjamin in his essay on collecting.[56] And I suspect that, to the extent that *The Picture Researcher's Handbook* does get its due in this book, it is at least partly an effect of my accumulation of six of its eight editions.

"Historical research nowadays is a dull business," the playwright Alan Bennett once mused about his abandoned research career in medieval history: "had I any sense I would have been . . . sifting through material other historians had ignored or discarded; it is seldom at the frontier that discoveries are made but more often in the dustbin."[57] Retrieving the handbook from obscurity, as its various editions languish regularly in the lower-price tiers of online secondhand booksellers, is itself an intermediary act of cultural judgment that extricates a piece of rubbish from the library discard pile in order to confer upon it the durability of a historical document.

Examining a specific copy of *The Picture Researcher's Handbook,* as opposed to reading it as a text, opens up a new perspective on the book as a "media artifact" of the sort that, according to Ernst, "carries cultural meanings . . . but is at the same time an archive of cultural engineering by its very material fabrication."[58] I realize a printed book from the 1970s is less paradigmatically engineered than the magnificent machines beloved (and collected) by bona fide media archaeologists.[59] Yet an illustrated book on picture research is, among other things, a product of the very process it describes, and a copy of an out-of-print book, its paper turned brittle and yellow with age, may as well as any sound or film recording offer an encounter with "the past as a form of delayed presence, preserved in technological memory."[60] Poring over the first US edition of *The Picture Researcher's Handbook,* I have had an unarticulated aim of "reverse engineering" the work of pre-digital picture research to identify elements of the process that might later be discerned as automated functions in the search engines and databases that have come to overtake, if not quite replace, picture researchers and picture libraries.[61]

The initial motivation for writing this book was my own experience as a picture researcher living through the period when digitization was changing the logic of work. The picture of the profession that emerged from the handbook supported my own recollections of pre-digital picture research as rich in paper, reliant on telephones and the post office, and deeply dependent on interpersonal skills and relationships. A more gradual realization has been that the same descriptions applied in equal measure to the world and work of pre-digital scholarship. The more carefully I have searched through the handbook, and the closer I have read the practical advice and technical instructions, the more I have found that these would have been perfectly useful and appropriate also to someone setting out to do historical research of all kinds, and certainly art-historical research of any kind, in the 1970s. If this book is an archive, in Ernst's previously cited meaning of the term, it is not just a sedimentation of social, cultural, and technical practices in the picture business; it is also an archive of pre-digitized research practices in general.

In his theses on "the work of research in the age of digital searchability and distributability," Smith argues that "the processual operations of the searchable and the distributable" have replaced "history as a form of knowledge."[62] The forming of that knowledge, as Bennett intimated, might require searching through dustbins in order to make a discovery and, as Smith would have it, subsequently transmitting that discovery in order for it to have an effect on the world. The achievement of digitization may in this sense be articulated as putting the "dustbin" online and making its contents searchable and distributable. "Up until just recently most of the on-line content we've seen has been 'dumped' from another source," wrote Microsoft founder Bill Gates in his 1996 memoirs, using computer-engineering jargon to picture the World Wide Web, implicitly, as a giant pile of rubbish.[63] It is precisely from the virtual, online equivalent of the remainders bin, rendered digitally searchable by feats of computer engineering, that I have been able to collect, and redeem, the specific, material research object of *The Picture Researcher's Handbook*.

Conclusion

"A picture library is a collection of pictures collected for a purpose," declared Hilary Evans in one of his publications on picture librarianship.[64] To put it another way, collecting is the means by which pictures get into libraries. This principle applies to all library pictures, even the most contemporary and up-to-the-minute stock. It is nevertheless most vividly materialized in collections of historical pictures, like the Mary Evans Picture Library, the contents of which have previously circulated in other networks before being absorbed into the modern-day picture industry. Research, on the other hand, is the means by which pictures get out of libraries again, to meet a viewing public. Again, this applies to all library pictures, regardless of storage medium and facility. Even when the library in question is a virtual platform specializing in digitally captured news photos, it requires looking-with-care to identify and retrieve a picture that matches a given purpose.

To make a library out of pictures and write a book about how to find them is to connect the purpose of collecting with the purposefulness of research. To collect, conserve, classify, and commercialize old and outdated pictures is to transmit the pictorial heritage of popular visual culture from earlier historical periods to potential new audiences in the present. To write an illustrated handbook on the craft of picture research is to produce a pictorial commodity that both embeds and embodies the skills and knowledge described within it. In doing all of these things, partly together with Nelki, Hilary and Mary Evans exemplify the work of picture librarians and researchers as human agents of intermediation, exercising aesthetic and intellectual judgment to create cultural and commercial value through the judicious accumulation, targeted extraction, and deliberate transmission of pictures.

We recall that their modest objective, in producing *The Picture Researcher's Handbook*, was to make the job of the picture researcher faster, more efficient, and more economical. In the 1970s, the most appropriate technology for helping picture researchers do their work more swiftly and cost-effectively was a handbook in the form of a printed codex volume. Over the years and decades that followed, other labor-saving technologies and devices would appear on the picture researcher's desk to further service that aim. As *The Picture Researcher's Handbook* was reissued in revised and updated editions through the 1980s and 1990s, without the further collaboration of Nelki, Evans and Evans regularly prefaced each new iteration with observations about current practices, potentials, and challenges in the picture business.[65]

A recurrent topic in these introductory remarks was the prospect and experience of ever-newer technologies that promised to fulfill the purposes of picture libraries and picture research better, faster, or more efficiently. In the next two chapters, which trace the developing discourses and practices of digitization in the 1990s and 2000s, we will examine some of these later incarnations of *The Picture Researcher's Handbook* for evidence of how professionals in the picture industry articulated hopes, fears, and expectations in encounters with a set of new technologies that would eventually reconfigure the very infrastructure of the pictorial economy.

II

Under Digitization

4

Approaching Digitization

In their 1992 introduction to the fifth edition of *The Picture Researcher's Handbook*, Hilary and Mary Evans identified an electronic device that had recently revolutionized working practices across the picture industry. "The widespread introduction of fax," they wrote, "has probably done more to change the face of picture research than any other technical innovation."[1] The editors went on to note how the medium had rapidly become the "preferred method of communication" between photo collections and their clients, before observing that "fax as we currently know it is doubtless only the first phase of a major revolution in telecommunication: it can only be a matter of time before the pictures themselves, to a quality suitable for reproduction, are transmitted electronically."[2] By the time the sixth edition was published in 1996, the editors could report that their prediction from four years earlier was in the process of coming true: "When our last edition was published, the fax was a relatively recent innovation: today it is generally regarded as the indispensable tool of the trade. With this edition, it is the prospect of digitized transmission which promises to transform, perhaps more fundamentally than any other change, the picture researcher's way of life."[3] Another five years down the line, as the seventh edition appeared in 2001, the accelerating implementation of "electronic transmission" led Evans and Evans to speculate that by the time "the next generation of researchers" had taken over, "the idea that pictures were ever obtained in any other way than electronically will seem as laughable as yesterday's brown paper and string seem to us."[4] These three excerpts, one from each of the handbook editions that were published between 1992 and 2001, signpost key moments in the history of picture research under digitization. As the subtitle of this second part of the book alludes, this and the next two chapters explore picture research both during and enduring digitization, undergoing, in other words, both a period and a process of technological change. Under digitization, research has been reconfigured as search and pictures have been recoded as computable information. Repositories of pictures have similarly been disintermediated as libraries and reintermediated as platforms.

This chapter considers the approach of digitization in the 1990s, when the idea of digital technologies taking command in the picture industry began to emerge. The next chapter explores how actual digitization manifested itself in the 2000s as a set of new or modified means of capturing, accumulating, extracting, and transmitting pictures, which would eventually bypass picture librarians as the human interface between collections and their users. The concluding chapter demonstrates how the seemingly automated services of online platforms continue to rely on the disavowed labor and unrecognized skills of human intermediaries. Together, the chapters that follow exemplify the specific debts that digital resources of picturable information owe to photographic cultures of accumulation and extraction, and reveal how the picture business enlisted digitization to serve its own purposes, yet ended up serving the purposes of digitization.

In the first edition of *The Picture Researcher's Handbook*, discussed at length in chapter 3, Evans, Evans, and Nelki gave a detailed outline of the several stages involved in a typical picture research project.[5] At each step, the authors' description focused on making appropriate use of sources, technologies, and infrastructures that were relevant for the task in hand. For instance, looking up preliminary information on a new topic meant consulting books and other printed publications in public libraries; obtaining the right pictures involved writing letters, making phone calls, or traveling to picture libraries to conduct on-site research; keeping borrowed materials safe and in order required systems of storage and record management; and returning all used and unused pictures to their respective sources, safely parceled up, demanded both wrapping materials and trips to the post office. Both picture libraries and picture researchers were constantly looking for ways to speed up or simplify any of these tasks, whether related to locating pictures, transporting them, or storing them.

Tools such as the *Picture Sources* directory and *The Picture Researcher's Handbook* were produced with the explicit objective of making it easier for researchers to locate and communicate with a wide range of sources. Brochures and catalogs were likewise printed and distributed by many picture libraries as a combination of advertisement of and finding tool for the specific contents of their own collections. The innovation of padded envelopes (such as the "Jiffy bag") improved transport safety for circulating reproductions, while filing cabinets were indispensable to the long-term storage needs of picture libraries and the short-term ones of picture researchers. These analog tools and technologies still dominated working life in the picture business for the best part of the 1990s, even as the industry increasingly anticipated the advent of digitization.

Focusing on the final decade of the twentieth century, this chapter takes an unashamedly teleological approach to the question of what picture libraries had, and what they did, that made both their contents and their working practices seem ripe for digitization. What capabilities could digital technologies provide that might enhance the work of picture libraries in capturing, accumulating, extracting, and transmitting pictures to a public? And what affordances did picture libraries have that might serve the purposes of digitization in return? To answer those questions I draw on evidence from three different kinds of period sources. First, the editors' introductions to the three editions of *The Picture Researcher's Handbook* published between 1992 and 2001 gave voice to hopes and expectations harbored by professionals inside the picture industry. Second, studies conducted by information scholars over the same period sought to identify how working practices in picture libraries might benefit from computational search and automated retrieval systems. Third, a television play produced at the end of the decade provided a popularized, fictional representation of a picture library and its employees that both explicitly illustrated the characteristics of picture research as intellectual work and implicitly expressed concerns over what the digitized future might hold.

Learning the Fax

The process of adopting new and computer-mediated ways of working was gradual and uneven in the UK picture industry. Computers had been introduced to help manage tasks like cataloging since the late 1980s, and the much-referenced Mosaic browser made the World Wide Web easily navigable from around 1993.[6] As late as 2001, however, when the seventh edition of *The Picture Researcher's Handbook* appeared, businesses were still making extensive use of the traditional infrastructures of telecommunication and postal services. New categories of information included in the handbook's directory of sources—from the inclusion of fax numbers as standard in 1992 to the introduction of email and website addresses in 2001—indicate how and when businesses embraced new communication media. The implications of such changes were further elaborated in the introduction to each volume, where the editors regularly expressed their views on recent developments in the business. In the two 1980s editions of *The Picture Researcher's Handbook*, Evans and Evans had bemoaned the chaotic number systems in telephone networks across the world. When the fifth edition appeared in 1992, the world looked, at last, to be "well on the way to a coherent international system" for telephone numbers.[7] The relative stabilization of this infrastructural component was one of the factors that enabled the worldwide adoption of fax as a means of instantaneous communication from around 1990.[8]

Faxing allowed the immediacy of the telephone to merge with the visual and documentary affordances of the postal letter, which in turn "benefitted the growth of visual culture," as the business historian Jonathan Coopersmith has argued, "by making the sending, receiving, and alteration of images easier and less expensive."[9] Just as importantly, fax users came to expect that all types of information, including visual kinds, would be "easy to acquire" and "simple to create and disseminate."[10] The fax machine's capacity to transmit facsimile inscriptions of documents, as opposed to transcriptions of their contents, meant that it disintermediated mail, courier, and telephone services for certain uses. These included both written communications, where an immediate or quick response in writing was desired, and communications that were more like instructions or messages that did not need an immediate reply.

For picture researchers submitting lists of topics or motifs to be searched for by picture librarians, for instance, a fax would be more convenient than a telephone call or answer service because it saved recipients the work of having to copy out the list in writing themselves. For businesses operating within global networks—as many picture libraries did—fax transmission also offered the same benefits as the telephone in overcoming spatial distances, without its disadvantages. Unlike telephone communication, which requires both parties to be simultaneously available, fax communication allowed senders to dispatch their messages when convenient (within office hours) at their end, and recipients at the other end, perhaps in a different time zone, could read and act on them at their own convenience. Regardless of geographical distance, however, the crucial benefit of fax over postal or courier services was that it eliminated physical transportation, and therefore delivery times, from the equation. For all its expediency, as Coopersmith notes, this also meant that "deadlines never ended," since the instantaneous delivery of fax "encouraged—or demanded—working up to the deadline."[11] During its heyday from 1980 to 1995, all these affordances of fax—diachronicity, instantaneity, picturability—prefigured a number of practices, from spamming to remote political activism, which in more recent years have been attributed to digital technologies.[12]

In this sense, the multiple applications of fax can be likened to the equally disparate and innovative uses of photocopying that Lisa Gitelman has found emblematized in the 1960s Xerox machine.[13] Yet xerography was primarily a way of saving a document by making a local record of it, regardless of whether or not the photocopy was to be shared with anybody else. Faxing, on the other hand, proved an ideal medium for sharing documents quickly and across huge distances, without necessarily expecting recipients to save them. (Indeed, in an office where I worked in the late 1990s, the incoming end of the fax machine was positioned straight over a wastepaper basket, for ease of junk fax disposal.) And just as Gitelman notes that "the relative ease of photocopying aided in the proliferation of documents," made more or less for the sake of documentation, so the relative ease and low cost of faxing aided in the proliferation of messages sent for the sake of messaging.[14] The lasting impact of the fax on working practices has more in common with Polaroid's impact on snapshot photography practices, in this respect.[15] Fax and Polaroid both gave users an early experience of cutting out the middle man—whether automatically receiving letters without waiting for the postal worker, or instantly receiving their own photographs without going to the drugstore—that was subsequently recognizable, and therefore immediately workable, when encountered in digital applications such as email and smartphone photography.

As previously noted, Evans and Evans made an explicit connection between fax and digital communications in their 1992 introduction to *PRH5*, and also made qualified predictions for the direction in which it would soon take off. The subsequent edition in 1996 showed that these had been largely fulfilled. Despite acknowledging the increasing importance of electronic communication forms, "electronic addresses" were nevertheless omitted from the directory entries in *PHR6* on the grounds that the systems and formats in operation were as yet too diverse, unstable, and liable to change to be of use in a printed publication. Again, Evans and Evans were prescient in predicting that "[t]here must come a time when on-line services are as compatible as are faxes." They further promised to include details of "E-mail, world-wide web, internet, and so forth" in due course, as soon as "digitized transmission and electronic communication are as routine as the phone and fax, and when the associated addresses are relatively stabilized and simple."[16]

Both editions of *The Picture Researcher's Handbook* published in the 1990s indicate that technological developments in these years were first and foremost experienced as affecting the ways in which picture sources and clients communicated about pictures, rather than the ways in which pictures as such were communicated or transmitted from sources to clients. Indeed, the possibility of electronic transmission of "the pictures themselves," which was felt to be just around the corner in 1992, had still not been fully realized by 1996. The editors noted then that "press and sports agencies for whom time is all-important, and some of the more competitive stock agencies," had begun to provide digitally transmitted image files, but that the majority of sources were as yet "holding back until the situation is clearer" because of the prohibitive cost involved, and the uncertainty over the longer-term viability of then-current technologies: "we know of one agency that bankrupted itself by spending too much, too soon, and another which has a dust-free humidity-controlled room full of expensive equipment which it never uses."[17] Picture industry professionals in the 1990s evidently harbored hopes that digitization would speed up and simplify the processes of extracting and transmitting pictorial goods for delivery and publication. As we see them articulated by Evans and Evans, these hopes were mainly tempered by fears of making the wrong call on substantial investments in machinery, rather than by concerns over the material integrity of the pictures to be circulated.

Picture industry professionals displayed little concern over the new technologies' impact on the supposed truth value of photographs, a topic that otherwise preoccupied much of public discourse on digital or electronic imaging around the same time. The explanation is of course that, with the exception of agencies exclusively committed to documentary photography and photojournalism, the picture industry as a whole was not invested in the "visual truth" of photography.[18] In fact, one could argue that parts of the stock photography business were heavily invested in anything but the truth. If it was the case that "the fact-based photographic currency" was being devalued by digitization, as one prolific writer on the topic suggested, this was of limited consequence for a business in which the primary function of photography was as a technique for capturing, accumulating, and transmitting visual commodities.[19]

Aside from the question of expensive equipment, the main challenge that digitization posed for picture libraries was related to the safeguarding of intellectual property across the promiscuous networks of the World Wide Web, as prefigured in the case of *Bridgeman v. Corel*, discussed in chapter 1. In *PRH6*, Evans and Evans acknowledged the value of the internet as "a communication resource," but expressed grave doubts about its suitability for "picture research" proper: "will a web site come to be considered an appropriate place for a picture library to display representative samples of its wares? Not every source would wish to be accessed by any stranger who takes the time and trouble to do so: many, I feel sure, will prefer to keep some measure of control over those who use their services."[20] A similar doubt was reported during an interview in 2008, when Rick, a manager at a large stock agency in the United Kingdom, was thinking back to the launch of their first searchable website in 2001: "At the time, many people were saying: 'Well, why would a researcher want to do all the work themselves researching from all these websites when they can do what they used to do, which was pick up the phone . . . ?'" Rick and his colleagues soon realized that, in fact, picture researchers "like to do the work, and not sit waiting for these things to come in."[21]

By the time *PRH7* came to be prepared in 2001, Hilary Evans, too, would have much revised his assessment of the internet's uses. In 1996, however, the sentiments expressed in the introduction to *PRH6* reflected the situation on the ground. In the mid-1990s paper-based print formats still overwhelmingly formed the final output of any library picture sold for reproduction, whether it was published as a magazine illustration, displayed on a book jacket, or incorporated in a piece of advertising. And for those purposes the most reliable means by which to provide photographs for reproduction remained, for the majority of regular picture libraries, analog materials and infrastructures like emulsion-based paper prints, color transparencies, padded envelopes, courier bikes, and postal services.

SEARCHING FOR AUTOMATION

The multiple editions of the handbook are testimony to the roles played by different communication technologies in carrying out the practicalities of locating, storing, and transporting pictures. These manual or mechanical tasks constitute what Craig Robertson would call the "information labor" performed by picture researchers and librarians, as distinct from the "knowledge work" involved in the intellectual processes of selecting, classifying, and interpreting pictures, which formed an equally significant part of their jobs.[22] It was in the routine tasks of information labor that picture librarians like Evans and Evans first and foremost saw the potential for new technologies to improve or facilitate existing practices in the 1990s. At the same time, researchers in the field of information science were studying the handling of picture requests in UK picture libraries with the aim of finding out how aspects of knowledge work, too, could be carried out faster and more efficiently through the adoption of digital technologies.

In 1993, Caroline McGregor and Peter Enser performed an "analysis of visual information retrieval queries" for the research and development department of the British Library.[23] The study focused on the processing of picture requests at the Hulton Deutsch Collection, which at the time was the most recent incarnation of the Hulton Picture Post Library, discussed in chapter 2. The researchers noted that clients submitted their request by phone, fax, or letter, while librarians responded to the queries chiefly by rifling through large quantities of prints in order to produce a suitable selection of results. The prints were organized in separate collections classified according to the two different schemes that had been inherited from two collections we recall from chapter 2: the library's founding collection, the Hulton Picture Post Library designed by Gibbs-Smith, and its largest acquisition, the library of the Keystone Picture Agency.

Having observed librarians navigating visually across these collections guided by the written or oral instructions provided by clients, McGregor and Enser concluded that, "in an environment such as that of the host library in this investigation, an extremely heavy dependency on the expertise and search time availability of the picture researchers in his/her role as intermediary must continue to be the norm."[24] A separate study published by Enser two years later addressed existing and potential solutions to the problem of using text-based finding aids to classify, search, and access visual materials. Discussing various attempts at creating "classification schemes for visually encoded knowledge," the author highlighted once again the Gibbs-Smith system employed by the Hulton for its dependence on "a picture researcher's knowledge of his or her stock," and the correspondingly "great emphasis given to browsing the picture collection within the search process."[25]

The attempts by information scientists to break down the job of finding a picture into discrete components belonged to a long tradition of productivity research that hails back to descriptive studies of mechanical labor from the early years of the Industrial Revolution. In such studies, the task of identifying all the separate operations involved in a work process—be it the production of pins in the 1750s or the retrieval of pictures from library files in the 1990s—was a first step toward determining which parts of the process might be usefully delegated to a machine. Warren Sack has documented the direct (if convoluted) line that runs from the illustrated descriptions of mechanical manufacturing processes in Diderot's and d'Alembert's *Encyclopédie* (1751–1766) to "what we know today as computer programming languages."[26] As Sack explains, the encyclopedists' accurate descriptions of manufacturing opened up a conception of work as a sequence of operations, rather than a mere product of expended energy. Establishing this idea made it possible, in turn, to conceive of a "division of labor," first among different kinds of workers, and then between workers and machines.[27] It is the same logic that underpinned efforts in the mid-1990s to produce "general categorizations of requests" that might be schematized and incorporated into what was then described as "the user interface of unmediated-query visual information retrieval systems."[28] In other words, what we now tend to call search engines.

Despite considerable efforts to devise computational and automated solutions to problems of picture research in the course of the 1990s, in 2000 Enser observed that the diversity and complexity of visual information processing meant that it was still difficult to bypass entirely "that highly capable, intelligent device known as the picture researcher":

> The picture researcher brings three fundamentally important attributes to the task of mediated visual information retrieval: collection knowledge, expert (domain) knowledge and world knowledge. In combination, they arm the human intermediary with the in-depth familiarity with the conceptual and physical attributes of a collection of image material, the underpinning expertise in a given subject domain and the tacit knowledge which informs our interpretation and signification of any given scene.[29]

This statement suggests why any amount of studying and describing the operations involved in picture research would necessarily reduce it to information labor, because it is in the nature of knowledge work as a mental form of processing to be idiosyncratic and ineffable. Enser's description is still as close as information scholarship comes to giving an accurate representation of picture researchers as cultural, rather than technical, intermediaries between pictures and their potential users or publics. Yet it would require a different medium than writing to convey fully the "intelligent device known as the picture researcher" in action, and the affordances of the picture library not just as a repository of pictorial information but as a visual and haptic environment of research.

Making Connections

Perhaps unexpectedly, it is the medium of television that has so far provided the most compelling representation of picture research and librarianship as knowledge work. A three-part television drama written and directed by Stephen Poliakoff, *Shooting the Past* (BBC, 1999), is set in a fictional institution in London, which traces its ten-million-strong photographic collection back to the nineteenth century.[30] When the show begins, its managers and employees are about to discover that the collection faces closure, due to the building having been acquired by an entrepreneur from the United States, who intends to repurpose it as a business school. Discovering that the collection managers have failed to sell off its contents as instructed, the new owner is both shocked and angry. He threatens the immediate destruction of all the photographs in the library, except for a few famous and financially valuable ones, which he intends to sell at auction to help fund the refurbishment of the building. A drama is then played out as the picture librarians must persuade the businessman not just to abandon the idea of destroying the millions of photographs but to preserve them all intact as a collection.

Despite being "obscurely set in a fusty library," as one critic has put it, *Shooting the Past* clearly resonated with audiences both when it was first aired and for several years after.[31] It was first broadcast on BBC2 in January 1999 to an initial UK audience of 2.5 million viewers, going on to receive a wide international distribution through network and cable television as well as DVD sales.[32] It was then repeated on BBC4 in 2006, and in 2007 was featured among the Top 50 Dramas of All Time in a poll conducted by the UK's Channel Four.[33] A contemporary reviewer described the drama as "a meditation on the nature of photographic images, a celebration of old-world English eccentricity at threat in a world of high-technology glossiness, and a reminder that nothing in our heritage is sacred."[34] As an example of what Robin Nelson terms "'high-end' TV drama," *Shooting the Past* has also attracted sustained scholarly attention for its evocative representation of "modernity, technological change and its effects on human experience."[35]

The setting of the picture library allowed Poliakoff to tell such a story in a way that was particularly suited to the audiovisual medium of television. In creative or poetic terms, the picture library made it diegetically plausible to use still photographs as a storytelling device within a television serial, making people, events, and objects from the past readily picturable within the present of the drama. In practical terms, the material means were afforded by the real-life Hulton Getty Picture Library,

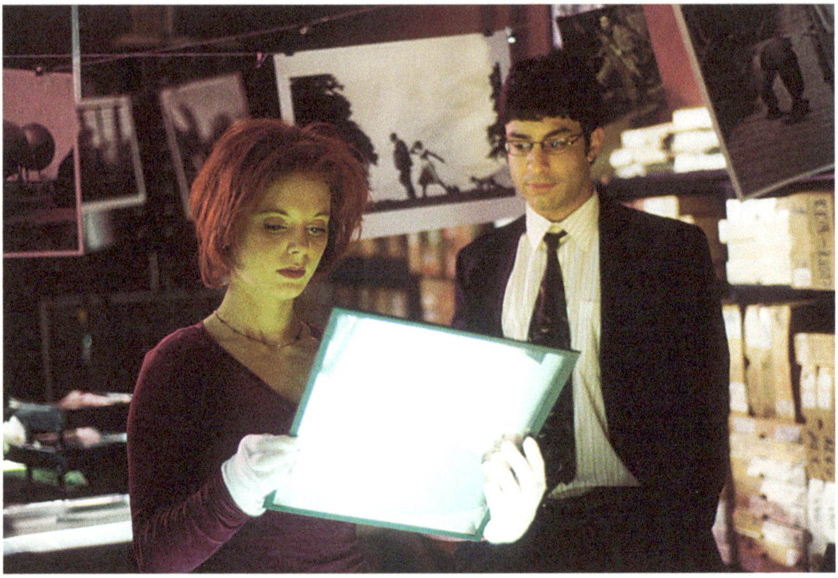

FIGURE 4.1
Still from *Shooting the Past* (1999). Emilia Fox as Spig and Arj Barker as Garnett. Props from the Hulton Archive. Photographer: Joss Barratt, BBC Photo Archive.

which lent photographs and library paraphernalia to furnish the set of the "Fallon Photo Library" (figure 4.1). For instance, the storage boxes that occupy the background in several scenes hail from the same Keystone Press Agency collection discussed in chapter 2 (see figure 2.2).[36] Most of the photographs displayed and discussed in the show can also be found among the historical holdings of the Hulton, where Poliakoff had carried out preliminary research for the production.[37]

From the first scene in the first episode, *Shooting the Past* is beset with "legacy" media technologies. The play opens with a monologue by the character Oswald Bates (Timothy Spall), who claims to be preparing to kill himself (figure 4.2). We see him recording his speech on an ancient Dictaphone and taking photographs of himself while talking, using a remote control to operate a still camera mounted on a tripod. Shown thus immersed in outdated recording media, this "chubby man, wearing a cardy—talking into a tape machine" makes it clear that what has brought him to this point are the events of the past few days, which we are about to have played out for us on the screen.[38] This opening scene

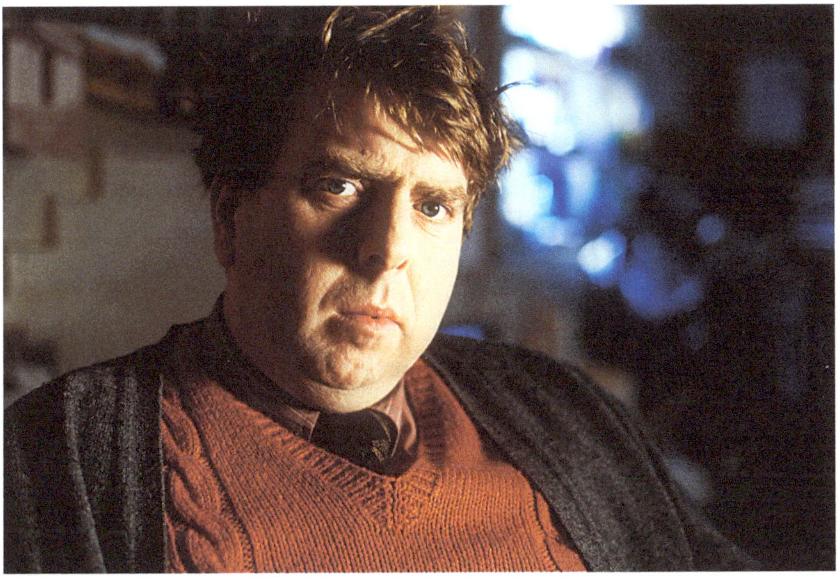

Figure 4.2
Still from *Shooting the Past* (1999). Timothy Spall as Oswald in opening scene. Photographer: Joss Barratt, BBC Photo Archive.

of a middle-aged man surrounded by outmoded technologies sets up the "wistful, some would say nostalgic, vision" that seems to pervade the show.[39] As the narrative will reveal, however, Oswald is in fact "a very modern person," whose "mind works very fast," so fast that he has foreseen what will happen once the new owners take possession of the library, and has taken what he deems to be the necessary steps to deal with it.[40]

From Oswald depicted in his own home, the camera cuts to a scene where two men in business suits are seen to be arriving at the picture library. Anderson (Liam Cunningham) is the new owner, and he is greeted together with his assistant, Garnett (Arj Barker), by the library manager, Marilyn (Lindsay Duncan); her deputy, Oswald; and three other staff members. Confrontation soon ensues as Anderson wants to know why the library holdings have not been moved out of the building, while Marilyn and Oswald insist they have never received the letters telling them to do so. Once the staff of the Fallon Library have grasped the gravity of their situation, they scramble to find a way of persuading Anderson to keep the collection intact.

The librarians first attempt to overwhelm their new owner with the wealth and range of pictures accumulated among its millions of items, insisting on taking him on a tour of the collection. The aim is to demonstrate that the real assets of the picture library are not "our prize fish, the Man Ray" and the few other masterworks by famous photographers that Anderson wants to put up for auction, but rather the totality of its enormous and eclectic collection.[41] This scene makes extensive use of photographic prints to create an impression of the picture library as a haptic and immersive environment, not least by having the actors weave through photographs suspended from lines strung among the shelves and filing cabinets. Such treatment of archival vintage photographs may cause real-life archivists and picture librarians to shudder, yet the prints pegged up on the lines are a visual trope of photographic materiality, which alludes to the wet processing of black-and-white emulsion photographs in darkrooms. In this case it also works as a visualization of the idea, familiar from Gibbs-Smith's description of the Hulton Picture Post Library in chapter 2, that picture librarians should be constantly soaked in pictures.

A scene at the very beginning of this sequence demonstrates just how immersed the librarians are in the collection's contents, as Oswald challenges Anderson and Garnett to ask him for a picture:

> OSWALD: I'll find anything you want—within seven seconds . . .
>
> ANDERSON: Seven seconds?
>
> OSWALD: Too long? Seven seconds is quite long you're right, we'll make it five.
>
> GARNETT: I take it you're computerised.
>
> OSWALD *(HIS VOICE RISING IN ASTONISHMENT)*: You think we have computers in here?—it'll take years to catalogue all this and get it on line . . . of course we have no computers, it's all in here. *(He taps his forehead.)*[42]

When eventually given the name of the street in the small town where Anderson grew up, Oswald sets off among the files and shelves (figure 4.3) to return, within seconds, brandishing the results of his search to the astonished American (figure 4.4). Shortly after, Marilyn displays her own intuitive grasp of the library's holdings to Anderson by pulling down a

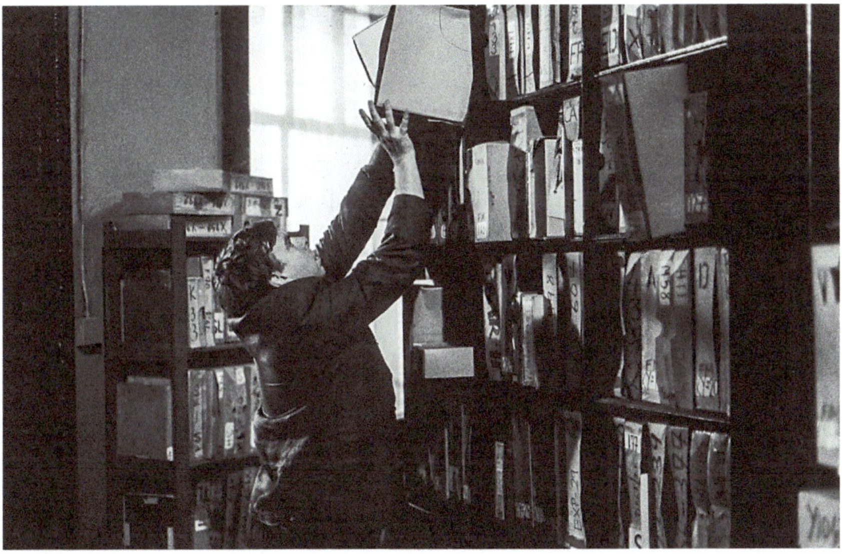

FIGURE 4.3
Still from *Shooting the Past* (1999). Oswald (Timothy Spall) among the files. Props from the Hulton Archive. Photographer: Gary Moyes, BBC Photo Archive.

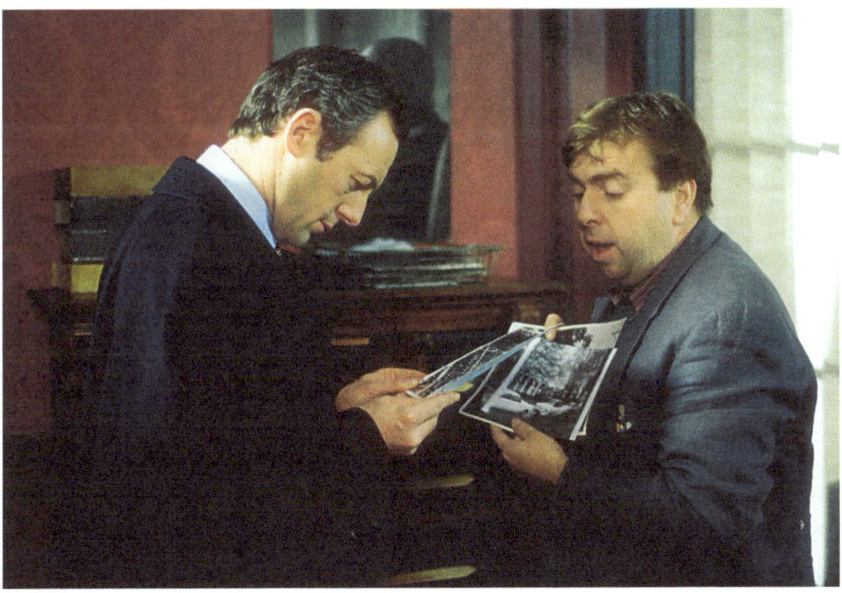

FIGURE 4.4
Still from *Shooting the Past* (1999). Liam Cunningham as Anderson and Timothy Spall as Oswald in the library. Photographer: Joss Barratt, BBC Photo Archive.

seemingly random box from a shelf and telling him its precise contents. In view of the fact that the fictional Fallon Library had been constructed with building blocks borrowed from the real-life Hulton, it is fitting that the picture librarians who are the heroes of Poliakoff's play should so forcefully demonstrate the value of being submerged in pictures.

When neither Oswald's rapid search result nor Marilyn's powers of persuasion succeed in moving Anderson to change his mind, the librarians change tactics. Appealing to his emotions, they present a story in photographs, compiled from across the collection, that documents the fate of a young Jewish girl growing up in Berlin in the 1930s. The story of Lily emblematizes both the horror of the Holocaust and the role of photographs in preserving the collective memory of its victims and survivors, as well as its enablers and perpetrators. It is presented in pictures ranging from amateur snaps, via Nazi-era documentation, to contemporary street photographs. Marilyn explains to Anderson how Oswald has managed to extract it, out of the millions of pictures in the collection, on the basis of an extraordinary gift for remembering faces and making visual connections between photographs. Although Anderson is moved by Lily's story—"a twentieth-century tale, caught like that"—he refuses to recognize it as a valid argument for preserving the entire collection.[43]

Oswald's compilation of pictures telling the true story of Lily has demonstrated the value of the photographic collection as a source of historical data. The creative and commercial potential in the collection is emphasized in a later scene, when Marilyn is trying to convince an advertising agency to buy the library before Anderson destroys it. "There are ideas here for a hundred campaigns," she tells the agency representative listening to her pitch, and as photographs borrowed from the real-life Hulton collection flow across the screen, she argues that the pictures will be sources of "constant inspiration" and "constant stimulation—not just providing surprising concepts for selling things, but they will also impress your clients as art objects in themselves."[44] This scene articulates the creative aspects of picture research as a method for making new and unexpected connections between pictures, in addition to uncovering already existing connections between the people or places depicted in them. Like Hilary and Mary Evans in real life, the picture librarians Oswald and Marilyn also operate as collectors, archivists, and conservators. In this capacity they are among "those few eccentrics" whose aesthetic judgment, according to rubbish theory, has the power to lift a piece of junk out of a pile and declare it a durable art object or a valuable historical document.[45]

In the end, it is precisely by sifting through piles and piles of pictures, exercising their skills and knowledge as interpreters of visual information, that the picture librarians manage to save the collection from destruction by extracting a sequence of photographs and newspaper clippings that turn out to have a direct connection to Anderson's personal history. Oswald and Marilyn reconstruct the extraordinary life story of his maternal grandmother, which happens to be documented in photographs scattered throughout the collection. The entire story has been assembled, with some unwitting help from Anderson himself, on the basis of one single photograph depicting his mother, which he carries in his wallet and is at one point persuaded to show Oswald. The latter sees a family resemblance in the mother's portrait to a face he already knows from the files: a woman named Hettie, whose adventurous life in the early 1900s is amply documented in the Fallon Library's archives of documentary, art, and news photographs. It is in this episode that *Shooting the Past* most compellingly conveys both the creativity and the intellectual effort involved in the work of intermediation performed by picture librarians.

In a final, virtuoso performance of his facial recognition skills, Oswald has identified the connection between Anderson and Hettie, via the photograph of his mother. Oswald then takes an overdose of pills, leaving behind a pile of materials and clues for Marilyn and the others to piece together. In the scenes that follow, Marilyn and her colleagues embark on what is effectively a historical research project, mobilizing all the picture library's affordances. Their archival search involves scrutinizing innumerable photographic images and other documents in a wide range of formats, from glass slides and acrylic-based negatives to paper prints and newspaper clippings, enlisting appropriate historical viewing equipment, such as lightboxes and projectors, in order to access the information they contain. The breakthrough occurs when Veronica (Billie Whitelaw), the oldest member of staff at the Fallon, accepts a client's request for pictures of all the UK prime ministers of the twentieth century. When Marilyn looks through the stack of pictures gathered by Veronica, in order to check that every prime minister from the twentieth century has been included, her eye alights on a detail in one of the photographs, triggering a visual connotation that enables her to fit the final pieces in the puzzle of Anderson's grandmother.

As depicted in the show, the process of deciphering Oswald's clues is, on the one hand, an exercise in picture research as rubbish-theoretical value creation through the judicious extraction of certain pictures, which have so far been languishing in the general obscurity of the collection, and imbuing them with a new and lasting significance. On the other hand, the same process demonstrates the significance of the picture library as a material "set" of data, in which each unit can potentially produce new and different meanings by being juxtaposed, compared, or contrasted with any number of other units.

This work of producing meaning from the assembly and juxtaposition of photographs is referred to in *Shooting the Past* as "making connections."[46] The characters frequently use this term to describe the way the human mind, and most specifically Oswald's mind, works to process the contents of the collection, extracting information from a variety of items and combining them in new and revelatory ways. The stories of Lily and Hettie exemplify two sets of "search results" of this visually led and largely intuitive process. In one scene this form of human intelligence is explicitly compared to the machine intelligence of a computer, when Oswald interrupts Garnett as he is working on his laptop:

> OSWALD *(COMING FORWARD, INDICATING LAPTOP)*: I'm very similar to that machine, you know—
>
> GARNETT: You are?
>
> OSWALD: Yes. *(He smiles.)* Yes, I think that's true. . . . It would be very interesting for me to take it on, my memory against its. . . . I'm very good at fuzzy logic . . . making connections. . . . I'll always *beat* it at fuzzy logic, and of course my database doesn't need constantly updating—it does that automatically.[47]

The same phrase recurs toward the end of episode 3, when Marilyn is sitting at Oswald's hospital bedside and thinking back to happier times, illustrated through a flashback scene set in Oswald's office some years earlier. Contemplating a pile of pictures on his desk, he asks Marilyn if she knows what he thinks "is so wonderful about our lives here," clearly referring to the picture library. When she says no, he explains: "What's wonderful is—we have a chance to dream . . . dream from looking at these pictures . . . let the mind float—make connections between things, daydreams, nightdreams. . . . We have space, time . . . no pressure . . . the most valuable things on earth."[48] Like the air or sea, alluded to by his use of the verb *float*, the Fallon collection is an environment that appears to envelop those who dwell in it. Inhabiting the environment of the picture library makes affordances available to Oswald, Marilyn, and their colleagues that are not just unavailable but imperceptible to visitors like Anderson and Garnett. The "fuzzy logic" that Oswald takes pride in is both a product and a requisite of his immersion in the material that constitutes the collection.

Since the late 1990s enormous efforts have been made in designing user interfaces and search engines that might "make connections" among pictorial data held in digital databases in ways that simulate the fuzzy logic, visual connotations, and sudden insights mobilized by human picture researchers like Oswald and his real-life counterparts. No computational search algorithm has yet been devised that entirely replaces the skill and judgment of the picture researcher, yet the work of library-based picture research was nevertheless reintermediated, from the early 2000s onward, as the screen-based browsing of results retrieved by a search engine from a database.

This development also seems to have been predicted by the fast-working mind of the anti-hero in *Shooting the Past*. In the final scene of the drama, we are made to understand that Oswald's overdose has left him with permanent brain damage, as he is shown in a clearly reduced state, sitting on a park bench with Marilyn. From her commentary it appears that the pills have been his way of throwing a spanner in the works and wrecking the Fallon Library's foremost tool for processing pictorial data: the machinery of his own memory. After his monumental feat of intermediation, extracting the story of Hettie from the files, he has disintermediated himself, preemptively, in order to avoid confrontation with the (lesser) computational technologies that he can see are about to replace the likes of him and his human intelligence.

The prospect of digitization as such is never articulated in *Shooting the Past*. As the play ends, its entire contents have been transferred to "an

American collection," where Marilyn hopes they will allow "some other Oswalds to make startling connections between things."[49] Yet there is no suggestion that digitization and online distribution might be enlisted to accelerate the commercial exploitation of the collection's assets, nor to enhance the potential for any other Oswalds to discover, explore, and make connections between its pictures. As for Anderson, he is clearly oblivious to the steady income from regular sales of reproduction rights, which constituted the basic business model of the picture library. And despite having just founded the American School for Business for the Twenty-First Century, he is evidently unable to foresee a market for digitized reproductions of historical photographs in the future that is about to unfold.[50]

Poliakoff's drama was of course not about the picture business as such; it merely used the picture library as an evocative setting in which to tell a story of existential threat that felt applicable to many historical cultural institutions in the 1990s. While the imminent digital transformation of workplaces in general, and of picture libraries in particular, remained unstated in the show, contemporaneous viewers immediately recognized the "world of high-technology glossiness" as part of that threat.[51] This impression was produced, paradoxically, through the conspicuous absence of actual digital devices from the screen, indicating the protagonists' unease around new technologies. This was underscored in dialogue sequences like Oswald's exchange with Garnett, quoted above, as well as in scenes showing Marilyn struggling to operate a borrowed mobile phone. In short, *Shooting the Past* contributed to a general cultural anticipation, tempered with apprehension, that greeted the rapid approach of digitization in the late 1990s.

The fictional representation of picture librarianship in *Shooting the Past* gave voices and put faces to a generation of cultural intermediaries whose specialized skills and knowledge looked set to be made redundant by new technologies of search and retrieval. In real life, such technologies were being developed in this period through newfound collaborations between computer scientists and information professionals.[52] How did the digitization of photographic collections affect working practices in picture libraries, and to what extent did the adoption of automated search and retrieval systems allow them to dispense with the intermediary services of staff, as hinted at in the television drama?

Improving Affordances

In their introduction to the 2001 edition of *The Picture Researcher's Handbook*, Evans and Evans recalled that in the early days of their career, the "only two ways a picture researcher could obtain a picture" were by personally visiting the location in which it was held or having it sent by post or courier. In both cases, the picture researcher would have to get their literal hands on the picture. Likewise, those employed in picture libraries would either assist visiting researchers in their on-site research or carry out file searches on their behalf on the basis of requests received by letter, phone, or fax, and then dispatch the results by post or in person. Until the mid-1990s, this pattern was reasonably consistent throughout the picture industry. In this respect, the fictional Fallon Photo Library in Poliakoff's *Shooting the Past* provides a broadly accurate picture of what "picture research" had looked like throughout the second half of the twentieth century. By 2001, however, the increased proliferation of "online search, access and retrieval," meant that picture research was increasingly starting to look like someone sitting in front of a computer screen.[53]

Digitizing photographic collections first of all changed the material character of the pictorial commodities that picture libraries offered for sale. Since many tasks were tied to the physical organization of their holdings, this had important ramifications for the practical work of the library staff. Some of these effects of digitization were documented at the turn of the century by Enser and colleagues, who had studied the predigital working practices of picture libraries some years earlier. In a report on "design and implementation factors in electronic image retrieval systems" from 2000, Tope and Enser included a case study of an anonymized commercial picture library, which had found that "the skills required by the company [had] changed" after the wholesale digitization of its holdings had introduced a "new system for locating images."[54] Once the library had established a web-based search engine open for direct access by clients, the latter no longer had to phone or fax the library with long picture lists in order to have research staff look through the files. New jobs were created for keyworders and other digitization workers, who were needed to maintain and improve the online resource, while picture researchers were increasingly taking on the same roles as sales staff, a function from which they had previously been rigidly separated. By the end of the digitization project, the very structure of the company had changed, with new departments set up and others downsized.

In a newspaper picture library studied in the same report, the researchers noted the same tendency of staffing ratios changing due to digitization. "Library staff are no longer needed to carry out searches on the user's behalf; rather the search is 'mediated' by the electronic image retrieval system," the authors observed, while emphasizing that staff would still be required "to mediate between the image and the system."[55] The digitized picture library, as described by Tope and Enser, was a very different physical environment from the pre-digital library conjured up in *Shooting the Past*. Its affordances of searchability, findability, and transmissibility would not have appeared as such to librarians in the mold of Oswald and Marilyn. Their skills of searching, finding, ordering, and interpreting had evolved within, and were therefore adapted to, the three-dimensional haptic space of a library with four walls, furnished with cabinets, shelves, and lightboxes. The digital environment of a database, accessed through the virtual window of a graphical user interface displaying a blinking search box or a grid of tiny thumbnails arrayed on a flat screen, afforded the ability to locate pictures by other means, to researchers equipped with other skills.

For the best part of the twentieth century, a picture library was a physical environment that afforded access to certain kinds of assets for certain kinds of actors. Photographs made up the bulk of these assets, of course, but the captions, catalogs, and indexes furnishing information about the photographs and what was depicted in them were also a key component of this category. These metadata were what made the pictures—or data—findable within whatever archival system a given picture library operated. They also made the pictures exploitable as commodities, as captions anchored whichever message a photograph was required to communicate, be it as documentation or illustration, and credit lines ensured that the correct rights-holder would be remunerated when it was reproduced. Findability and exploitability were, along with searchability, mobility, and transmissibility, the key affordances that characterized photographic libraries as environments in which picturable information was preserved, and from which it could be extracted as pictorial data. The actors who performed this work of preservation and extraction were largely professional picture librarians and researchers, who made use of all these affordances in their capacities as intermediaries between pictures and their users.

Both commercial picture libraries, relying on regular sales in order to remain in business, and professional picture researchers, looking to do their job as efficiently as possible, were well disposed toward new tools and technologies that might enhance the searchability, mobility, and transmissibility of library pictures. Not least were they keen to adopt tools that would speed up or alleviate the more tedious and time-consuming tasks such as copying out picture requests from clients, keeping records of pictures lent or borrowed, wrapping and dispatching picture parcels, and other tasks. When faxing became both practicable and affordable around 1990, researchers and librarians alike embraced this labor-saving device, which enabled them to communicate both instantly and visually with suppliers and clients across the globe. The enthusiastic adoption of fax habituated workers in the picture industry to the instant, yet diachronous communication of visual information to and from anywhere in the world. This primed them, in turn, to recognize and appreciate the prospect of digitized image transmission, which became increasingly viable toward the end of the 1990s.

The potential for digitization in the picture business emerged in conjunction with developing apparatuses for digital image capture (themselves derived from photographic machinery) and stabilizing display technologies for computer graphics.[56] Once pictures were digitized they afforded visibility to machine vision—a computer's way of "seeing" visual data—which is profoundly different from human vision. This subsequently enabled various elements of picture (re)search to be articulated as problems for computing to solve.[57] Once the work of processing images had been configured as a task for computing, the pictorial commodities residing as prints and transparencies in the files of picture libraries and archives became recognizable as exploitable sources of computable data.

Creating digitized surrogates of both the photographic assets and informational affordances of picture libraries made it possible to converge them in online platforms, where access could eventually be mediated by search engines rather than researchers. The establishment of such platforms around the turn of the twenty-first century might be ascribed to technological developments and advances in computer and information science. As we shall see in chapter 5, however, it would in practice be driven by actors previously external to the industry, who were primarily invested in developing new technologies, which would in turn make profit extractable, in new ways, from already existing assets.

CONCLUSION

The three different kinds of texts analyzed in this chapter—handbook introductions, research reports, and television drama—all approach the work of picture research and the institution of the picture library from diverging points of view. For picture librarians Evans and Evans, and the readers of their handbook, a picture library was a business, and picture research a way to make a living. When the editors predicted in 1996 that digitized transmission would transform the picture researcher's way of life more than the fax had done less than a decade earlier, this was by and large a hopeful proposition. It welcomed the power of digital technologies to cut through the layers of intermediation involved in the routine information labor of communicating with clients and transmitting pictures. For information scientists like Enser and colleagues, picture libraries were knowledge institutions, and picture research was a form of idiosyncratic knowledge work. They sought to identify ways to break down the complexity of tasks like searching, finding, interpreting, and selecting pictures appropriate to a given topic into discrete information-labor operations that could subsequently be automated. Finally, for a screenwriter and director like Poliakoff, a picture library was first and foremost a location with certain affordances that made it suited for television, and picture research was physical performance that brought this location to life on screen. Through the eccentric character of Oswald, personifying the intelligent device of the picture researcher as a distinctly human intermediary, the achievement of this performance was to exemplify aspects of picture libraries and picture research that would resist disintermediation by digital technologies.

As I have read these texts, the handbook introductions and research reports expressed hopes and expectations about what digitization could do *for* workers and businesses in the picture industry, whereas *Shooting the Past* mobilized anxieties about what digitization would do *to* them. Although the explicit prospects of digitization remained unarticulated in the television drama, its scenario anticipated how new technologies would soon produce a crisis of how we were to understand work in general, and the work of intermediation in particular.

5

Making Digitization Work

Five years after declaring the fax machine as an essential tool for picture research in 1996, Hilary and Mary Evans acknowledged that "the computer has become an indispensable part of the researcher's life."[1] The two had of course coexisted for some time in many workplaces; however, by the turn of the twenty-first century networked computers had taken over most of the fax machine's tasks in the UK picture industry. When the seventh edition of *The Picture Researcher's Handbook* appeared in 2001, the editors nevertheless expressed skepticism about moving the entire research process online: "How cheerfully does a picture researcher contemplate finding the illustrations for an encyclopedia by searching website after website, downloading hundreds of images from scores of suppliers onto her on-screen lightbox?"[2]

The response from actual researchers was more positive. Some years later, in 2008, I interviewed a seasoned freelancer, Julia, who had worked in picture research since 1974 and told me that "nothing is like being able to open ten libraries, have their windows there in front of me and just search on all of them simultaneously. It's just great."[3] Similarly, Marie-Louise, a staff picture editor with experience going back to the 1980s, recalled that "overnight my whole world was revolutionized" when the main picture supplier of her specialist magazine launched its searchable website in 2002: "I thought it was the most wonderful thing that had ever happened because suddenly I was back in control of what I was searching."[4] Having spent the early part of her career visiting picture libraries to carry out research on-site (in the manner recommended by the first edition of *The Picture Researcher's Handbook*, as we recall from chapter 3), Marie-Louise had found it frustrating when, in the 1990s, her role had demanded that she mainly work over the phone, and she had to rely on library staff to interpret her picture requests. Far from feeling despondent, both these picture professionals positively relished the sense of control and efficiency that web-based, self-service picture research seemed to offer.

In the meantime Evans and Evans, too, had come round to the fact that "today's marketplace is made up of websites."[5] When the eighth and final edition of their handbook was published in 2006, the editors not only acknowledged that "picture research has changed more since our last edition than in all the 31 years since our first"; it was also clear that their own compilation work for the handbook had been largely conducted on the internet.[6] By this time, picture researchers were less likely to be put out by the routine task of trawling through thousands of pictures on websites than by the idea of working on an obsolete print product like an encyclopedia.

In fact, the fate of the printed encyclopedia—that flagship commodity of the book publishing industry, disintermediated by a crowd-sourced website—exemplifies the profound impact that digitization visited, in the early years of the twenty-first century, on all the print-based sectors of the pictorial economy served by the picture business. It is possible to see its demise as the sad passing of a tried-and-trusted medium for the preservation and transmission of general knowledge. It is also possible to see the online encyclopedia Wikipedia and its various avatars as more viable technical solutions to the perennial problems of encyclopedia publishing, such as updating information, correcting errors, and restricting the scope and size of entries. Viewed from this perspective, digitization solved specific problems that were associated with the encyclopedia as a cultural form, but which had in fact been caused by its historical instantiation in the material device of the printed codex. In the process of solving those problems, digitization simultaneously disintermediated encyclopedia publishing as a viable business model. Considering picture research from the same angle reveals that digitization also solved specific problems inherent to the work of accumulating, extracting, and transmitting pictures. And the particular solutions that digitization offered had consequences, in turn, both for the business models of picture libraries and for the work of picture research.

When speaking of digitization in the 2000s it makes sense to think of it as two distinct but interdependent processes: on the one hand, making pictures available in digital formats on platforms where users could find and receive them and, on the other hand, providing users with access to the digital tools and networks they needed in order to do so. In the first process, digitization made new kinds of work for employees in picture libraries, producing digital surrogates for both pictures and researchers. In the second, picture researchers made digitization work for them, enlisting its tools in the service of getting the job of finding a picture done. In both cases, digitization eliminated or alleviated some kinds of work, and created or magnified other kinds. In the digital environment of online search and delivery, picture librarians and research staff at picture sources largely disappeared from view. At the same time, it required a lot of work behind the screen to give those sitting in front of it the impression that they were doing it all by themselves.

In the picture industry as elsewhere, the digitization of work could be achieved only by making digitization work. The previous chapter showed how digitization in the 1990s became thinkable as a set of technological solutions to problems of picture research, a form of knowledge work that information scientists sought to reconfigure as information labor fit for computers. In the early 2000s, these efforts bore fruit in the sense that digitization became workable as a set of tasks and practices. Paying particular attention to the disruptive impact of Getty Images on the picture industry in this period, this chapter draws on firsthand accounts by experienced picture researchers and contemporary evidence from relevant editions of *The Picture Researcher's Handbook* and other printed sources to explore both the new kinds of work that digitization was making and what workers in the picture business made of digitization.

The Platformization of Pictures

As I suggested in the introduction to this book, it is impossible fully to disentangle the material production of digitized content from the cultural expectation that content should be available in digitized form. From both these aspects, digitization in the picture industry must also be seen as part of the wider restructuring of contemporary capitalism around the core unit of the "platform," as opposed to the "firm."[7] Around 2000, the web-based platform emerged as an infrastructural device of disintermediation across a wide range of industries. Platforms seemingly provided consumers with direct access to any number of goods from any number of suppliers, whether the trade was in pictures, airfares, hotel rooms, books, or antiques. Transactions could now be carried out without the intervention of traditional human intermediaries like library staff, travel agents, booksellers, or auctioneers, whose functions were replaced by automated approximations in the shape of e-commerce applications and search algorithms.

In the same way that digital disintermediation in the early 2000s seemed to produce, or favor, or coalesce around one or two hegemonic platforms in each sector—think Amazon, eBay, or Expedia—the picture industry saw the establishment of Getty Images and Corbis Images as twin behemoths. From the mid-1990s they "competed for supremacy in the picture market," as Estelle Blaschke puts it, each company representing "a mirror image" of the other.[8] Notwithstanding their mutual rivalry, these two actors established the industry-standard platforms against which all other purveyors of pictorial commodities were forced to compete, and with which virtually all picture researchers sooner or later had to deal.

Indeed, Getty and Corbis were perceived almost as a double act among picture professionals in this period, both on account of their relative similarity vis-à-vis the diversity of traditional picture libraries and because smaller operators in the industry were doubly pressurized by their combined presence. We recall from chapter 1 how Corbis started out trying to license digitized surrogates of works of art for domestic consumption before realizing there would be more money in a digital version of the tried-and-tested picture library model. As Corbis has been the topic of numerous studies already, including a definitive one by Blaschke, cited above, I will focus my discussion of platformization in this chapter on Getty Images, which in any case ended up absorbing its main rival and thus emerging victorious from their struggle for hegemony—albeit not until 2016.[9] I will nevertheless refer to "Getty and Corbis" in contexts where it would be misleading to suggest that Getty Images was the sole actor involved.

In the same edition of the handbook where they declared the computer as indispensable, Evans and Evans identified Getty Images and Corbis Images as "the most prominent examples" of what they called a new breed of "mega-sources."[10] From their point of view, the most obvious characteristic shared by these new consolidated sources was that they made "essentially the same pictures available on a global basis."[11] As we have seen in the preceding chapters, of course, neither consolidation nor global distribution was in itself a new phenomenon in the picture business. The long-established syndication agreements among libraries and agencies had for decades ensured that "the same pictures" were available to clients across the world. Distributing them by digital means only meant that more pictures could be distributed faster to more clients at the same time. The true impact of the Getty and Corbis platforms on the picture industry, however, came not so much from harnessing the distributive power of computational networks to provide the same pictures everywhere as from providing instant access to all kinds of pictures in one and the same place.

In the pre-digital period the picture business was comparable to an old-fashioned high street in a European town or city, where different picture purveyors operated out of their own separate shops. Stock photographs were held by certain libraries and historical pictures by others, while travel pictures, fine art reproductions, and animal photographs could each sustain entire businesses on their own. By the 1970s, this virtual townscape made up of general and specialist sources had grown bewildering in its breadth and diversity, prompting Evans and Evans, as we recall from chapter 3, to publish the first edition of *The Picture Researcher's Handbook* as a finding tool conceived along the lines of a travel guide. When Getty and Corbis around the year 2000 both launched digital platforms that gave researchers instant access to substantial collections of pictures in most of the general as well as specialist categories, it had a similar effect on independent businesses in the picture industry as the opening of two out-of-town shopping malls would have on local shops in a city center.

The "fragmented" character of the picture business was in fact what first made it an attractive investment prospect for eponymous cofounder of Getty Images, according to a profile of Mark Getty published by *The*

Economist in March 2000.[12] An investment banker and scion of the petroleum-enriched Getty family, Getty had created Getty Images in 1995 together with fellow banker Jonathan Klein. Neither partner had any previous experience of the picture industry before actively setting about disrupting it through the targeted deployment of digital technologies. According to *The Economist*, Getty was casting around for an area of business in which to set up a firm of his own when he settled on the stock photography market both because its innumerable traders in intellectual property appeared underappreciated by other investors and because he had identified "scope for increasing efficiency by digitizing the business and putting it on the Internet."

Picture libraries had been routinely merging and consolidating for decades, as previously noted, yet in the pre-digital picture market mergers and acquisitions had tended to happen among collections that were similar in kind. A typical example would be the Hulton Picture Post Library absorbing other historical press libraries like the Keystone Press Agency, as discussed in chapter 2. The approach of Getty Images to consolidation followed a different logic: within the space of five years the company had acquired the already-consolidated historical archive that originated with the Hulton Picture Post Library; the global general stock photo franchise the Image Bank; Tony Stone Images, a highly successful supplier of contemporary high-end stock; and the Liaison Agency, which specialized in photojournalism.[13] Making pictures from all these extensive collections of very different kinds available in the form of digital surrogates through the same web platform certainly created a mega-source, as Evans and Evans put it, but more importantly it produced a meta-source of pictures, a digitized collection of collections.

Creating this meta-source in the shape of a digital platform required Getty to invest heavily in what *The Economist* termed "electronic infrastructure," exemplified by "data centres and websites," as well as "thick pipes for downloading images." Such investments "raise[d] the fixed cost of the business" on top of the running costs involved in day-to-day digitization tasks like scanning and keywording. According to the 2000 profile, the estimated cost of Getty Images' infrastructure investment over the two preceding years had been USD30 million, while the cost of digitization could be broken down to a figure of USD45 per picture when scanning and keywording were included. These numbers were put into perspective by the information that by early 2000, Getty Images had thus far processed just over one third of the three million pictures it was planning to put online. "Small firms cannot afford that sort of investment," *The Economist* laconically noted.

This observation was precisely in line with the assessment that Evans and Evans had offered some four years earlier, in their introduction to the 1996 handbook. Reflecting on recent examples of "rash institutions" committing themselves "prematurely" to newfangled systems of digital transmission, the editors had noted that "[f]ew can afford to invest substantial sums in systems that may be out of date in a couple of years."[14] In the event, the large-scale adoption and development of digital computational technologies for picture-industrial purposes was led (and bankrolled) by investors who had specialized in computationally mediated trade or management of information: investment banking, in the case of Getty and Klein, and software engineering, in the case of Corbis founder Gates. It stands to reason that individuals from these backgrounds could recognize the potential for information technologies to transform the management and exploitation of photographic collections. "Stock photographs are information," as Paul Frosh has observed, and "[m]ore to the point, they were always information, even before the advent of digital technologies."[15] Digital platformization, as exemplified in this chapter by Getty Images, first and foremost amplified the volume, accelerated the speed, and extended the reach of existing practices within the industry: the aggregation and syndication of collections, the exploitation of pictures as intellectual property, and the globalized distribution of pictures.

The new online platforms functioned both as repositories of digital surrogates produced through technical digitization and as finding aids whereby anyone with the required access privileges—not just experienced picture researchers—could search for and retrieve pictures from those repositories. In practice, the work of interpretation, which had previously been performed by picture library staff (like Oswald, Marilyn, and Veronica in *Shooting the Past*) in response to individual picture requests, was now built into the database as an algorithmic operation performed by a search engine. Sifting through a comprehensive vocabulary of keywords and search terms, which designated keyworders had attached to each picture file, the engine would automatically retrieve any picture that matched the search terms entered by the researcher.[16] Converging both the storage and the search functions of picture libraries in one and the same interactive interface, Getty and Corbis thus offered intermediation as an infrastructure rather than a service. And by setting the pace and standard for the provision of digitized content by picture libraries, these two platforms also taught picture researchers to expect digital search and delivery from other purveyors. In this respect the platforms were as instrumental in creating a demand for digitization as they were in supplying the digitized content to satisfy it.

The impact of digital platformization as promoted and pioneered by Getty and Corbis hit the UK picture industry with full force in the course of 2000–2001. With the exception of news and sports agencies, which had already gone fully digital by the end of the 1990s, libraries serving clients in advertising, book publishing, magazine publishing, and documentary production had been able to carry on throughout the 1990s more or less in the same way as in previous decades. Once the meta-sources Getty and Corbis had established their online one-stop shops for all manner of visual content, including high-quality stock photography and historical archive pictures, it nevertheless became clear that digital search and delivery was no longer the preserve of agencies serving the fast-moving market for news and sports photographs. The marketplace for pictures had moved definitively online, and any picture library wishing to stay in business must make the contents of their archives available in digital formats, one way or the other.

The Work of Digitization

Moving picture research onto the internet was not a simple matter of building a website and expecting researchers to come, however. The establishment of a fully-fledged digital platform like Getty Images involved substantial investment beyond the means of small businesses, as underscored in *The Economist* article cited above. Therefore picture libraries had to approach the work of digitization in different ways, depending on their size, economy, and inclination. Regardless of scale, the technical processes of digitization required some form of access to both dedicated hardware, such as scanning equipment and servers, and specialized software, like search engines and asset management systems. So-called wetware, in the form of skilled human operatives, was equally important to each step of the process. On a general level, picture libraries that turned a large profit or formed part of an international franchise were able to take a factory-like approach to transforming their holdings from analog to digital formats, employing dedicated scanning operators and keyworders for the purpose. Less profitable and/or smaller-scale operations were more likely to organize the work of digitization along the lines of a cottage industry, adding tasks of image processing and metadata input to the workloads of existing staff, or putting it out to trusted individual associates.

The case of the commercial picture library studied by Tope and Enser, which was discussed in chapter 4, provides an example of a wholesale digitization project conducted according to factory principles.[17] The anonymized stock photo library, which aimed its pictures primarily at advertising and publishing clients, had prior to digitization held its stock in 35-mm slides and relied on printed catalogs to promote its images. The new web-based resource for image search and retrieval was intended to replace the catalogs as "a finding tool for customers," partly at the initiative of the IT director and partly as "a response to rising customer expectations after the creation of websites by other picture libraries."[18] From the viewpoint of their clients, this picture library went more or less overnight from having no online offering to having a fully operational platform for digital search and download. Behind the scenes, however, the official launch of the website marked the result of three years' labor.

The kinds of work that went into this project included lengthy preparatory stages of selecting and prioritizing pictures for digitization; an extensive period of scanning, indexing, and keywording each digital file; and a full year of testing before the actual website went live. The kinds of workers involved included library staff and sales executives during the selection process in the United Kingdom, technical operators at the international franchise's designated facility in the United States, where the scanning and original file processing took place, and various web designers, programmers, and other IT staff engaged in the design, testing, and implementation phase back in the United Kingdom. The project also affected the working conditions of employees both during and after its completion. During the main processing phase operators at the US scanning facility had been put on extended hours to keep on top of the workload (even factoring in overtime pay, it had reportedly been cheaper to transport the 35-mm slides to the US and back than to establish a separate scanning operation in the UK). And as already noted in chapter 4, once the searchable website was up and running many library staff members at the UK site found themselves redeployed in the capacity of sales representatives, since their research tasks had been disintermediated by its automated search engine.

A small and family-run picture business like the Mary Evans Picture Library (MEPL) did not have the financial muscle to undertake the complete digitization of its holdings in one fell swoop. It nevertheless managed to establish what a member of staff called "a reasonable online presence" more or less at the same time as the major actors in the UK picture industry.[19] Exemplifying the cottage-industry approach to digitization, MEPL responded to the rapid development of online picture research in the years 2000–2001 by producing a parallel library of digital surrogates, in the form of low-resolution scans from duplicate transparencies, which picture researchers could consult online. The work was entrusted either to employees on-site or to former employees in possession of a good-quality scanner as well as familiarity with its collection. This gradual approach to digitization was partly necessitated by MEPL's status as a small, independent company and partly due to its owners' faith in the affordances of the transparency.[20]

The library's filing cabinets full of dupes continued, meanwhile, to serve as its main repository of publication-grade pictures for some time into the 2000s. MEPL had a long-established practice of distributing photographic reproductions to clients in the compressed, yet high-resolution format of 6 × 4.5 cm color transparencies, which were produced on-site using specialized photo-reprographic equipment acquired for the purpose. There were three sets of duplicates that made up the circulating part of the picture library, allowing the original prints, vintage photographs, journals, and books from which reproductions were made to remain securely stored in the library's archives.

The smoothness with which Evans and Evans were able to move their picture library online was in several respects an unintended consequence of their earlier investment in this analog apparatus for the multiplication and preservation of pictures. In the immediate context of the UK picture business in the early 2000s, maintaining analog transparencies as "hi-res" versions of the low-resolution image files offered to view on the website was a pragmatic way to satisfy clients' increasing demand for online picture research and delivery. In a wider perspective, this workaround also illustrates how digitization in this period did not disrupt or replace photographic storage and transmission media so much as it was supported and enabled by them.

Undoubtedly, digitization had some of the same effects on picture librarians' work at MEPL as it did at libraries that had undergone a more comprehensive digital transformation, such as the commercial stock library referenced earlier. Enabling clients to consult the collection online meant fewer searches to carry out on their behalf, but more processing of scanning requests, and negotiation of usage fees for items that clients had located themselves. Library staff were nevertheless also closely involved in the various processes of digitization, owing to the fact that it happened more gradually, and largely within the premises of the library itself. From an employee's point of view, the MEPL approach must have made it easier to welcome digitization as simply another set of faster and more efficient tools for helping pictures do their job, rather than to fear it as an assemblage of automated machinery that would soon relieve you of yours.

The approach that Evans and Evans took to the digitization of their own library was grounded in what they called "the question of quality," which was tied to an explicit distinction between "intelligent" and "unintelligent" picture sources.[21] Acknowledging that each served different purposes within the picture industry, the handbook editors suggested that any of the "giant stock libraries" with their "unintelligent" automated search and download facilities would probably do if you were merely looking for "a straightforward image of a tropical sunset or a portrait of a showbiz celebrity." These were the kinds of things that unintelligent sources could provide in abundance. If, on the other hand, "your need is obscure, or you are illustrating a complex text, the personal expertise and guidance provided by a specialist source may prove indispensable." An intelligent source was, in other words, one in which knowledgeable people did the thinking and searching.[22] Even while fully "embracing the internet," Evans and Evans adhered to their belief that serious picture research required skilled and educated human intermediaries.[23]

This was further evidenced by a brochure printed and distributed in 2004 to promote the MEPL website. Its introductory text explicitly identified the brochure as "an invitation to visit www.maryevans.com" and "a taster of the many pictures in our collection."[24] The opening paragraphs served to introduce MEPL and its website to prospective clients, but perhaps more importantly to remind existing clients that its collections were now available online. Although it primarily promoted the website, the spiral-bound, forty-eight-page volume also provided clients with the tactile affordances of a printed catalog, thus enticing them to search out pictures on screen by demonstrating how attractive they appeared on the printed page. The bulk of its pages was devoted to presenting sample illustrations in full color, printed on high-quality paper stock, organized around themes that were hinted at in encyclopedia-style running headers (another nod to a paper-based cultural form that had played a significant role in sustaining the pre-digital picture business). Thus personalities were sampled "from Archimedes . . . to Zola" (with an additional insert headed "via Napoleon"), while professions were represented "from blacksmiths to bureaucrats," children "from growing pains to playing games," fashion "from frock coats to farthingales" ("via hats"), and religion "from Adam and Eve to Zoroastrian fire worship." For all that the work of finding pictures by 2004 was largely being carried out online, printed paper artifacts would for some years yet remain the predominant publication context for library pictures. Thus the brochure—complete with its allusion to the printed encyclopedia—attested to the longevity of paper as a valued medium of exchange in the pictorial economy, even as its contents indicated that the transactions of that economy were, and should be, increasingly taking place through screens.

As a printed artifact promoting a website, the MEPL brochure from 2004 is a curious document that attests to a specific moment in the history of digital disintermediation in the picture industry. Reproduced on the final two pages of the brochure were photographs showing staff at work in the library, handling paper-based originals, preparing transparencies for scanning, or consulting the MEPL website from desktop computers. Aside from illustrating the variety of work that went on in an establishment that prided itself on "successfully combin[ing] the latest technology with the traditional values of a professional, friendly, long-established picture library," these pictures also shored up the reassuring statement that clients contacting the library, whether in person or via the web, would always encounter "responsive human beings to remind you that picture research doesn't have to be a dialogue between robots."[25] This dismissive reference to roboticized picture research evidently confirms the impression, outlined earlier, that Evans and Evans remained committed to employing human intermediaries in their library. It also suggests that they ascribed to their clients a skepticism toward fully digitized search and retrieval that was similar to their own.

The MEPL brochure offers a glimpse of how a picture library at this time "imagines its users"—borrowing a phrase from Gitelman—as both eagerly seeking out pictorial content online and reluctantly giving up in-person, hands-on research.[26] While its primary purpose may have been to advertise the contents and features of the website, it was equally meant to reassure clients that services offered online were in addition to, rather than in replacement of, the library's personal services. As a historical artifact, this item printed on high-quality paper further belongs to a moment in time when the affordances of websites were not yet deemed equivalent to those of the printed page for the purpose of showcasing pictures that were themselves ultimately destined for print. Nor did this equivalence suddenly emerge with the appearance of a single, newfangled feature or technology. It had to be gradually produced, both through technological improvements to the processing, search, and display capabilities of photo library websites and by habituating users to the experience of working with screen-based interfaces. Producing a printed brochure to advertise a website was one way of contributing to this process of habituation, which in turn was yet another way of making digitization work.

Digitizing Research

The picture library run by Evans and Evans had three crucial elements in place that worked in favor of digitization once they decided to embark on it. First, the circulating picture collection consisted of duplicate transparencies that were easily scanned in low resolution. Second, the library had an existing computer catalog from which it was possible to extract good metadata about its holdings. And third, the original source materials for the duplicates were still preserved in the archives, from which the MEPL was able to provide clients with high-resolution scans on request. Restricting its web presence to a modest resource limited to low-resolution picture files, the MEPL could pace its investment in equipment and infrastructure, while still meeting picture researchers' expectations of being able to consult an online image database. It had become vital by the mid-2000s to meet these expectations, as Evans and Evans admitted in the 2006 eighth and final edition of their handbook, where they saw fit "to include only sources which can be accessed by e-mail and preferably also via a website."[27] The now pervasive logic of web search was detectable down to the design and organization of the handbook itself, where the main division into sections of "General," "Regional," "National," and "Specialist," consistently applied since the fourth edition in 1989, had been replaced by a purely alphabetical order of subject keywords, similar to those one might enter into a website's search box. These editorial changes reflected the fact that the global marketplace for rented pictures had by 2006 moved definitively online, and that the handbook was by now addressing a constituency of picture researchers fully habituated to a digitized work environment.

In the winter of 2007–2008 I conducted a series of interviews with typical members of this constituency, professionals in the UK picture industry who had begun their careers sometime between 1960 and 1990 and who were still working or had recently retired from the business at the time of our meeting. Our conversations focused on firsthand experiences of how digitization had affected the picture business in general and their work in particular. Although their individual trajectories were very different, there were clear consistencies across the various accounts, both on key points of chronology and on what they deemed the most significant impact of digitization on the practical work of picture research. Most interviewees agreed, for example, that digital technologies began to make themselves felt sometime after 1995 and that the major changeover to digital technologies and working practices occurred around 2001–2002. There had been computerized systems of administration in place for several years before that, but the work relating to the pictures themselves did not begin to move online until the last half of the 1990s.

On the one hand, interviewees affirmed that digital technologies had "kind of democratized" picture distribution, as one of them put it, by enabling photographers and smaller picture suppliers to connect directly with a large customer base and thus cut out the intermediary agencies with their large international networks.[28] On the other hand, there was a concomitant sense that the worldwide market was dominated by the two major platforms, Getty Images and Corbis Images. Rick, a manager in a large but independent picture library in London, described this as "a supermarket philosophy" where, especially in the newspaper segment, "researchers are forced to buy all the images from a few, large, preferred suppliers."[29] While digitization in theory had enabled photographers and small agencies to sell their pictures directly to newspapers, in other words, the largest actors like Getty Images operated with economies of scale that, as in other retail markets, enabled them to push prices down. At the time of our interview in 2008 Rick estimated that "the average sale price for a photo is half of what it was three years ago," a development that he explicitly attributed to the pricing policies and market position of Getty Images.

Aside from confirmation of the hegemonic position of Getty Images at the time, I identified across these conversations three main manifestations of the impact of digitization on the practical work of picture research. One was the almost total computerization of a job that had previously involved a wide range of tools and technologies. Another was the disintermediation of picture librarians and research staff at picture sources. The third can best be described as the changing temporalities of research, experienced as working not just against the clock of ever-diminishing deadlines but in concert with the time lags and redundancies of digital transmission.

In pre-digital days the job had involved a lot of legwork, often a good deal of travel, and mainly direct communication either in person or over the phone. These aspects were remembered fondly by interviewees Marie-Louise and Julia, who had both been researching for the book publishing industry in the 1980s. In each of our meetings they individually emphasized the joys of visiting picture sources in person. "I actually got out to libraries, museums, talked to authors, looked at endless images," explained Marie-Louise, who started out researching for picture books in 1986.[30] As for Julia, she laughed that, "I was thin in those days—I was literally running around London most of the time. Just running around."[31] Julia also shared memories of overseas trips to Berlin and New York, in order to research and collect large amounts of pictures for a long-running publishing project: "all the [relevant] pictures were in Berlin in those days and I had to fly in on the last plane. The text had just been written so I had to go in with the text, . . . rush off to the first picture library, gather all the pictures, get a taxi to the second one, gather all the pictures, get the plane back, so the thing could be laid out and designed the next day."[32] Some years later, she had been required to travel to New York to consult the Bettmann Archive and another large New York agency, Black Star:

> It was a murder thing for [a magazine publisher] and the only way I could get the pictures in those days was to actually go there and physically research in two major libraries, UPI Bettmann and the Black Star library. . . . Bettmann themselves were incredibly slow. They knew I was coming, they knew that I was taking the material. I was doing something like twelve issues for the magazine in one week which was pretty heavy research and I didn't really have much text or anything. . . . I ended up with a big pile of pictures and I couldn't get them to book them out for me. And I kept saying, "Please could you do these today?" And it got nearer and nearer to my departure and I really had to have them on the plane because I knew they would forget about them. And they said something that really surprised me because I was going, "This is New York, this is supposed to be really fast," and they said "No, London's the fastest place, not New York." And that was an incredible surprise to me.[33]

Julia's anecdotes vividly conjure up the ambulatory character of pre-digital picture research and underscore the point repeatedly made by Evans and Evans in their handbook, that the picture business was always international in remit. The episode from New York draws additional attention both to local differences in working practices and to the potential for confrontation between researchers and librarians, two of the less pleasant intermediary elements that were largely eliminated with the move to automated online search and download.

The disintermediation of picture librarians from the search process was regretted by some and considered a relief by others. "Digitization has taken some of the buzz out of the office," regretted Rick; the phones had fallen silent because the website had taken over as first port of call for researchers, and the filing cabinets—which the researchers had previously climbed over each other to rummage through—had been removed to the basement.[34] While Rick seemed to find it a pity that the library's own intermediaries were no longer in demand, picture editor Adam felt that the advent of searchable picture library websites had improved his own research experience. In the pre-digital days, Adam explained, "I was relying on another person at the other end of the phone understanding my brief and not having a bad day so that they would pull out the right thing from the files. Now I can do that myself."[35] The same sentiment was expressed by Marie-Louise, who had researched extensively on-site in picture libraries early on in her book-publishing career, and found it frustrating when moving into magazine publishing that the shorter deadlines required her to rely on briefing picture librarians over the phone. As quoted at the start of this chapter, Marie-Louise felt that digitization put her "back in control of what [she] was searching," as she had been when going through a library's physical picture files by herself.[36] Julia, the freelance picture researcher who had been so frustrated by the slow service at Bettmann in New York, also relished the feeling of "being in control" once she learned how to use the websites and, not least, was able to search across several of them at the same time.[37]

These reactions are a reminder that, long before the construction of automated search engines, picture researchers had relied, for a great deal, on locating pictures by inputting keywords into an apparatus the workings of which they could not control. Whether picture requests were sent by letter (as recommended by Evans, Evans, and Nelki in 1975), fax (as had become standard by 1992), or listed up over the phone, the keywords, phrases, and descriptions provided by picture researchers had to be decoded and interpreted by the library research staff to match up with the classification and cross-reference systems according to which their particular holdings were organized. To give one example, a request for "conjoined twins" to the Keystone Picture Agency in the 1950s would have sent picture librarians searching through the boxes labeled "Freaks," whereas in the Hulton Picture Post Library they would probably have gone looking under "MED" for "medical."[38] The picture researcher who had placed the request would have to trust the library staff to know where to look, and what alternative terms or categories to search under if nothing came up. While each collection's idiosyncratic "archival script" would often be embedded in the metadata when pictures were digitized and made available for online search, they would normally also be supplemented by new keywords, in order to make them retrievable by as many clients as possible and, as in the case of the long-since disbanded "Freaks" category, updated to remove offensive descriptions.[39]

The feeling of being in control of the search, expressed by Adam, Julia, and Marie-Louise, was mainly due to being able to search using variations and combinations of terms limited only by their own imaginations rather than by somebody else's. That is not to say the users of online platforms fully trusted the pre-interpretation built into the keyword infrastructure to incorporate every possible concept or idea that they might associate with a given picture. Despite admitting frustrations over keywording standards and practices across various platforms, and missing the personal contact with librarians and archivists, however, none of the researchers I interviewed was nostalgic for the pre-digital system of human-only intermediation.

At the time of our interview, Julia considered the greatest frustration with online picture research to be the slowness of transmission due to lack of computing power or bandwidth. Waiting was of course nothing new in picture research (as her own account of getting impatient at the Bettmann Archive attested) but when waiting times were measured in hours or days it was possible to call other sources or go out to libraries for on-site research while pictures were being couriered or sent in the post. Once all sources were to be accessed through the same computer terminal, it meant one search could slow down all the others, as Julia described it:

> I think one of the really frustrating things about starting to work online was the minute that you got the hang of it, because most companies didn't have very good broadband access, everything was so slow. . . . When the system goes down or is very slow it's still deeply frustrating because you're onto the next kind of ten searches; the others are lagging behind.[40]

This experience of the computer simply not keeping up to speed with the work rate was also highlighted by freelance picture researcher Susi, who explained that each download of a high-resolution file was taking more than a minute:

> Now, in effect, it is probably still quicker than me having to ring up an agency and say, "Have you got this image?" and them having to post it to me. But there is an element of I'm actually just sat at the machine. . . . So what I now have to do is I will have to work out before I download the picture what part of my job should I leave during the picture being downloaded.[41]

While Susi conceded that one-minute downloads were not really slow "in the great scheme of things," she suggested that online workflows had changed perceptions of speed and accessibility: "I think people, when they expect [it] this instant, it is instant but it's a different kind of instant." The two kinds of instantaneity could be compared to the difference between Polaroid photography and digital photography. In its time, Polaroid was described as "instant photography," even as part of the excitement of using it was waiting for and watching the image that emerged from the green-gray emulsion of the print.[42] Compared to handing in a roll of film at the chemist's and waiting for it to be processed, the minute or so it took for the Polaroid to appear was instantaneous. Yet this was clearly "a different kind of instant" to that of the smartphone snapshot, which appears on the screen in fraction of a second, and next to which the formerly instantaneous Polaroid appears more like an analog version of a slow digital download.

Working to tight deadlines was nothing new in publishing, as testified both by Julia's stories of whistlestop trips abroad and by the account in chapter 4 of how faxing had encouraged twenty-four-hour work cycles and last-minute submissions across working life in the 1990s. Accordingly, when Evans and Evans in 2001 had referred to "the shorter deadlines that have become today's norm," this was a development that had been ongoing since pre-digital times.[43] To the extent that digital search and transmission encouraged even shorter deadlines, this was less significant than the way digital workflows produced other kinds of "dead" time, for instance, when waiting for files to download or search engines to complete their processes. The improved efficiency promised by digitization was further compromised by picture libraries with searchable websites that did not necessarily provide direct-download facilities. Sometimes this was due to deliberate access restrictions, as in the case of large aggregated sources like Getty Images, which, as Susi explained, provided direct download to subscribers but required non-subscribers to place orders for individual transmission. In the case of smaller outfits such as the Mary Evans Picture Library, as we have seen, the lack of download options was due to low-res website pictures being the only digital versions in existence at first, as high-res files were scanned and supplied on demand from transparencies. In either case, it was necessary to contact the picture source in question and have somebody transfer the high-resolution file separately, again incurring waiting times and delays, which revealed the idea of instantaneous picture delivery over the internet as still more of a promise than a reality for many users.

Picture researchers may have experienced more control of the process of locating pictures once picture librarians had been digitally disintermediated, but this effect was in part counteracted by the technological reintermediation of the process of retrieving publishable file sizes of those pictures. This was the downside of digital disintermediation that several interviewees noted: the reduced number of staff, both on picture desks and in picture libraries. Marie-Louise regretted that there was "no people contact anymore"; Julia said she missed the "endless cups of tea"; while Adam described how he saw the intermediary functions of picture libraries changing in the following terms: "There will be fewer jobs in agencies as everything can be run on skeleton staff—I mean, people don't run the telephone exchanges anymore! You only need people when something goes wrong." Adam's prediction in 2007 echoed the earlier prognostication by Tope and Enser, cited previously, which in 2000 had foreseen that digitization would affect staff levels as well as skills requirements in picture libraries. As the information scientists had envisaged, the work of intermediation was less frequently taking place between pictures and clients, and more often between pictures or clients, on one side, and online search and retrieval systems, on the other. The infrastructure of intermediation constituted by automated and aggregated digital platforms still relied on intermediaries, but in the capacity of technicians rather than librarians.

Even though interpretive schemas and structures were necessarily preprogrammed by each platform at keyword level, the digital disintermediation of picture librarians relieved picture researchers of experiencing their own ideas and search terms being individually interpreted and filtered by another person's imagination. At the same time, digital reintermediation introduced new obstacles to efficiency, such as repeated waits for search engines to return results and unpredictable delays in the transmission of files. Digital platforms offering direct access to library holdings may have eliminated the handling, dispatching, and filing of physical pictures, thus freeing up more time for picture researchers to focus on the creative knowledge work of research: the looking at and thinking about pictures that usually drew picture researchers to the profession in the first place.[44] Digitization nevertheless created its own forms of routine and mechanical tasks, including the constant typing of search terms, the endless clicking through search results, the repeated downloading of picture files, and the clerical challenges of routing them through the temporary and virtual archives of digital picture management systems. Although the work was performed across the graphical user interfaces of networked computers, it was still tedious information labor.

Conclusion

Throughout the twentieth century emulsion-based photography had been the recording and transmission medium of choice in the picture industry. During the first decade of the twenty-first, it was replaced by digital technologies of image capture and distribution. For this replacement to happen it was necessary for digital images first to assume an equivalence with photographs and then to gain an advantage over them. In the early 2000s the technical quality of digital photographs was poor compared to emulsion photographs, and it required enormous computing resources to create and store digital files that were even approximate to a 35-mm slide in data richness. The small size of digital images could also be an advantage for digital distribution, however. Providing low-resolution digital surrogates online required no waiting times between search and retrieval, and thus represented an improvement of service to picture researchers who used to place orders by phone or fax. Online searches could also be carried out without incurring either mileage or travel expenses, making it both more efficient and more economical than going out to libraries in person and sifting through their files on site.

The work of picture research has always entailed going through vast quantities of material in order to retrieve a small selection of items for actual use. In the early days of digitization it was therefore still acceptable to wait for a few hours or days for a limited number of high-resolution reproducible photographs to be delivered by post, courier, or file transfer, once the time-consuming selection process had been conveniently performed online. Once the networked computer had replaced the filing cabinet or catalog as the researchers' primary picture-finding tool, however, expectations of digital delivery were not far off. It was only a matter of time before the web also became the libraries' main channel of picture distribution. This nevertheless required a series of concerted efforts to produce digital technologies as equivalent to photographic ones, and visual content platforms as equivalent to picture libraries. This, too, was work generated by digitization.

By the turn of the millennium, Getty and Corbis had taken the lead on this development by both acquiring substantial collections of stock and archival photographs and building the digital infrastructures that were needed in order to monetize them by electronic means. "Intellectual property is the oil of the 21st century," Mark Getty was quoted by *The Economist*, going on to compare "the richest men a hundred years ago," who had "made their money extracting natural resources or moving them around," to contemporary magnates—perhaps like his business rival at the time, the software magnate and picture-industrialist Bill Gates—who "have made their money out of intellectual property."[45] It was this extractivist business logic that underpinned Getty's project to acquire and disseminate pictorial commodities across worldwide networks on an unprecedented scale in the early 2000s.

In one sense, this was no different from how picture libraries had always made their money by intermediating between picture buyers and picture sellers.[46] Yet the value to be extracted from visual content platforms was not limited to percentages collected for the smooth management of reproduction rights on behalf of photographers or archival collections. The sheer traffic in photographs sustained by these platforms yielded an equally valuable by-product in the form of data generated simply from users' interactions. There were no search fees on online platforms because users paid with the data to be harvested from the search procedure itself, even when they decided not to buy any pictures. These data could be analyzed and used for improving search algorithms or expanding sought-after content, thus improving the likelihood of more researchers finding relevant pictures to download from the platform in question, or they could be sold for any number of other uses by any number of other data analytics companies. In this way a mega-source like Getty Images not only developed infrastructures for a web-based picture industry; it built an interface between an established pictorial economy and an emerging informational economy.

Elsewhere in the picture industry, smaller and more local actors set about producing equivalences between their established library services and the online resources they were beginning to offer, in response to the digitization challenge laid down by the likes of Getty and Corbis. The 2004 brochure produced and distributed by the Mary Evans Picture Library is a most evocative manifestation of this phenomenon. It was created as a paper-based, illustrated print product that promoted the benefits of the picture library's website, reassuring clients that an online search was just as good as visiting the library itself. It explicitly promoted equivalence between website and library by underscoring that both were staffed by the same humans—and not by robots. By the very design of its material support, however, the brochure also evoked the haptic and aesthetic differences between pictures reproduced on the screen and on the page. The implicit audience for such an artifact was, as I have suggested, the picture library's imagined users, picture researchers who by and large shared Evans and Evans's passion for print culture and ambivalence about digitization.

The interviewees who voiced the picture researchers' perspectives in this chapter were clearly not among those imagined users, in the sense that they mostly expressed satisfaction with the digitization of their working practices. I have highlighted both the advantages they reported that digitization had brought them (searching across multiple websites, being in control of the search process) and the drawbacks that were frequently mentioned (slow data processing, delayed or unavailable downloads). I have not yet addressed a further point that came up in some of these interviews, namely, the concern that picture research itself was disappearing as a profession. Noting that the work of locating pictures was increasingly being reassigned to designers and subeditors, now that anyone with a registered account could search for and download pictures online, Susi put it this way: "We're like the drummers in a band. You've got a machine that can do it now and the keyboard guy will do it."[47] This somewhat jaded quip alludes to another equivalence, between researcher and search engine, that the digitization and platformization of the picture industry appeared to produce. It is yet another iteration of that old story of modernity, already told several times in the preceding chapters of this book, which invariably predicts that this will kill that, labor will be mechanized, and people will be replaced by machines.

And yet many bands still avail themselves of a drummer, just as press, publishers, advertisers, and media production companies still hire the services of dedicated picture researchers.[48] In effect, the drum machine did not so much replace drummers as it gave a wider range of people the ability to (re)produce the sounds of drumming. Similarly, the exponential proliferation of online picture sources since the early 2000s has made it possible for virtually anyone with an internet connection both to carry out picture research and to distribute their own pictures, whether for personal, public, or commercial purposes. In this respect digital technologies have, to a certain extent—as Rick put it—democratized aspects of both the music and the picture industries.[49] No drum machine or online visual content platform could be made to work, however, without data from which to synthesize the sounds and images they offer. These data have been derived from records and documents that together inscribe and embody the accumulated legacies of skills, knowledge, and practices developed and performed over generations. The final chapter of this book turns to examine how those legacies can be seen to endure in and beyond digitization.

6

Enduring Digitization

In May 2011, subscribers to Getty Images' wire news photo service and visitors to the news section of its website were treated to sixty-seven pictures that all shared the tagline "An Inside Look at the Hulton Archive" and carried the same basic caption (figure 6.1):

> London, England—May 13: The vast collection of historic photographs stored in the Hulton Archive on May 13, 2011 in London, England. The comprehensive archive contains pictures created at the birth of photography in the early 1800s and covers every era and event through to the 21st century. Staff at the Hulton Archive are employed on a wide range of jobs including: conservation, retouching, hand-printing, scanning and archiving. (Photo by Oli Scarff/Getty Images)

The caption followed the strict conventions of news photography, in which everything that is worth reporting must be defined as an event and therefore specified by date and location. Yet the fact that a "vast collection of historical photographs" was being "stored" could hardly be classified as headline news. Rather, the series by Oli Scarff, a Getty Images staff photographer at the time, was an example of self-promotion bundled in with the picture library's regular supply of news coverage and features to clients in the press, similar to the Keystone photographs from 1951, analyzed in chapter 2. The photographs and their accompanying captions illustrated and described the work performed by picture library staff, and in several instances also showcased the contents of the historical picture collections housed by the Hulton Archive. In this way, Getty was using the medium of news photography to remind wire service subscribers to visit the archival section of its online platform, much like the Mary Evans

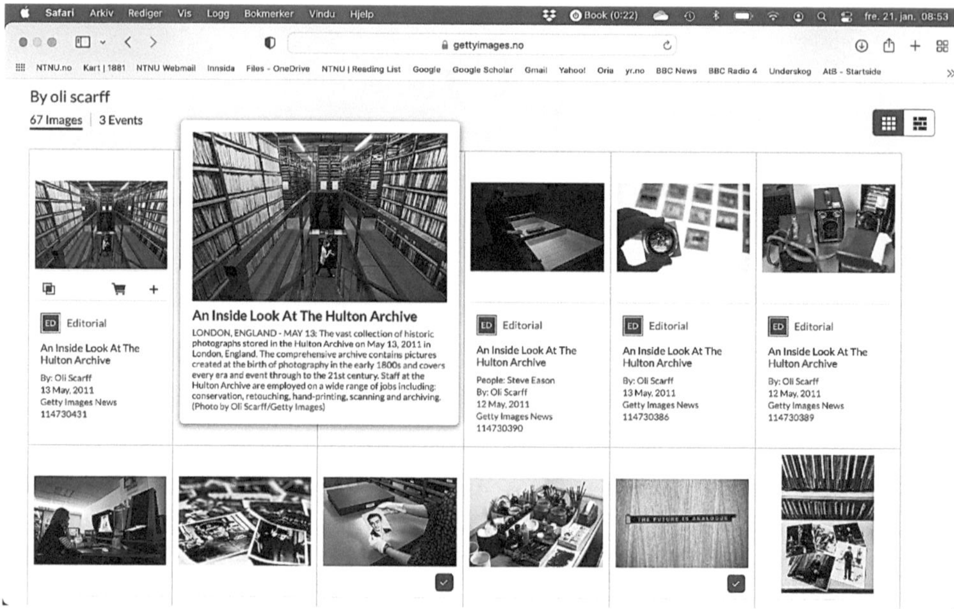

FIGURE 6.1
"An Inside Look at the Hulton Archive" (screenshot January 21, 2022). Getty Images, https://www.gettyimages.no/photos/an-inside-look-at-the-hulton-archive?assettype=image&family=editorial&phrase=%22An%20Inside%20Look%20at%20the%20Hulton%20Archive%22&sort=oldest.

Picture Library, as we recall from chapter 5, had employed the printed medium of the brochure to direct clients to its website.

Scarff's pictures offered detailed views of the pre-digital infrastructure of picture libraries, as it was still preserved at the Hulton Archive premises in 2011: rows upon rows of filing cabinets, shelves upon shelves of box files, sheets upon sheets of transparencies (figure 6.2). These are the long-established tools and furniture of picture librarianship, which by the 2010s had been further supplemented by the tools and furniture of digitization, in the form of drum scanners, negative scanners, and hooded computer screens (figure 6.3). Several photographs showed people making use of either analog or digital equipment, depending on the particular task they were performing. They represented the picture library as a thoroughly "post-digital" workplace, in Florian Cramer's sense, where employees were simply "using the technology most suitable to the job," whether that job was conserving, archiving, hand-printing, retouching,

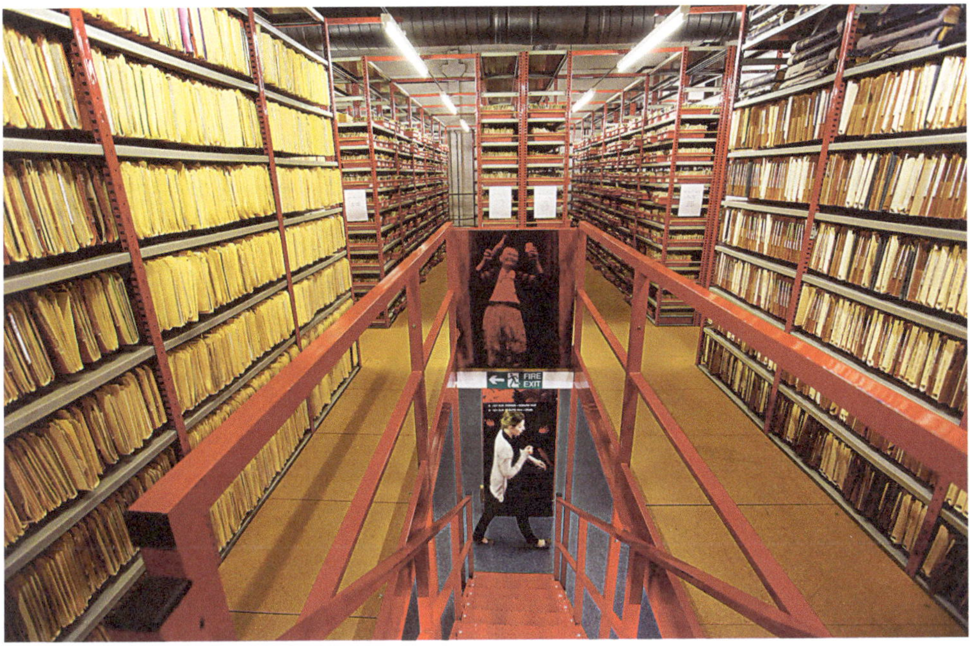

FIGURE 6.2
"The vast collection of historic photographs stored in the Hulton Archive." May 13, 2011. Photo by Oli Scarff/Getty Images. Original caption from Getty Images.

or scanning.[1] Together, the photographs and their captions pictured digitization as a set of domesticated technologies, rather than disruptive ones. Far from disintermediating the work of picture library staff, the tools and tasks of digitization appeared simply to have been absorbed into their existing workflows of intermediation.

This look inside the Hulton Archive presents the post-digital picture library as a place in which both people and photographs endure digitization. It depicts picture library workers engaged in digital scanning, retouching, and archiving, enduring (and by all means possibly enjoying) digitization as a job to be done. It also shows a selection of pictures undergoing digitization, being subjected to the multiple stages of a transformative process. In presenting this work as permanently ongoing, moreover, the pictures indicate that digitization will never be fully done. Coming from Getty Images in 2011, this amounted to an admission of sorts. It revealed that the company, which in the early 2000s had been instrumental in "digitizing the [picture] business and putting it online,"

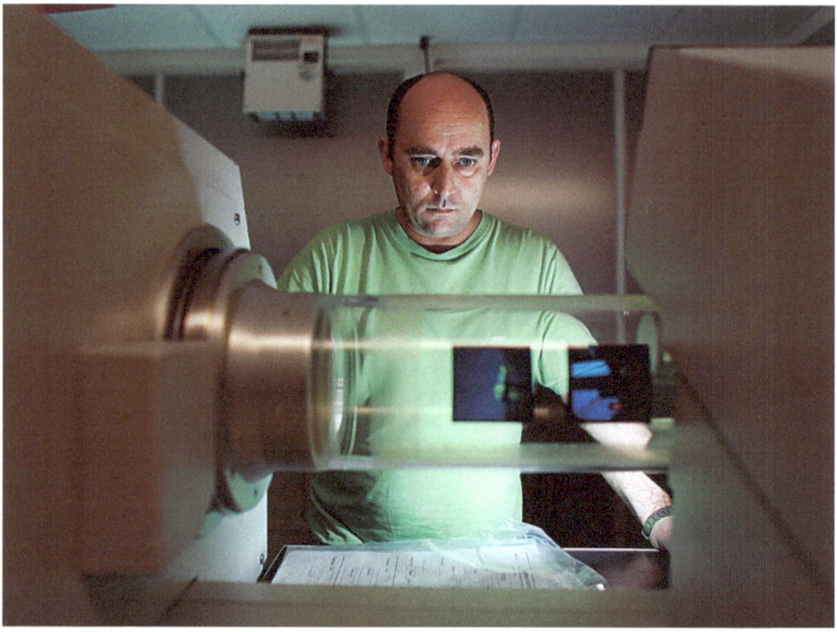

FIGURE 6.3
"Scanning Supervisor Richard Davis performs a high-resolution drum scan of a picture from the vast collection of historic photographs in the Hulton Archive." May 12, 2011. Photo by Oli Scarff/Getty Images. Original caption from Getty Images.

was still making use of the analog machineries of capture, accumulation, extraction, and transmission in the 2010s.[2] Yet by doing so, it was preserving the legacies of photography by ensuring that its objects, skills, and practices would endure beyond digitization.

This chapter explores the work of reintermediating photographs through digitization in the 2010s by analyzing examples from two highly dissimilar digital repositories, serving quite different constituencies. One of these examples is the series of pictures from the Hulton Archive, introduced above, which in early 2022 was still available to view for free and download for a fee from Getty Images. The other one is a digitized transparency of a medieval tapestry that belongs to a collection of ecclesiastical art, which also at the time of writing was accessible and downloadable for free through Unimus, the open-access online research portal shared by Norwegian university museums.

Both of these examples are representations of photographs that in their turn are representative of different fields of photographic practice: news and documentary photography, in the case of Hulton pictures, and museum photography, in the case of the tapestry reproduction. The websites through which they are distributed are also representative of two different kinds of online repositories: in the case of Getty Images, a profitable commercial platform of a global brand specializing in monetizing all kinds of visual content, and in the case of Unimus, a publicly (under) funded resource set up by a national consortium of knowledge institutions to meet politically defined demands for democratized and remote access to cultural heritage. Analyzing these two disparate examples alongside each other illuminates the several kinds of labor that lie congealed beneath the surface of a digitized photograph, accessed through the interface of a digital platform. In both cases, digitization calls attention to itself as an intermediating process involving emulsion-based photographic originals and human operators. Each of them also illustrates, in radically different ways, the skill and judgment required to produce and maintain the digitized sources derived from analog photographs that had become ubiquitous by the 2010s.

The labor of digitization "is understood as being a menial one for its repetitive character and low level of complexity," according to Beate Löffler and Tino Mager, and for that reason it is often outsourced to "anonymous staff members with . . . sparse and/or performance-related payment," as we have seen examples of in chapters 4 and 5.[3] One of the cases explored in this chapter contradicts that narrative, while the other confirms it. Together, they broaden our understanding of the social and political conditions that have been, and still are, shaping the digitized sources of visual cultural heritage that picture researchers, scholarly researchers, and internet users in general have long since come to take for granted.

Picturing Post-Digitization

In the previous chapter, we learned how the picture business went digital very suddenly, with the main marketplace having moved online sometime between 2000 and 2002. We also saw how different actors in the picture business in the course of the 2000s endeavored to make digitization work for their own ends, whether as established picture librarians, disruptive technology entrepreneurs, or professional picture researchers. By the 2010s, digitization no longer seemed especially promising or threatening, but more of a permanent condition affecting both commercial industries and public institutions of culture. Digitization, it turned out, was work that never ended.

The fact that it was also "a very costly business" was largely disavowed,[4] however, amid a prevailing consensus that digitizing the contents of libraries, archives, and museums constituted "a cultural and moral imperative and obligation."[5] The force of this cultural obligation drove the massive-scale digitization of books, documents, and photographs from public collections in the first decade of the twenty-first century, just as commercial picture libraries were being driven by business imperatives to go digital. A result of this "digitized turn," as historian Lara Putnam has called it, was what I call the phenomenon of post-digitization.[6] The term describes a pattern of behavior among internet users that seems to rest on the erroneous assumption that everything—at least everything of interest, relevance, or importance to anyone interesting, relevant or important—has already been digitized, and if it has not, this is an unfortunate omission that should be rectified immediately.

The concept of post-digitization serves a different purpose than the more established term *post-digital,* which denotes a general accommodation of and acclimatization to digital tools and objects in everyday life and work, as illustrated in the Hulton Archive pictures introduced above.[7] I build this differentiation on the distinction drawn by Putnam between the "digital turn" and a concomitant "digitized turn" in historical research and scholarship, which to my mind is applicable far beyond the discipline of history.[8] The digital turn refers to the use of specific research methods that have been developed thanks to digital computation, "specialized techniques like text mining and distant reading," as a supplement to established historical research methods and sources.[9] Post-digital practices in the pictorial economy are those that exploit specifically digital imaging technologies—from drone vision to facial recognition software—in addition to making, storing, and distributing pictures using whichever method, analog or digital, that is most convenient for the task in hand. The digitized turn, on the other hand, denotes what "all historians, however traditional, are enacting" whenever they are using digital search engines and reading digitized historical sources in order simply to perform the age-old historians' task of what Putnam calls "finding, and finding out."[10] This corresponds to my conception of post-digitization in the pictorial economy, which means the only pictures being looked at, and looked for, are those that have been reproduced and disseminated as digital surrogates.

The boundary between the post-digital and the post-digitized is not hard and fast, as most digital research practices in the historical disciplines require huge repositories of already-digitized historical data. A paradigmatic example that straddles this divide is Google Books. On the one hand, it was one of the large-scale and high-profile projects of mass digitization in the early 2000s that had ushered in the digitized turn and helped create an illusory state of post-digitization by the 2010s. On the other hand, it played an equally significant part in the digital turn by assembling a vast digital corpus of data that invited the application of computational research tools.

Established in 2004, Google Books involved collaboration with a number of university libraries to scan millions of books, page by page, and then render the textual content of those digitized pages searchable.[11] Although it was far from the first to devise and execute an ambitious digital library project, Google pioneered book scanning technologies that were operable "on an industrial scale."[12] It harnessed its considerable assets of technology and infrastructure, from search algorithms and data processing to server parks and scanning facilities, in order to ingest as much as possible of the cultural data hoarded by libraries. In this process, the tech company not only raised the bar for factory-style mass digitization projects; it produced a digital repository fully integrated with its own hegemonic search engine.

This made Google Books supremely visible to users and contributed significantly to establishing the expectation that all libraries (and archives and museums) would make their books (and documents and artworks) digitally accessible in the same way. "I cannot imagine working, now, without Google Books," the historian Emma Rothschild declared in 2011.[13] Any number of scholars in art history, media studies, and visual culture would by then have said the same about Google Images, with the important difference that while Google Books is a repository of digitized documents, Google Images is a specialized search engine that directs searchers to other repositories.

Working from reproductions was not in itself a new experience for historians or art historians, who had already for several generations been accustomed to reading archival documents and old periodicals via microfilm and microfiche, and studying works of visual art through photographic prints and transparencies. These secondary sources were nevertheless rarely obtainable from the comfort of one's own desk. Many an academic researcher practicing in the mid- to late twentieth century would therefore have nodded in recognition at Hilary and Mary Evans's previously cited observation, in the first *Picture Researcher's Handbook*, that it was "hard to appreciate the sheer quantity of time and trouble needed to find a single, apparently simple, illustration," if you had not personally done the work of looking for it.[14] The digitization of artworks may not have obviated the need for art historians in the 2010s to seek out original works on site, any more than the photographic "museum without walls," theorized by André Malraux in the 1950s, had done in the preceding century.[15] Digitized reproductions in combination with digital search tools, however, made the work of looking for them faster and easier. This was where Google Images came into its own, not so much as an online picture library but as a digital replacement for finding tools like *The Picture Researcher's Handbook*.

Getty Images had a comparable effect on the field of professional picture research in the early 2000s to the one Google Books had on library-based research in the same period. Neither of these repositories was an adequate replacement for analog libraries—whether of books or pictures—but they were instrumental in habituating researchers to the immediate digital availability of books and pictures. We recall the "supermarket philosophy" that picture library manager Rick ascribed to Getty Images in chapter 5: by providing a one-stop shop for everything from daily news photographs to creative stock via historical illustrations and highlights from the history of photography, the Getty platform was an obvious starting point for any picture researcher. And its subscription model, which allowed publications to pay a fixed monthly rate in return for unlimited downloads, encouraged users to stay within the platform.

Researchers working with minimal budgets would therefore try to tailor their picture requests to the content available from Getty, rather than seek out alternative sources that incurred additional costs, even though they might provide more relevant material.

Google and Getty Images did not have the same motivations for keeping users within the confines of their respective online environments. The ad platform Google was giving free access to content in exchange for enormous amounts of user data that would be translated into advertising revenue, while the meta-source Getty was monetizing the "long tail" of stock photography by offering all kinds of pictures for all kinds of purposes, while siphoning business off from competitors through its competitive pricing and subscription plans (and then not infrequently acquiring those competitors).[16] Despite the differences in their business models, both platforms saturated their users with digitized content at an unfathomable scale. This abundance invited readers, researchers, and viewers to indulge in the fantasy of post-digitization, the idea that any historical document or picture worth consulting would already have been digitized.

Regardless of the fallacy inherent in post-digitization, the digitized turn irrevocably turned the knowledge work of research almost exclusively into "a desk discipline," as Putnam calls it.[17] In order for knowledge workers like scholars and picture researchers to do their jobs via networked computer terminals on desks, however, other workers had to perform the information labor of "scanning, storing, labelling, keywording, and meta-texting," in short: the labor of digitization.[18]

Preserving Photography in the Hulton Archive

We saw in chapter 5 how digitization changed the character of picture librarianship by largely replacing the intermediary functions of library research staff with the intermediary interface of the searchable website. The series of pictures introduced at the start of this chapter, presenting "an inside look at the Hulton Archive," illustrated that, even so, there was still work to be done in the picture library.

The caption that accompanied all photographs in the series listed scanning as just one of a range of activities routinely performed by employees.

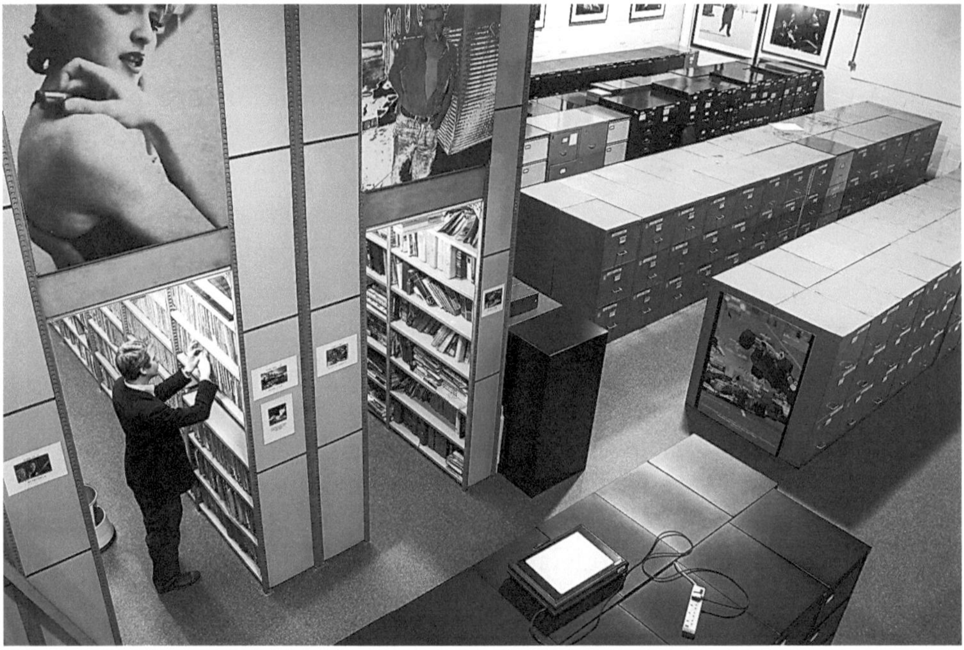

FIGURE 6.4
"A man looks through the vast collection of historic photographs in the Hulton Archive." May 12, 2011. Photo by Oli Scarff/Getty Images. Original caption from Getty Images.

Other tasks included conservation, archiving, and the production of fine photographic prints for exhibition display or the collectors' market. Indeed, work at the Hulton Archive in 2011 appeared as focused on preserving the legacy of photography as a historical medium of both archival storage and fine art as on producing digital surrogates for the rapid distribution of archival photographic content.

Views of boxes, shelves, and filing cabinets containing historical photographs (figure 6.4) conveyed both the scale of the picture library's holdings and the variety of physical storage solutions that over the years had been adopted by the different archives assembled within the metacollection of the Hulton Archive. Although it was not detailed in the caption, the preservation of these different systems also required maintaining the knowledge of how to search them, which in turn meant rehearsing, on a regular basis, the various archival scripts that constituted

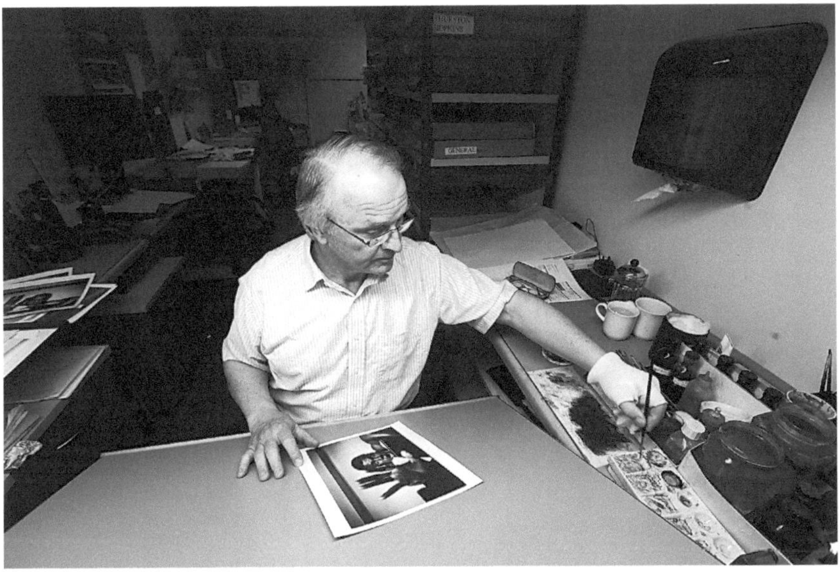

Figure 6.5
"Retoucher Peter Gamble uses inks to 'spot' hand-made black and white prints made from the historic photographs in the Hulton Archive." May 12, 2011. Photo by Oli Scarff/Getty Images. Original caption from Getty Images.

the pre-digital search protocols for each collection. The pictures showing equipment and activities pertaining to the practice of hand-printing and retouching (figure 6.5) likewise documented the work of preserving the intangible darkroom skills of emulsion-based photographic print production, the simulated effects of which had long since become embedded in digital tools of image capture and display.

The practical work of digitization did not appear significantly different from photographic tasks detailed in the series. Most of the pictures followed a traditional photojournalistic pattern of showing people at work with their tools, whether it was a scanning supervisor performing a drum scan or a technician carrying out digital image restoration with the help of Photoshop (figure 6.6). Apart from one anonymous "man look[ing] through the vast collection of photographs," who posed in some of the general views of the archival space, all the people included in the photographs were identified by name and job title in the captions. Using the genre of the picture-led news story, Getty Images thus presented their

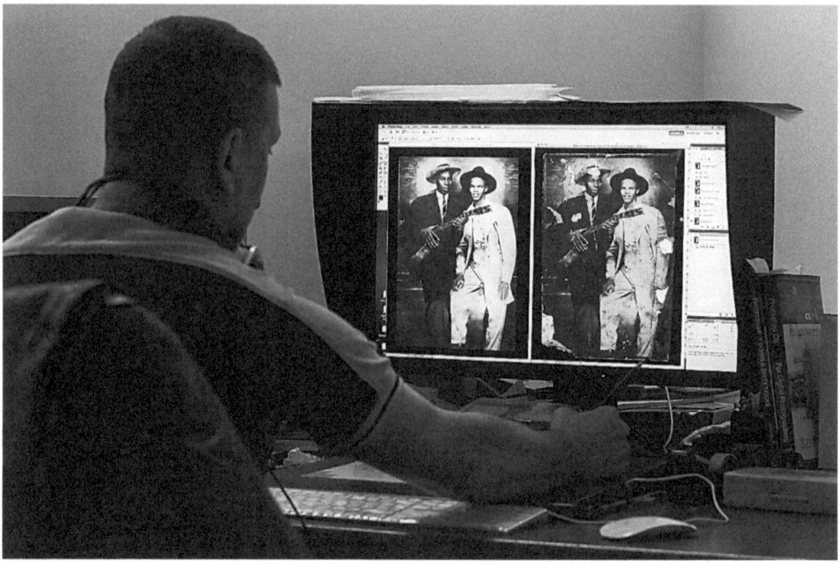

FIGURE 6.6
"Scanning technician Matt Green uses Photoshop to restore a badly damaged picture from the vast collection of historic photographs in the Hulton Archive." May 12, 2011. Photo by Oli Scarff/Getty Images. Original caption from Getty Images.

subscribers with documentation of their skilled employees performing a number of specialized tasks involved in the conservation and archiving of photographs, as well as in both the chemical and digital processing of them. In these pictures, the tasks of digitization seemed to have been absorbed into the workings of the picture library, as opposed to the tasks of the picture library having been obliterated by digitization.

This picture story was, as already indicated, doing the same job as the photograph and extended caption from Keystone in the 1950s that I analyzed in chapter 2: it was explicitly showing and telling customers how the picture library worked, and it was implicitly pointing out to them that there was a considerable amount of human labor, skill, and judgment priced into the reproduction fees that the library charged for its pictures. In the 2010s, when clients were usually doing the job of searching for, finding, and transmitting (i.e., downloading) pictures all by themselves, there may have been even further cause than in the 1950s to explain how value was added to the visual commodity "behind the scenes."

Looking through the full set of sixty-seven pictures nevertheless produces the impression that the overriding purpose of photographing employees at their work, writing explanatory and promotional captions to go with the pictures, and distributing them along with the daily output of news photographs was for the commercial digital platform Getty Images to assert its credentials as a bona fide custodian of analog photographic heritage. This effect was achieved by a twofold visual strategy. First, as in the examples discussed above, several pictures (thirteen, to be exact) detailed the practical work of chemical photographic processing, from darkroom printing to retouching by hand. Second, an even greater number of pictures (twenty-nine) featured photographic prints or transparencies from the collection that were either photographs of famous historical figures or events or pictures produced by famous photographers.

The caption for a picture in the latter category began, "A black and white print of a couple kissing in Times Square on VJ Day, taken by Alfred Eisenstaedt," and the print displayed in the digital photograph (figure 6.7) was one of the iconic press photographs of the twentieth century, a photographic celebrity in its own right.[19] In his 2011 photograph of Eisenstaedt's photograph from August 1945, however, Scarff angled his lens in such a way as to render the image itself blurred out in the background, while the typescript caption stuck to the bottom of the print was in focus. This drew attention away from the content of Eisenstaedt's photograph—a photographic visualization of joy and relief at the end of the Second World War—and onto the form in which it had circulated. Under the headline "V-J Day in New York" (in all caps), the caption read: "5. Photo shows: New York City went all out in its celebration resulting from the announcement of Japan's surrender to the Allies." The number five at the start of the caption indicated that this photograph had been the fifth in a series (of which the others have been largely forgotten), while the assortment of stickers and stamps surrounding the glued-on strip of paper were signs to where and by whom it had been handled through the years, with the red dot signaling that it had been digitized by the Hulton Archive.

Scarff's rendition of Eisenstaedt's photograph highlighted the single photographic press print as an individual material object that "bears the marks of its own history."[20] At the same time it also bore witness to the

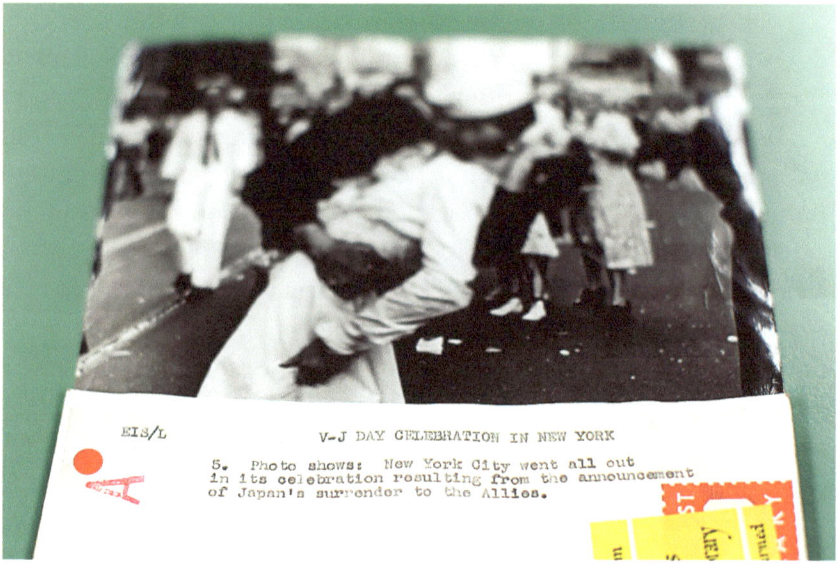

FIGURE 6.7
"A black and white print of a couple kissing in Times Square on VJ Day, taken by Alfred Eisenstaedt, is laid out from the vast collection of historic photographs stored in the Hulton Archive." May 13, 2011. Photo by Oli Scarff/Getty Images. Original caption from Getty Images.

material practices that characterized the particular sphere of the mid-twentieth-century pictorial economy occupied by the news publishing and picture industries. In short, while Scarff's photograph was none-too-subtly informing subscribers and users that they could license Eisenstaedt's photographs from Getty Images, it was also enlightening them about the historical material culture of news photography. The digital news photograph from 2011 was showing its viewers what a press photograph used to look like in 1945.

Other compositions involving "celebrity" photographs from Scarff's series used the accoutrements of analog picture librarianship to highlight the material condition and visual appearance of vintage prints or transparencies from well-known historical events. Two examples are reproduced here: one is a color print of the 1967 moon landing by NASA's Apollo 11 crew (figure 6.8), and the other is a 35-mm color transparency capturing Diego Maradona's "Hand of God" goal in the quarter final

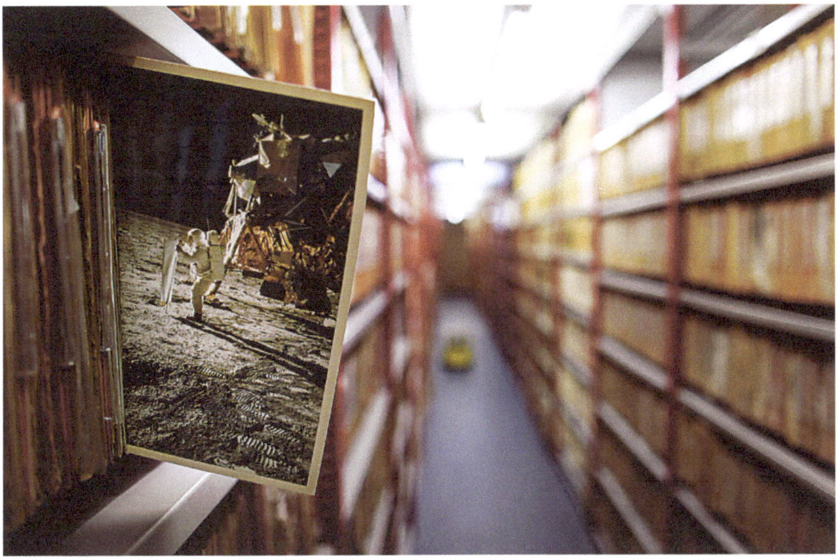

FIGURE 6.8
"A color print of the moon landing is seen in the vast collection of historic photographs stored in the Hulton Archive." May 13, 2011. Photo by Oli Scarff/Getty Images. Original caption from Getty Images.

against England during the soccer World Cup of 1986 (figure 6.9). The print is shown sticking out from a hanging file in a vast shelving system that stretches, out of focus, into the far distance of the background. The transparency is picked out through the lens of a loupe, pinched between two fingers and sharply focusing the tiny translucent picture against the blurred background of a slide sheet resting on a lightbox. Using the loupe as a framing device cannily demonstrated one of the basic tools of picture research and editing in the transparency era, while the shelves surrounding the moon landing print emphasized the paper-based infrastructure of pre-digital search methods.

Like the Eisenstaedt photograph, the moon landing print and the "Hand of God" slide both document events that have been regularly referenced and memorialized in mainstream media since they first occurred. Accordingly, it is safe to assume that both of these analog archive photographs, like the red-dotted VJ Day print, had already been digitally reproduced and made available for download on the Getty Images platform

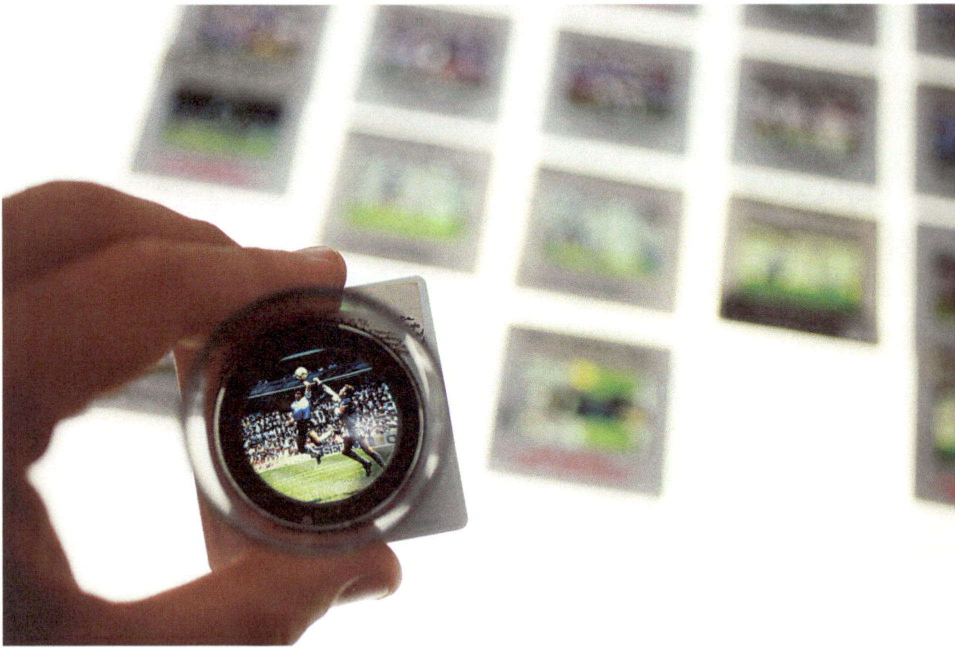

FIGURE 6.9
"Color slides of Diego Maradona's infamous 'Hand of God' goal are laid out from the vast collection of historic photographs stored in the Hulton Archive." May 13, 2011. Photo by Oli Scarff/Getty Images. Original caption from Getty Images.

long before 2011. Yet those digital reproductions would have simply recaptured and retransmitted the image content of the print and the transparency, disintermediating their original material supports. Scarff's born-digital compositions restored to the frame the archival apparatus of storage and retrieval, which had preserved the photographs in their print and transparency forms, yet been disavowed in their digital surrogate forms.

All these three photographs of famous historical photographs could be cited as examples of Getty Images capitalizing on its own history, or at least the histories of picture libraries it had acquired or absorbed. This has always been a common strategy for purveyors of stock photography, as Abbott Miller observed in chapter 2.[21] The same photographs could also be read as metapictures of the series as a whole, in the sense that they visualized how the objects, technologies, and practices of analog photography were nested within, or propping up, the products of digitization. As "photographs of photographs of photographs" they playfully illustrated the work of digitization as, essentially, rephotographing photographs from the archives.[22]

Although outnumbered by pictures of traditional photographic activities, Scarff's series also contained several detailed depictions of staff in the process of scanning and digitally enhancing photographs. The captions specified the various roles of those appearing in the photographs as archive research manager, curator, darkroom technician, retoucher, scanning supervisor, or scanning technician, and also provided their individual names. In view of the previously cited tendency to outsource digitization to anonymous and low-skilled support staff, this recognition seemed to set the Hulton Archive apart from other sources of digitized historical documents. Nowhere to be seen, however, were the caption writers and keyworders whose information labor made digitized Hulton Archive collection items findable and viewable through Getty Images' web-based platform—and who would in fact have captioned and keyworded every one of the sixty-seven photographs before they were put online.

There is an obvious aesthetic argument in favor of this omission, since the work of caption-writing and keywording is not visually distinguishable from any other office job; it looks like someone sitting in front of a computer. So does picture processing in Photoshop, however, and there were at least two photographs in the set showing that activity. Yet those pictures, which included views of digitized historical photographs on screen, constructed an equivalence between photographic and digital picture processing that served to underscore the main function of these carefully composed pictures from inside the Hulton Archive. This was to promote Getty Images as a keeper of the photographic flame, a company that, having set the pace of digitization in the picture industry, and in the process helped turn it into a branch of platform capitalism, nevertheless took it upon itself to preserve not just an important historical collection of photographs, but the historical legacy of the photographic medium itself. Communicating this to subscribers and website visitors by means of a picture story implicitly reassured existing and potential clients that the fees charged by the platform were not just lining the pockets of its investors but safeguarding the future of photography's past.

Getty Images was able to assume both the moral responsibility and practical burden of looking after the durable objects of photographic heritage because it was at the same time trading transient digital commodities on a massive scale, within the post-digitized pictorial economy it had been instrumental in creating. In the public and nonprofit sectors of that economy, however, the effects of post-digitization were rather different. The digitized turn in scholarship from the early 2000s framed the mass production of digital surrogates for cultural objects as a progressive, technopolitical tool of democratization. Combined with the general fallacy of post-digitization, that everything has or should already have been digitized, this contributed to the establishment of digitization as a goal in itself across publicly funded libraries, archives, and museums.

Like the commercial picture-industrial platforms that emerged in the 2000s, online museum resources developed in the same period also derived most of their visual content from existing reproductions in photographic media. In the same way that prints, slides, boxes, shelves, filing cabinets, darkrooms, lightboxes, and scanners in the Hulton Archive were shown by Scarff to underpin the online offerings of historical photographs available on the Getty Images platform, the catalogs and archives of museums represented the raw material from which digital repositories of art reproductions were built.

The reproduction histories of paintings and other visual works of art have for decades been considered worthy of study by art historians as evidence of the reach and reception of particular works or artists.[23] Working through the digitization history of one specific slide reproduction of a work of art, from online version to original 35-mm transparency format, is a way of reverse engineering this approach to uncover the convoluted processes of institutional and technical intermediation that go into to producing a seemingly disintermediated digital surrogate.

The Tapestry and the Transparency in the University Museum

It is often remarked that the discipline of art history—"developed and taught largely with photographs and printed books"—owes its existence to the reproductive and remediating capacities of photography.[24] Just as published reproductions have performed the work of intermediation between artworks and their publics, photographic reproductions held in the archives and slide libraries of museums, schools, and universities have intermediated between items in their original material forms and in their "documented forms" as objects of learning, teaching, and research.[25] An original art object becomes a document through the process of having information about itself recorded and inscribed in a catalog. Photographs created as part of this process of documentation occupy a space "between art and information," as Elizabeth Edwards and Christopher Morton have put it.[26] Within museums, such photographic reproductions have been "dehistoricized as both documents and collections" as curators and conservators have considered them "as illustrative props for other classes of object" rather than "as knowledge-objects in their own right."[27]

This functional transparency of photographic documents—we see through them in order to look at something else—is mirrored in the material characteristic of the photographic transparency, most frequently encountered in the popular format of the 35-mm slide. Photographic slide reproductions have functioned as visual surrogates for original sources within a variety of contexts, from documentation and research to teaching and publication. For the purposes of art-historical argument, for instance, "slides are accepted as paintings," as Robert S. Nelson has noted in a much-referenced study on slide projection as a fundamental tool of art history.[28] This acceptance was produced through rhetoric, as Nelson shows, but it was also reliant on the see-through-ness that made it possible to enlarge the compact-sized yet visual-information-rich slide by electric light projection. In short, for all the purposes detailed above, the most significant quality of the slide was its transparency, the see-through surface allowing access to an apparently immediate visual experience.

For the same technical reasons that they performed this intermediating task so well, by providing compact storage of an almost infinite amount of visual data, photographic transparencies also proved highly convenient sources for digitization, as we have already seen in the context of the commercial picture industry, discussed in chapter 5. And once the contents of slide libraries had been digitized, and the physical libraries themselves disintermediated by online repositories of digital surrogates, computer screens and their graphic user interfaces assumed the

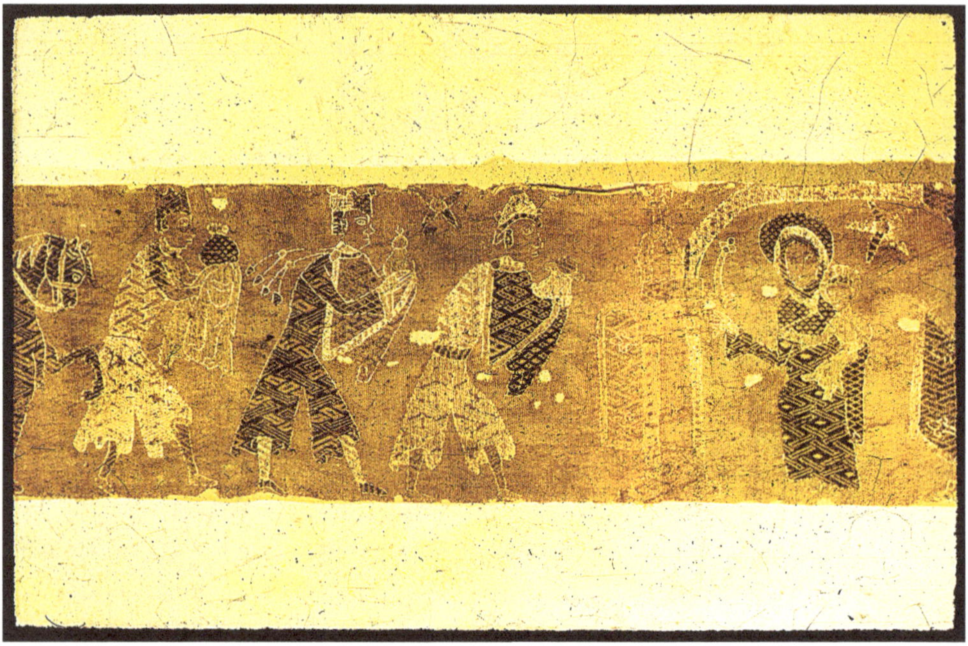

FIGURE 6.10
Digitized reproduction of slide depicting Høylandsteppet (the Høylandet tapestry) (n.d.). From the photographic archives of the University Museum, Trondheim. CC BY-SA 4.0.

transparent qualities of slides as media that we habitually look through. More than occasionally, however, flaws or characteristics belonging to the specific copy of an item that has been selected for digitization are carried over from the primary medium of reproduction, for example, photography, into the new surrogate. This is precisely what has happened in the case of the digitized slide reproduction of a medieval tapestry that forms the focal point of my final analysis in this chapter.

The Høylandet tapestry (figure 6.10) is a surviving fragment of an embroidered textile depicting an Adoration scene, which is thought to date from the late twelfth century.[29] It measures about 210 cm × 44 cm and is as of this writing in the ecclesiastical collection of the University Museum in Trondheim, Norway. In 1866, the fragment was discovered bundled together in a corner of the village church loft at Høylandet in the Trøndelag region of Norway, where it may have been languishing in obscurity ever since the Reformation in 1537. Today, the original textile is kept under controlled climatic conditions in the museum stores and is viewable only by appointment. Two different reconstructions of it were made in the 1980s and 1990s: one for the village church at Høylandet, which was made by an amateur in the local parish, and another for the Nidaros Cathedral in Trondheim, which was produced by a professional textile artist. Access to the Høylandet copy is restricted to hours of worship, while the Trondheim copy is kept in a part of the cathedral that is closed to the public. As with so many significant works of art, then, the Høylandet tapestry must for the most part be viewed, appreciated, and studied through photographic or photography-derived reproductions.

My first encounter with the tapestry occurred in 2018 through a web-based portal for university museums in Norway, which is aimed at scholars and students, and thus not calibrated for commercial exploitation, like Getty Images. The photograph reproduced in figure 6.10 (K3/109) came up first out of a total of five results, all derived from the photographic archives of the University Museum in Trondheim. Looking closely at this digitized version of the tapestry on my computer screen, I was immediately struck by the faithfully rendered photographic characteristics of the original reproduction. A distinct color cast and traces of dust seemed to suggest that the photograph, which clearly was the source of the digital surrogate, had deteriorated in a manner not dissimilar to the work of art it was supposedly standing in for. The strong yellow cast perceptible in the digitized photograph, for instance, was consistent with the chemical degradation that typically occurs in color transparency emulsions over time. Random markings suggested either scratches on the emulsion surface or specks of dust trapped inside the slide mount, both of which could signify a lack of care in the storage and handling of the transparency.

If my access to this picture had been limited to the post-digitized realm of remote research, I would not have got much further in establishing which elements of the digital surrogate were accurate representations of the tapestry and which were artifacts of the photographic reproduction and its technical properties. Since both the transparency and the tapestry are preserved in the museum of my own institution, however, I have easily been able to consult the non-digitized sources in their real-world

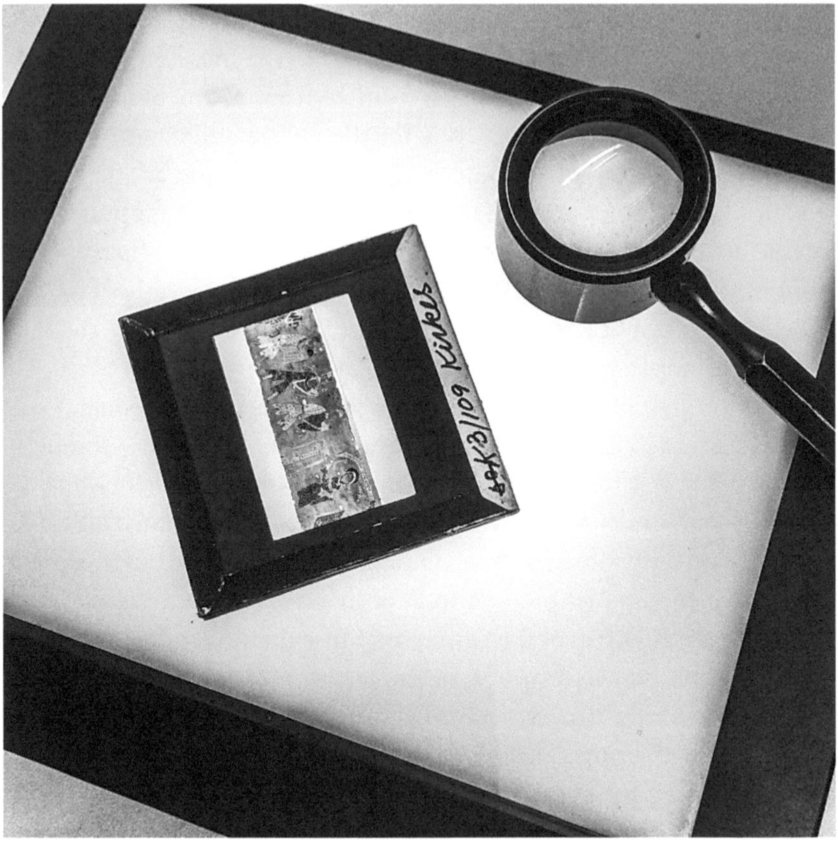

FIGURE 6.11
Original slide of Høylandsteppet on lightbox in the University Museum, Trondheim (2019). Photo by author.

settings. Inspecting the original transparency in a study room at the University Museum (figure 6.11), some of my assumptions about its material condition were confirmed, and other details came to light. The mount turned out not to be the usual 35-mm plastic frame mount but instead a 5 × 5 cm glass mount, possibly intended for lantern slides, the projection format that preceded the 35-mm photographic slide carousel. The uneven edge running alongside the top and bottom of the digitized image resulted from the black 35-mm card mount that had been inserted into the glass one to keep the exposure in place inside a slide mount of the wrong proportions.

In keeping with most of the University Museum's photographic documents from the pre-digital era, this slide carried no textual information about itself beyond a number identifying its physical place in the photographic archive. The handwritten label read "K3/109 Kirkes.," indicating that the photograph was (and still is) kept in slot no. 109 inside storage box K3, and that the item depicted belongs to the museum's ecclesiastical collection (Kirkesamlingen). Apart from this, no further information was to be gleaned from my inspection of the single original slide. When I asked museum staff for a qualified estimation of when slide no. 109 had been produced, their assessment was mainly based on circumstantial evidence such as the known dates on other slides in the same box.

One suggestion was that the slide could have been produced in connection with a major exhibition of ecclesiastical art put on in 1953 as part of celebrations of the 800th anniversary of the establishment of the first Norwegian diocese in Trondheim in 1153. This would have provided a pleasing symmetry with the theory that the investiture of Norway's first archbishop may have been a likely occasion for the tapestry to have been brought there in the first place.[30] Examining the photographic object itself for technical clues indicated, however, that the slide was made at a later date. The 35-mm color transparency format made it more likely to have been produced in the 1960s or later. As for the visual content of the transparency, an experienced museum photographer alerted me to the possibility that the fragment had been photographed while lit from below by a light table, explaining the unusual luminosity of the textile as it appeared in the photograph. This forensic lighting scheme would have highlighted tears and holes in the fabric, and was a strong indication that the photograph had been made as a visual aid for technical conservation, probably as part of the documentation work for the making of the reconstructed version of the tapestry in the late 1980s.

On the basis of these investigations, I concluded that the K3/109 photograph was likely to have been produced with an exclusive audience of professional textile conservators in mind. As mentioned, however, this photograph was just one out of five digitized reproductions of the tapestry that my original search had returned. Two of these were stored alongside K3/109 in the box labeled K3, which was stored in the basement vault that houses the museum's photographic archives. The box contained photographic records of items ranging from archaeological and architectural heritage sites to paintings and illuminated medieval manuscripts. It also included a handwritten list of contents as well as a photocopied typescript letter, with added handwritten notes, dating from the 1960s (figure 6.12). The letter detailed problems with recovering certain slides from a former employee and had clearly been included in the box to explain why some photographs indicated in the contents list were missing. Together with the lack of consistency in the labeling of slides, this letter testified to an unsystematic approach to recordkeeping when it came to photographic documents within the University Museum.

As Edwards and Morton have observed, "associated information" about museum photographs has tended to be stored mainly "in the heads of the curators who produced and kept them," and rarely been considered worthy of inscription beyond "the most cursory identifier or description of content on or around the image support."[31] The contents of box K3 bore out this observation. Seeing slide K3/109 in its storage box did not help fix a specific date or even year of production, and the arbitrariness with which it was archived testified to an indifference within the museum to the value of its photographic records as historical sources. Beyond cursory identifiers inscribed on the slide mounts, the museum's registration data related to photographic documents was limited to the card catalog linking collection items to their respective reproductions, which were stored separate from the transparencies themselves.

In the pre-digital era, the University Museum had considered management of the photographic archives and catalog to be a clerical task, rather than a curatorial one. Potentially relevant associated information had therefore more likely been kept in the heads of secretaries rather than curators. When the character of clerical work was changed by computerization in the course of the 1980s and 1990s, the traditional "office ladies" were not replaced upon retirement and so did not have occasion to transmit whatever tacit knowledge they may have had about the catalog system and its contents to successors.[32] In this respect the photo archives of the University Museum are representative of similar archives across any number of museums, in which photographic documentation was considered on a par with typing and filing as a mere administrative support for the actual work of collection management and conservation.[33] The idea

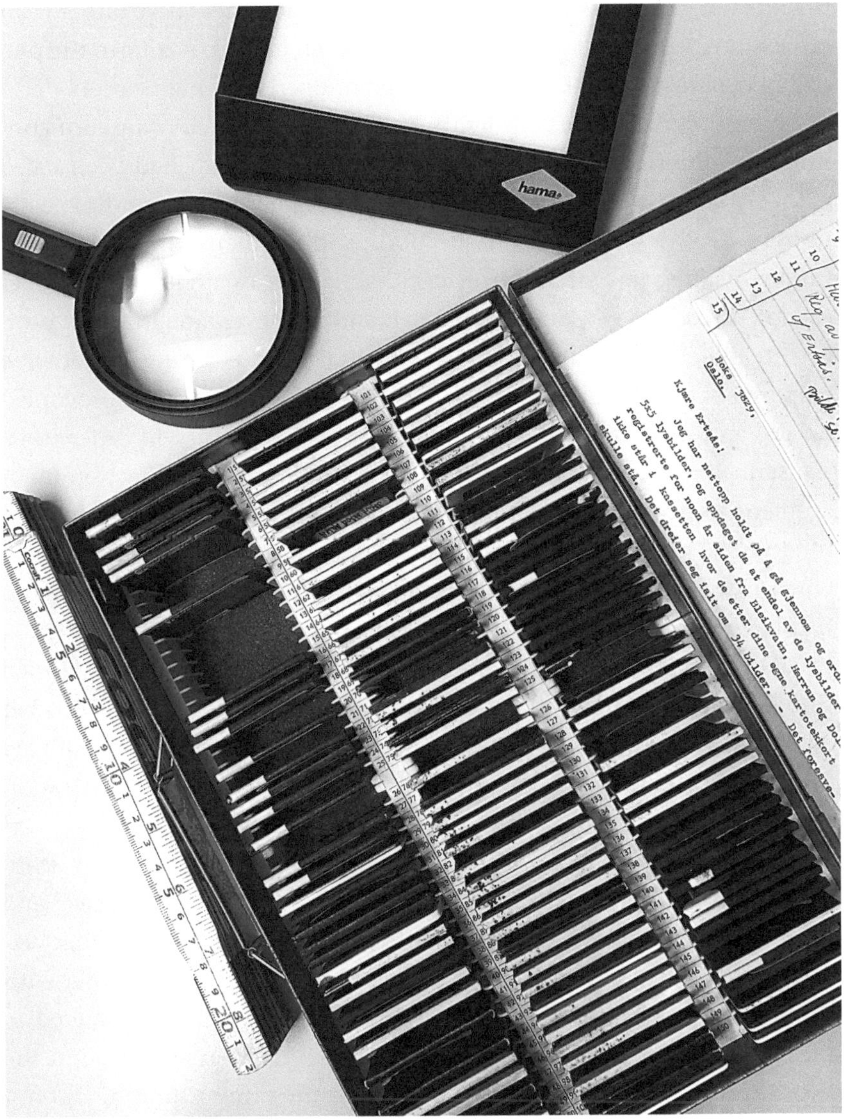

FIGURE 6.12
Box of 35-mm slide mounts in the photographic archive at the University Museum Trondheim (2020). Photo by author.

that documentation was the work of technical-administrative rather than professional-curatorial staff seems to have been carried over from the predigital era into the recent and contemporary period of digitization.

The disjointed history of digitization at the University Museum confirms this impression. In the early 2000s, the museum had been faced with a combination of pressure from funding authorities and expectations from users to digitize its collections, and like many knowledge institutions in the same situation, it decided to start by digitizing its paper catalog cards. The work began in 2004, and like several digitization projects in the Nordic countries it was undertaken as part of a nationwide employment scheme for job-seekers.[34] The cards were first photocopied on-site and then shipped to another part of the country in order to be transcribed into a digital format legible to the museum's collection management software. This digitized information then sat on the system for nine years, still as disconnected from the photographs as it had been when it was stored in the card catalog. In the meantime, the museum had been awarded a major revitalization project, which ran from 2006 to 2015. Like the catalog digitization scheme, this was partly funded through cross-financing from unemployment schemes, and in 2013 it enabled a substantial number of photographs to be scanned and linked to the metadata files that had been created in 2004 from the digitization of catalog cards.[35]

During neither the digitization of the catalog in 2004 nor the scanning of photographic slides in 2013 was there any attempt to recover and record additional information about the photographs beyond what was inscribed in the paper catalog. The bits of paper preserved together with the transparencies inside box K3, for instance, were not considered as metadata pertaining to either photographs or items, at any stage in the two separate digitization processes. Likewise the project funding did not cover the capacity of museum staff to check the accuracy of the digitization work performed by a constantly changing crew of temporary trainees before it was put online. As a consequence, mistakes and anomalies introduced by the digitization process have been discovered only randomly and in retrospect.

One example is the digitized version of another transparency from box K3, labeled K3/34 (figure 6.13), which shows a detailed view of one

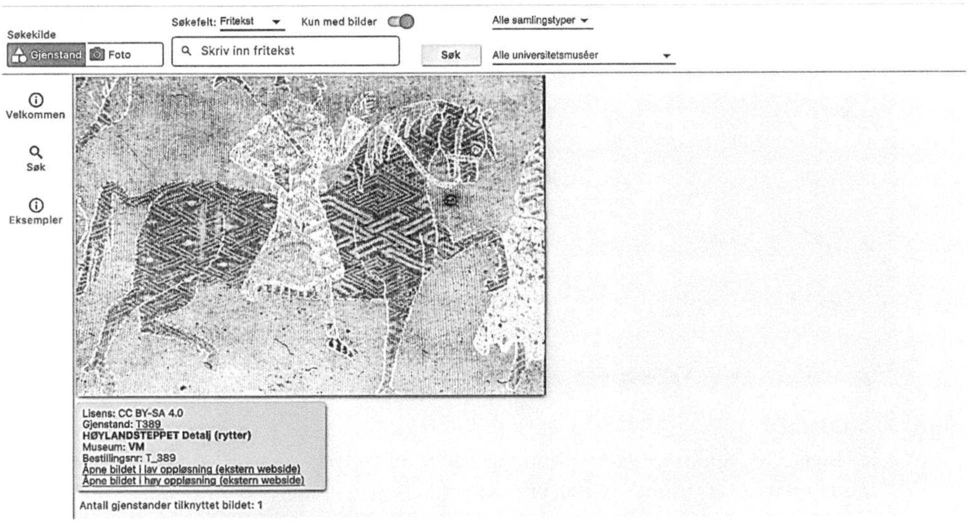

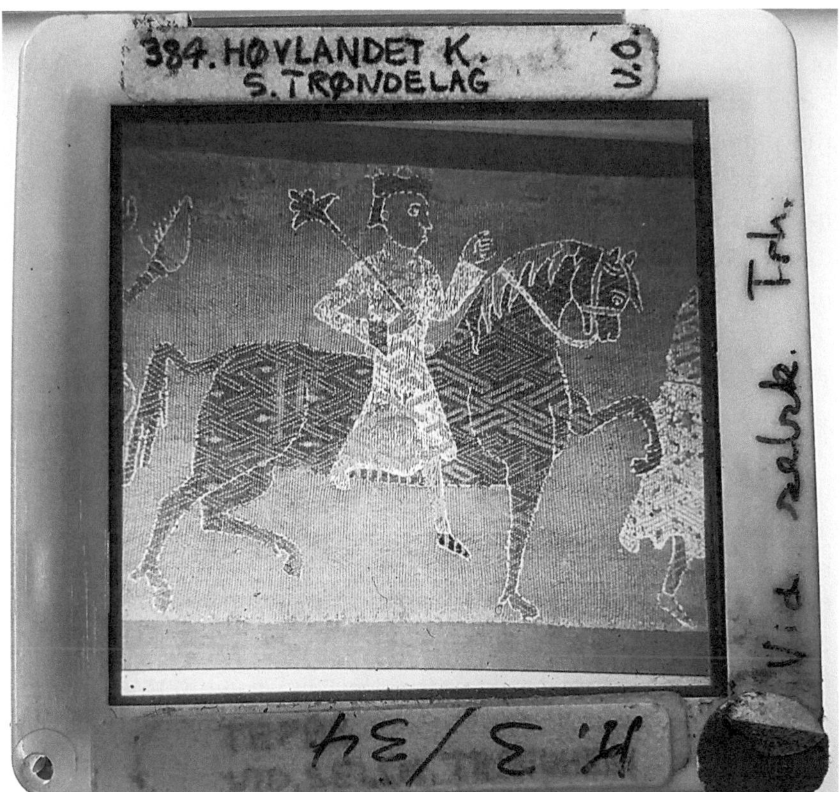

FIGURE 6.13
Top: Digitized version of slide K3/34 as it appears on the Unimus portal (screenshot March 1, 2022). Unimus, https://www.unimus.no/portal/#/photos/410ec0cb-bfb7-4f49-abda-feff528e92d3. *Bottom*: Original transparency in the University Museum, Trondheim (2020). Photo by author.

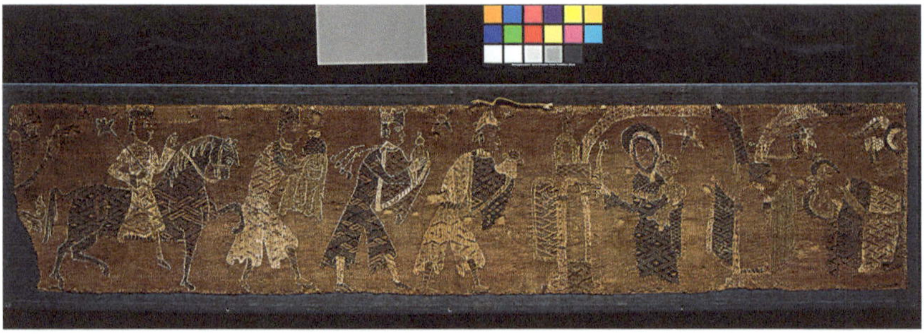

FIGURE 6.14
The Høylandet tapestry. Digital photographic record with gray card and color scale. 2017. Displayed on Unimus portal. Photo by Åge Hojem, University Museum, Trondheim. CC BY-SA 4.0.

of the kings depicted in the Høylandet tapestry but is missing a significant portion of the human figure—the head—which is clearly visible on the original slide (figure 6.14). This virtual decapitation probably resulted from the slide being fed through the scanner by an operator without adequate training or technical knowledge to adjust the setting according to differently formatted transparencies. This can only be a qualified guess, however, for the decisions made by anonymous and temporary digitization workers are rarely documented, as Löffler and Mager have noted, and thus remain a "black box" for researchers consulting digital surrogates.[36]

As an individual digital reproduction, this example represents an error of very limited consequence. It is nevertheless symptomatic of the "minor politics" that characterizes digitization as a material process involving individual operators, who in order to get the job done are constantly having to make small, practical decisions, which may in turn "unintentionally [modify] the content of the source material."[37] Since neither the decisions themselves nor the names of those who make them tend to be recorded, Löffler and Mager argue that the "digital authorship" of visual datasets like digitized picture collections cannot be established in a way that facilitates traditional "source criticism."[38] Indeed, the only reason I detected the missing head from the digitized detail of the tapestry was that I had managed to negotiate access to the slides from which the digital surrogates had been made, an opportunity that the effects of post-digitization have made it increasingly difficult for researchers to obtain.

Following the digitized turn, funding models and workflows across both scholarly and editorial research positions encourage, if they do not downright require, researchers to focus on the post-digitized opportunities for searching across multiple online archives and libraries from their own efficiently equipped workstation, at the expense of seeking out "the still-existing world of non-digitized sources."[39] The framework of post-digitization thus limits the range of sources from which visual and historical information is gathered, even as the post-digital approach to research expands the range of methods for producing historical as well as visual knowledge. It also prevents researchers trained exclusively within this framework from developing forms of technical and historical knowledge that would enable them to recognize the kind of digital artifacts that derive from previous processes of reproduction.

This is the kind of technical and historical knowledge—derived in my case from having trained as a photographer, worked as a picture researcher, and studied art history in the age of the photographic slide—that allowed me to diagnose the color cast, scratches, and dark bursts of dust visible in the scanned version of slide K3/109 (figure 6.10) as artifacts of emulsion-based photography. For researchers without this knowledge (anyone training as photographers, starting out as picture researchers, or studying art history after the late 2000s), seeing the digital surrogate of slide K3/109 displayed online alongside a much more recent born-digital photograph of the Høylandet tapestry (figure 6.14) will not make much sense. While the digital reproduction offers a seemingly immediate, transparent view of the tapestry in its true colors (or rather the colors it has faded to over the centuries), the digitized transparency effectively obscures the artwork it depicts by the sheer visual force of its photographic materiality.

This archived transparency was first produced, as we have established, to serve as a working object for conservators and researchers in order to reduce handling and display of the fragile original tapestry. The online digital surrogate that was created in 2013 replaced the transparency as a working object in this regard, responding to the requirements of post-digitized habits of work and research. En route from primary to secondary reproduction, however, the historical source—the tapestry fragment—has faded into the background of its photographic representation, which by virtue of the digital reproduction process has been turned into a historical source in its own right. Yet how would a post-digitized researcher looking up the tapestry online know any of this?

No information about the sources and processes of reproduction, whether photographic or digital, is provided alongside the University Museum's digitized photographs on the Unimus platform. On the one hand, this is in keeping with the already-mentioned general lack of interest, on the part of museums, in recording and recognizing museum photography as a constituent practice of the modern institution. Like the dearth of contextual information and reliable metadata about the transparencies in box K3, the failure to acknowledge the photographic origins of digitally displayed museum items betrays the same "symptomatic carelessness" toward the intermediating work of museum photographers that Georgina Born identified back in 1998, which still "sits oddly with the museum's obsessive archival functions."[40] On the other hand, it is a missed opportunity to expand the remit of the museum's role as custodian of cultural heritage by including the legacies of its own material practices of intermediation.

Condensed in this digitized slide lie "the embedded skills, techniques, and knowledge" of all those that Sean Cubitt insists we recognize as "our ancestors."[41] Starting in the twelfth century, the tapestry itself embodies the weaving techniques and embroidery skills of anonymous craftspeople entrusted with the production of sacred textiles in medieval Scandinavia.[42] The transparency is a reproduction of the textile that exemplifies both a prevalent photographic format and a professional visual documentation technique commonly mastered by museum photographers in the late twentieth century. The unidentified photographer was in this case, moreover, facilitating the work of another set of skilled professionals, the textile conservators tasked with repairing the tapestry in the 1980s and 1990s. The slide was then labeled and archived by administrative staff at the museum before being extracted from the files for digitization in 2013 by another anonymous figure, the scan operator enlisted as part of a work-to-welfare scheme to create a digital surrogate of the transparency.

All these layers of labor are present when viewing the picture labeled as the Høylandet tapestry through a web browser materialized on a computer screen, which is itself a sedimentation of dizzyingly deep ancestral know-how. Leaving aside the original ecclesiastical display context for the tapestry, on which even historians of medieval art can only speculate, each stage in its technical reproduction and dissemination has involved the work of unrecognized intermediaries, whose skill, knowledge, and judgment to varying degrees have left their traces on the working object of the digital surrogate. More than they impart "information about the object's origins," as Jasmine Burns notes, "surrogates reveal contemporary practices regarding the mode in which the data is constructed and transferred."[43] As my detailed account of a single photographic slide reproduction has illustrated, this is not a phenomenon that has arisen with digitization. Within the contemporary research regime of post-digitization, however, it can have greater than ever ramifications for the production of knowledge, when it becomes ever harder to test that knowledge against the original objects that it purports to describe.[44]

To sum up, the case of the digitized transparency of the Høylandet tapestry exemplifies how digital museum collections build on preexisting collections of photographic reproductions, with provenances that are not necessarily acknowledged in the online repositories that after the digitized turn are the first (and increasingly only) port of call for scholarly and picture researchers alike. It also exemplifies how public institutions of cultural heritage are dependent on the intermittent availability of temporary and precarious staff to perform the labor of mass digitization, with predictably unpredictable consequences for the consistency and reliability of the resulting resources. Finally, it suggests that the conservation and reproduction histories of artworks must start to incorporate the conservation and digitization histories of their reproductions, too.

Conclusion

Writing in the 1980s about the costs and charges involved in the commercial exploitation of a picture collection, picture librarian and *Picture Researcher's Handbook* coauthor Hilary Evans listed all of the tasks and jobs involved in setting up a picture library in the first place, and then implementing the various systems and procedures required for it to provide its services, before making the following observation: "In short, a number of people have done a great deal of work. Who is going to pay for it all?"[45] This rhetorical question referred to the search and service fees that picture libraries in the pre-digital era charged for their work of intermediation; however, the examples discussed in this chapter have illustrated that it might as well be asked in relation to the online repositories of post-digitization.

The recurring tasks of filing, searching, selecting, packaging, and posting that in the 1980s had been required in order for a picture to meet its public had in the 2010s long since been disintermediated by the World Wide Web, at least if the picture either was born digital or had already been digitized. In the latter case, the intermediating work of digitizers—among them scanners, catalogers, and keyworders—had come on top of the collecting, classifying, cataloging, captioning, and cross-indexing already performed by the custodians of the original analog archives. A number of people, in other words, had first done a great deal of work to ensure the establishment of a pre-digital picture library, and then a number of other people had, at a later stage, done an equal amount of work to create a digital platform providing direct search and download of all the visual contents from that library. The resulting platform consequently incorporated and embedded the accumulated labor, skill, and judgment of all those people.

The photographs by Oli Scarff from the Hulton Archive, analyzed in the first part of this chapter, depicted the tools and tasks of a pre-digital picture library, which in a historical archive still needed doing alongside the additional operations of digitization that had become routine by the 2010s. The captions furnished by Getty Images also identified by name the individual professionals engaged in the work of making photographs from the preceding 150 years conveniently accessible to audiences in 2011. I have suggested that this series of self-promoting pictures served two purposes: alerting existing subscribers to archival photographic content that they might not otherwise go looking for, and asserting the company's cultural capital as a custodian of photographic heritage, enabled by the economic capital it accumulated as a commercial online platform for visual content of all kinds and genres.

If Scarff's series from the Hulton Archive demonstrated the added cultural value that Getty Images clients were getting for their money, the digitization history of the Høylandet tapestry illustrated the low value and status attached to the intermediary roles of both photographers and digitizers within the University Museum. Despite contributing to what

Löffler and Mager term the digital authorship of visual datasets available from the Unimus research portal, the welfare-to-work interns engaged on a short-term basis to scan items from the museum slide collections were not granted recognition of either skill or identity. Their congealed labor nevertheless endures in the resulting digital repository, along with the visible signs of photography's historical function and material characteristics as a technology of capture, accumulation, and transmission within the museum.

Digitizing historical photographs means ensuring they endure in digitization, whether they were works of photography to begin with, like the Hulton Archive's classic press photos, or photographic representations of other works, like the University Museum's transparency of a tapestry. Edwards and Morton have noted how the "presence" of photographs "sprawls across museum collecting and curatorial practice," having been accumulated sometimes intentionally, and sometimes accidentally.[46] In a similar way the presence of photography's material history lingers in digital surrogates that have been made from museum photographs.

The University Museum may only inadvertently have preserved evidence of historical photographic practices in digitized form, as a by-product of unsupervised processing and unclear decision-making during the 2013 digitization project. Getty Images, by contrast, has continued to position itself as the champion of photographic preservation. In early April 2020, nine years on from Scarff's "Inside the Hulton Archive" series, a headline in the art and design section of the London-based newspaper *The Guardian* declared that "Getty uses remote working in effort to preserve photo archive."[47] "Millions of images," the article reported, "are being preserved remotely as one of the largest photography archives in the world attempts to prevent damage during the Covid-19 lockdown."

This dramatic opening seemed to imply millions of photographs being whisked away for safekeeping during a global pandemic, yet once again it was an example of Getty adopting the event-based format of the news story to promote its archival content, this time pegged to "the use of remote temperature and humidity controls" to maintain a stable environment for its holdings of more than 80 million prints and negatives at its state-of-the-art archival facility for the long-term conservation of emulsion- and paper-based materials. The link to lockdown and the pandemic appeared spurious, as an archival facility housing photographs and film stock, which had already survived in less than ideal conditions for the best part of a century, could hardly be at risk of immediate disintegration just because nobody was around to double-check the automatic thermostat every few minutes. It was, however, a new and topical angle on the same story that Getty Images had sought to promote in 2011: "We're not just a commercial archive, we're looking after our cultural heritage."

The words were attributed to Matthew Butson, who has been in charge of UK archival operations at Getty Images throughout its several iterations and name changes over three decades. Expanding on the significance of the archive's mission, he further declared that "you're losing history if you don't look after this stuff." Butson then offered examples from the recent past of how archival photographic material had attained sudden relevance for news and current affairs reporting. Aside from the 2020 pandemic having led to a resurgent interest in material from the 1918 outbreak of the Spanish flu, he cited the unexpected rise to political prominence of former UK Labour leader Jeremy Corbyn in 2015 and the election of US president Donald Trump in 2016 as prominent examples of how "about 80% of Getty's archive work was driven by personalities becoming relevant again."

Illustrated by a supposedly "rare shot of Marilyn Monroe," the story was first and foremost an example of how the photographic—and not least photographed—past can be made relevant to the present on the most unexpected pretexts. "You're always telling a different story," as one of the quotes from Butson ran: "It's not reinvention, you're simply shedding more light on an event or topic or person." Just like the picture story from 2011, the press release from Getty Images that must have instigated the newspaper item in 2020 was doing precisely the same thing: telling a different story about historical photographic archives by shedding more light on the work that goes into looking after them. The same could be said about this book, which has shed light on the historical work of intermediation performed by librarians, archivists, and researchers, in order to tell a particular story about the systems, processes, and technologies that since the 1830s have been making pictures available to an ever-expanding public.

Conclusions and Implications

Every week, an email drops into my inbox with the offer of a "free stock image," available for download if I log onto Shutterstock.com. This is an online platform for buying and selling a diverse range of "content," and at the end of the year 2021 it boasted "more than 400 million images" available for download through its website.[1] In addition to stock and editorial pictures, sourced from both amateurs and a range of established news agencies, it carries videos and music. It can also furnish a host of design templates for customers to use when publishing pictures, videos, and music on other web-based platforms, whether these have been licensed from Shutterstock or not. "One library, millions of ways to tell your story," is how it pitches itself to customers.[2] "Share your work and start earning," it promises potential contributors, who are invited to "join Shutterstock's global community of contributors and earn money doing what you love."[3]

Welcome to the latest incarnation of the picture library as a "lean platform," an Uber or Airbnb of the pictorial economy, which owns no property and employs no staff, except the intellectual property of the software and data analytics that make up the platform itself, and the staff needed to run the extractive operation of percentage collection and data analysis.[4] Welcome also to the creative gig economy, based entirely on the mutually supportive fallacies that doing what you love is not really work at all and that being paid per piece or task is the bright future of work under capitalism, rather than a hideous throwback to its past.[5] Just as Uber, Airbnb, and Deliveroo encourage us to think of driving, dwelling, and cycling—things we do anyway—as potentially monetizable services, so Shutterstock and other "microstock" platforms lead us to see the smartphone photos that attract likes on our social media accounts as potential assets to rent out, rather than share for free.[6]

Shutterstock sends me these emails not because I used to be a picture researcher but because, in many ways, I still am. In fact, as I observed in the introduction to this book, we are all picture researchers now, whether we like it or not. Over the past few years, the standard templates and formats that many of us use to produce working documents and semi-official publications of various kinds have increasingly begun to include or invite some kind of default illustration. Now, my presentations and publications tend to include pictures anyway, because as a scholar and teacher of visual culture what I have to say is usually directly related to or occasioned by some sort of image. Yet more and more I find myself also feeling obliged to "liven up," or emphasize by visual means, information that is purely textual, such as the title of a lecture, a key quote from a work of theory, or the submission date for an essay. Somehow, all this basic information appears to need accompaniment by a photograph, or what the stock industry calls a "vector" (a computer-generated drawing) in order to merit the requisite attention.

I use pictures to ease my navigation of the online teaching space, too: when running three different courses on the same online learning platform with the same user-unfriendly interface, it helps no end to have a banner at the top with an immediately recognizable visualization of each course topic. In order to comply with standards of intellectual property rights within my institution, however, I must fill these spaces either with pictures to which I personally own the copyright, pictures in the public domain, or pictures that have been duly licensed from another source. So if I am not prepared to be my own stock photographer, I have to be my own picture researcher—on top of the teacher and researcher that I am already employed by the university to be, full time. Hence my signing up for a limited-period subscription to Shutterstock's services a few years ago, providing them in the process with my email address, and thus the means by which to provoke me, every week, with their disingenuous offer of a supposedly free picture. For as readers of this book will have gathered by now, there really can be no such thing.

The successive chapters of this book have detailed the varied work of intermediation that over decades of reproducing, archiving, captioning, cataloging, copying, searching, and re-searching has built the aggregated collections of visual data and textual metadata that, by the early 2000s, could be rendered into computable information through the technical processes of digitization. The legacies of this work are still embedded in the online picture repositories and search engines that define the post-digitized pictorial economy of today. We encounter them explicitly, as visual metaphors like the gridded display of thumbnail image search results, which emulates the layout of a 35-mm slide sheet, and as textual metadata in the form of captions or credits, identifying the provenance of pictures from long-defunct publications or news agencies. We also encounter the legacies of picture research and librarianship implicitly, as the product of generations of appraisal. The digitized resources we consult today are, in the first instance, the sum of judgments made about what to capture and preserve by photographic means and, in the second instance, about which photographic reproductions to extract for recapture and transmission as digital surrogates. Even though most of the content we see online today is born-digital, rather than dumped from an analog source (to paraphrase a quote from Bill Gates cited in chapter 3), the post-digital and post-digitized pictorial economy of the 2020s still relies on the market-making mechanisms of intermediation, which this book has traced back to the pre-photographic trade in paper-based visual ephemera that flourished in the 1830s.

The figure of *The Connoisseur* (figure 1.1)—a woman made out of pictures—that we first encountered in chapter 1 can be reinvoked here as a visual summary of the examples discussed throughout this book, and a metapicture of the key issues raised in each chapter. In all the versions of *The Connoisseur* currently circulating online, the lithographic print that was first produced through the joint efforts of Spratt, Madeley, and Tilt, working at the cutting edge of imaging technologies of their day, appears remediated on the screen by the sedimented layers of nearly two more centuries of technological development, human ingenuity, and physical labor. As such, it embodies what Cubitt calls "the dead still present in the automata of technology."[7] It does this neither more nor less than any other lithograph dating from the same period that has been digitized and transmitted through the same online networks. What distinguishes *The Connoisseur* from other prints, however—even ones from the same series, like *The Conchologist* or *The Entomologist*—is that it also helps us visualize the complex relations among labor, skill, and technology, in both its own time, the 1830s, and its future, which is our past and present.

In its original historical context, discussed in chapter 1, this lithographic print of a contemporary caricature illustrated the democratized access to art enabled through the constellation of Enlightenment ideas and industrial reproduction technologies in the early 1800s. It also embodied the distributed authorship of pre-photographic mass-produced picture commodities in the early nineteenth century through its explicit recognition of drafter and printer, as well as publisher. This arrangement acknowledged and institutionalized the mutual dependency of artists and reproducers within a legal system of copyright that accorded protection of an original design only once it had been subjected to the work of intermediation performed by engraver and printer. Although the picture industry that developed in the twentieth century was technologically enabled by photography, it was made economically viable by this legal recognition of the value added by the intermediaries who orchestrated the actual encounter between pictures and their publics.

Chapter 2 detailed the ascendancy of this industry in the early 1950s, when *The Connoisseur* would have been an apposite visualization of the picture librarian "soaked" in her material, in the manner recommended by Gibbs-Smith in his account of the storage and retrieval system at the Hulton Picture Post Library. Clearly gendered as female, the character might also have been recognized as an ancestor by the women librarians surrounded by photographic prints in the Keystone files (figure 2.3), where pictures were allegedly pouring in from all over the world, seeking to be rapidly connected with audiences through the intermediary offices of the picture library's skilled and efficient staff.

The further fortunes of the lithograph in the latter half of the twentieth century would also speak to Keystone founder Bert Garai's idea, outlined in the same chapter, that the value of a picture can be enhanced by the label attached to it. This was certainly case with the copy that ended up in the files of the Mary Evans Picture Library in the 1970s, where comanager and chief caption writer Hilary Evans retitled it "The Picture Library Girl." Under that name it was adopted as a totem of the library's mainly female staff and an alter ego of Mary Evans herself, exemplified by the printed invitation to visit the eponymous picture library "at home" in its new premises. The character could just as well have graced the cover of Evans and Evans's coauthored *Picture Researcher's Handbook* as a visual metaphor for the diligent picture researcher who was always prepared to go out and look for pictures in person. Above all, however, it would in that context unambiguously have signaled the picture researcher's work of cultural intermediation as a practice of connoisseurship, the acquired ability to exercise independent aesthetic judgment and recognize value in pictures that others may have overlooked or rejected.

In the booming pictorial economy of the 1970s, the first edition of *The Picture Researcher's Handbook* taught a generation of researchers how to do their job by explaining the tools and knowledge needed to attain that ability. Then, in the late 1990s, the BBC television drama *Shooting the Past* demonstrated to a general audience how a picture library had worked for the best part of the twentieth century. As discussed in chapter 4, Stephen Poliakoff's scenes, set in the fictional Fallon Photo Library, were built with props from the real-life Hulton Picture Post Library, illustrating yet another way of picturing picture librarians immersed in their collection. Like *The Connoisseur,* who carries an entire picture collection on her person, Oswald in *Shooting the Past* carried the millions of images in the Fallon collection inside his head, and could entrust the spatial memory and fuzzy logic of his brain to retrieve, within seconds, the individual, material pictures from the precise, actual locations in which they were filed away. On screen, Oswald embodied the picture librarian as an "intelligent device," the intellectual operations of which information scientists in the 1990s were beginning to study and describe with a view to transforming the knowledge work of intermediation performed by humans into automated information labor that could be executed by computers. Through the setting of the picture library, *Shooting the Past* conveyed an apprehension that was felt among cultural intermediaries far beyond the picture industry.

When digitization took hold of the picture industry in the course of the 2000s, as we saw in chapter 5, online repositories of digitized pictures increasingly became the default starting point of any picture research process, and technologies of intermediation, in the form of digital platforms and automated search engines, relieved library staff from much of their intermediary functions. Against this background, *The Connoisseur* could be reinterpreted once again, this time as a late Georgian steampunk vision of a mechanical picture librarian: an automaton programmed for the aggregation, retrieval, and display of pictures, with its handheld lorgnette intriguingly pre-figuring the now-ubiquitous magnifying-glass icon of digital search.

Finally, in chapter 6, *The Connoisseur*'s human face and hand, peeking out from under the pile of pictures, could be read as an allegory of the bodies and minds that scaffold the pictorial cornucopia of post-digitization since the 2010s. In that chapter we encountered representations and traces of the human intermediaries that have been, and still are, performing the labor and supervising the machineries of capture, accumulation, extraction, and transmission that make digitized repositories of photographs and other pictures appear online as if by magic. This work of reintermediation amounts to a form of "digital authorship," as Löffler and Mager put it, which nevertheless goes as unacknowledged in the online interfaces of digitized collections of visual research data in the twenty-first century as did the work of hand coloring lithographs performed by women or girls in the nineteenth century.[8]

A host of similarly anonymous and therefore uncreditable digital coauthors made it possible for me to write this book. I have gathered my examples and case studies from the digital platforms and physical archives of commercial picture libraries and public museums, from the digitized and physical holdings of public libraries, from broadcast and print media, from the online circuits of the secondhand book trade, and from conversations with picture researchers and librarians. With the exception of the picture story from the Hulton Archive in chapter 5, all of the pictures and texts I have analyzed are "born-analog" items, which in one way or another have been processed by digital technologies in order to reach me. This means that I have often consulted digital scans of pictures or pages of text, sometimes in addition to, and often instead of, consulting the paper or emulsion-based original document. In other cases it means that I have got hold of an analog item or real-life person by communicating through a digital platform. This way of conducting research is now par for the course in the humanities, where digitization "has speeded up" scholarship, as the historian Emma Rothschild notes, by increasing the amount of time that can be spent actually consulting sources compared to that spent searching for them or gaining admittance to the archives, libraries, or museum stores that hold them.[9] In compiling a history of the work of intermediation in the picture industry, I have in other words benefited from (or perhaps I should say suffered under) the disintermediated environment that characterizes both picture research and academic research in the era of post-digitization.

It used to be that the main difference between professional picture research and scholarly research on or about pictures could be summed up in the distinction between search and research, drawn by library scholar and photo historian Estelle Jussim decades before either of them were digitized: "Unlike research, which is usually the investigation of the relationship between two or more variables, a search simply accomplishes the finding of a wanted item [and] represents a one-time need, unrelated to any scientific structure of investigation."[10] Since the purpose of picture research is, in most cases, to discover the most suitable illustration of a given subject in a given context, it stops once the discovery has been made, and the picture has been chosen. Scholarly research, by contrast, often starts with a discovery or choice—a single picture that intrigues an art historian, for instance—and then finds its purpose in the gathering of a number of other variables, as Jussim calls them, through which to search and re-search for evidence of relationships, which in turn may lead to other discoveries requiring more gathering and searching, and so on.

Disintermediation by digitization has blurred the boundaries between search and research, between picture research and scholarship. Because there is so much available to search through (400 million images on Shutterstock alone!), at no perceptible cost to the researcher, picture researchers can end up endlessly sifting through potentially relevant stuff, unable to make a definitive decision because the algorithmic mechanisms of the database throw up ever more suggestions. And scholars can decide to stop looking and ignore other potential variables as soon as the picture they had in mind, the document they knew existed, or the citation that confirms their hypothesis turns up in the search results.

Both these behaviors are ways of coping with the digital overwhelm at human scale. They are also symptoms of the post-digitized condition that limits—or infinitely expands—search and research to the already digitized. Research "that is powered by patterns in the digitizable detritus of the modern world," as Putnam phrases it, will at some level also reflect the patterns of power that enabled digitization of that detritus in the first place, as well as those that regulate access to it.[11] I have accounted in this book for some of the work of intermediation that is involved in the processes of digitization, performed with the aim of producing the pleasurable illusion of disintermediated search. The pleasure and ease with which it is possible to use online resources, however, is also due to another kind of intermediation, which is no less crucial to the practical functioning not just of post-digitized research but of online searching and browsing in general.

Digitization has not done away with the need for human intermediaries in the pictorial economy, but they are frequently doing the opposite of the traditional work of intermediation in the picture industry. Where the picture researchers and librarians we have met in this book helped pictures do their job of being looked at in a visual material culture dominated by editorial media, the new intermediaries have their work cut out looking at pictures in order to stop others from having to see them. Generally known as content moderators, they work "to evaluate and adjudicate online content generated by users and decide if it can stay up or must be deleted," as Sarah T. Roberts has documented, and this work is intentionally left "imperceptible to the users of the platforms that pay for and rely upon this labor."[12] It is the labor, skill, and not least judgment of commercial content moderators that stand between us and "some of humanity's worst expressions of itself."[13] Yet they are treated as part of the infrastructure of digital social media, and their interventions are frequently attributed by users to an algorithm. You can be sure that any commercial platform that invites user-generated content from and for a general audience relies in some measure on the services of paid content moderators, even a high-end purveyor of glossy stock imagery like Shutterstock. Unlike the contributors of content to that platform, however, moderators would probably be hard pushed to say they are getting paid for doing what they love.

The intermediary work of content moderators suggests another response than my earlier provocation at the notion of pictures being "free," as in given away for nothing. As we have seen, there are any number of authors and coauthors who have laid down their labor in the production of both the picture that is offered and the machineries through which it is being circulated and exploited. This labor may have been "freely given," as Cubitt writes of the contemporary mass image, but it is nevertheless "purloined as forced labour in the form of machinery."[14] Even if I could be *free to* download any one of the 400 million Shutterstock images without imparting with money, however, it is the intermediary work of content moderators that ensures I can exercise that freedom while remaining *free from* exposure to offensive or hateful pictures. In the apparent free-for-all of the post-digitized pictorial economy, human intermediaries are no longer required to make pictures meet their public, but they are very much needed to keep the public safe from certain pictures. The work of intermediation is never done.

Notes

Preface

1. Walter Benjamin, "Unpacking My Library," in *Illuminations* (London: Pimlico 1999), 63.

Introduction

1. W. J. T. Mitchell, *Picture Theory* (Chicago: University of Chicago Press, 1994), 6. Original emphasis.

2. Sean Cubitt, *The Practice of Light: A Genealogy of Visual Technologies from Prints to Pixels* (Cambridge, MA: MIT Press, 2014), 1.

3. Lisa Gitelman, *Paper Knowledge: Toward a Media History of Documents* (Durham, NC: Duke University Press, 2014), x. See also Michel de Certeau, *The Practice of Everyday Life* (Berkeley: University of California Press, 2011), 131–132.

4. Stephen Bann, "Photography, Printmaking, and the Visual Economy in Nineteenth-Century France," *History of Photography* 26, no. 1 (March 1, 2002): 16, https://doi.org/10.1080/03087298.2002.10443249. See also Stephen Bann, *Distinguished Images: Prints in the Visual Economy of Nineteenth-Century France* (New Haven, CT: Yale University Press, 2013).

5. Deborah Poole, *Vision, Race, and Modernity: A Visual Economy of the Andean Image World* (Princeton, NJ: Princeton University Press, 1997), 8.

6. A similar perspective appears to inform Diana Kamin's approach in a book published too recently for me to engage directly here. See Diana Kamin, *Picture-Work: How Libraries, Museums, and Stock Agencies Launched a New Image Economy* (Cambridge, MA: The MIT Press, 2023).

7. Friedrich Balke, Bernhard Siegert, and Joseph Vogl, eds., *Medien der Bürokratie*, Archiv für Mediengeschichte (Paderborn: Wilhelm Fink Verlag, 2016).

8. John Tagg, *The Disciplinary Frame: Photographic Truths and the Capture of Meaning* (Minneapolis: University of Minnesota Press, 2009), 3.

9. Tagg, 3.

10. Matthew Kirschenbaum, *Track Changes: A Literary History of Word Processing* (Cambridge, MA: Belknap Press, 2016), 16. See also Gitelman, *Paper Knowledge*, 21–52.

11. John Durham Peters, *The Marvelous Clouds: Toward a Philosophy of Elemental Media* (Chicago: University of Chicago Press, 2015), 289.

12. Peters, 264.

13. Diana Kamin, among others, has noted "a linguistic shift over time" in favor of image over picture as a standard denotational term for visual representations, which in turn seems connected to discourses on the "dematerialization" of objects in the digital era (a topic to which we will return in chapter 5). See Diana Kamin, "Picture-Work: On the Circulating Image Collection" (PhD diss., New York University, 2018), 11.

14. W. J. T. Mitchell, *Image Science: Iconology, Visual Culture and Media Aesthetics* (Chicago: University of Chicago Press, 2015), 16.

15. Christine L. Borgman, *Big Data, Little Data, No Data: Scholarship in the Networked World* (Cambridge, MA: MIT Press, 2015), 18.

16. My concept of the picture industry diverges slightly from that proposed by Walead Beshty et al. in a volume that includes both scientific research and contemporary art under the umbrella of this term. See Walead Beshty, *Picture Industry: A Provisional History of the Technical Image, 1844–2018* (Zürich: JRP Ringier, 2018).

17. J. Abbott Miller, "Pictures for Rent: From Stereoscope to Stereotype," in *Design Writing Research: Writing on Graphic Design*, ed. Ellen Lupton and J. Abbott Miller (London: Phaidon, 1999), 121–133. See also Helen Wilkinson, "'The New Heraldry': Stock Photography, Visual Literacy, and Advertising in 1930s Britain," *Journal of Design History* 10 (1997): 23–38.

18. Paul Frosh, *The Image Factory: Consumer Culture, Photography and the Visual Content Industry* (Oxford: Berg, 2003); Matthias Bruhn, *Bildwirtschaft. Verwaltung und Verwertung der Sichtbarkeit* (Weimar: VDG, 2003).

19. Michelle Henning, *Photography: The Unfettered Image* (London: Routledge, 2018), 43.

20. Marshall McLuhan, "Address at Vision 65," in *Essential McLuhan*, ed. Eric McLuhan and Frank Zingrone (London: Routledge, 1997), 220.

21. McLuhan, 221.

22. Joanna Sassoon, "Photographic Materiality in the Age of Digital Reproduction," in *Photographs, Objects, Histories*, ed. Elizabeth Edwards and Janice Hart (London: Routledge, 2004), 186.

23. As Sean Cubitt explains, the chip must be "drained" between each exposure, through a complex process of conversion from charge to voltage to a digital format that can be stored in the device's memory. See Sean Cubitt, *The Practice of Light: A Genealogy of Visual Technologies from Prints to Pixels* (Cambridge, MA: MIT Press, 2014), 100–102, 276n4.

24. Henning, *Photography: The Unfettered Image*, 42.

25. Frosh, *The Image Factory*, 176.

26. Elizabeth Edwards and Janice Hart, "Introduction," in *Photographs, Objects, Histories: On the Materiality of Images*, ed. Elizabeth Edwards and Janice Hart (London: Routledge, 2004), 1.

27. Edwards and Hart, 14.

28. Sassoon, "Photographic Materiality in the Age of Digital Reproduction," 189; Joan M. Schwartz, "Un beau souvenir du Canada: Object, Image, Symbolic Space," in *Photographs, Objects, Histories: On the Materiality of Images* (London: Routledge, 2004), 18.

29. Nina Lager Vestberg, "Archival Value: On Photography, Materiality and Indexicality," *Photographies* 1 (2008): 60.

30. Elizabeth Edwards and Janice Hart, "Mixed Box: The Cultural Biography of a Box of 'Ethnographic' Photographs," in *Photographs, Objects, Histories: On the Materiality of Images* (London: Routledge, 2004), 47–61.

31. Geoffrey Batchen, "Ere the Substance Fade: Photography and Hair Jewellery," in *Photographs, Objects, Histories*, ed. Elizabeth Edwards and Janice Hart (London: Routledge, 2004), 32.

32. Edwards and Hart, "Introduction," 2. See also Frosh, *The Image Factory*, 11–12.

33. Estelle Blaschke, *Banking on Images: The Bettmann Archive and Corbis* (Leipzig: Spector Books, 2016); Kamin, *Picture-Work*; Diana Kamin, "Cards, Cabinets, and Compression in Early Stock Photography," *Information & Culture* 56, no. 3 (November 2021): 229–250, https://doi.org/10.7560/IC56301.

34. Nadya Bair, *The Decisive Network: Magnum Photos and the Postwar Image Market* (Berkeley: University of California Press, 2020); Zeynep Devrim Gürsel, *Image Brokers: Visualizing World News in the Age of Digital Circulation* (Oakland: University of California Press, 2016), http://search.ebscohost.com/login.aspx?direct=true&db=nlebk&AN=1196937&site=ehost-live.

35. Peters, *The Marvelous Clouds*, 21.

36. Daniel F. Spulber, "Market Microstructure and Intermediation," *Journal of Economic Perspectives* 10, no. 3 (1996): 150. I am grateful to Terje Gaustad for this reference and for giving me a crash course in intermediation and disintermediation from an economics perspective.

37. Jennifer Smith Maguire and Julian Matthews, eds., *The Cultural Intermediaries Reader* (London: Sage, 2014), 1.

38. The term "cultural intermediaries" was coined in the English translation of Pierre Bourdieu, *Distinction: A Social Critique of the Judgement of Taste*, trans. Richard Nice (Cambridge, MA: Harvard University Press, 1984), 91, 323–327. Aside from Frosh's brief use of the term to characterize the functions of "advertising art directors and picture editors" within the "hegemonic framework" of stock photography, I have been unable to find references to the specific work of picture research or picture editing in the literature I have surveyed on cultural intermediaries. See Frosh, *The Image Factory*, 5. See also Sean Nixon and Paul Du Gay, "Who Needs Cultural Intermediaries?," *Cultural Studies* 16, no. 4 (July 1, 2002): 495–500, https://doi.org/10.1080/09502380210139070; Keith Negus, "The Work of Cultural Intermediaries and the Enduring Distance between Production and Consumption," *Cultural Studies* 16, no. 4 (July 1, 2002): 501–515, https://doi.org/10.1080/09502380210139089; David Hesmondhalgh, "Bourdieu, the Media and Cultural Production," *Media, Culture & Society* 28, no. 2 (March 1, 2006): 211–231, https://doi.org/10.1177/0163443706061682; Jennifer Smith Maguire, "Bourdieu on Cultural Intermediaries," in *The Cultural Intermediaries Reader*, ed. Jennifer Smith Maguire and Julian Matthews (London: Sage, 2014), 15–24.

39. N. Katherine Hayles, "Intermediation: The Pursuit of a Vision," *New Literary History* 38, no. 1 (June 6, 2007): 104, https://doi.org/10.1353/nlh.2007.0021.

40. N. Katherine Hayles, *My Mother Was a Computer: Digital Subjects and Literary Texts* (Chicago: University of Chicago Press, 2005), 31, http://ebookcentral.proquest.com/lib/ntnu/detail.action?docID=530439.

41. Hayles, 31.

42. Alina M. Chircu and Robert J. Kauffman, "Strategies for Internet Middlemen in the Intermediation/Disintermediation/Reintermediation Cycle," *Electronic Markets* 9, nos. 1–2 (1999): 109–117.

43. Elihu Katz, "Disintermediation: Cutting Out the Middle Man," *Intermedia* 16, no. 2 (1988): 30–31. See also Daniel Dayan and Elihu Katz, *Media Events: The Live Broadcasting of History* (Cambridge, MA: Harvard University Press, 1992), 215–217, 229–230; Michael Strangelove, *Post-TV: Piracy, Cord-Cutting, and the Future of Television* (Toronto: University of Toronto Press, 2015).

44. Katz, "Disintermediation," 31.

45. Chircu and Kauffman, "Strategies for Internet Middlemen," 109.

46. See, for instance, Craig Standing and T. Vasudavan, "The Impact of the Internet on the Role of Travel Consultants," *Participation and Empowerment: An International Journal* 7, no. 8 (December 1, 1999): 213–226, https://doi.org/10.1108/146344499 10303595; Alan Ching-biu Tse, "Disintermediation of Travel Agents in the Hotel Industry," *International Journal of Hospitality Management* 22, no. 4 (December 1, 2003): 453–460, https://doi.org/10.1016/S0278-4319(03)00049-5; José I. Castillo-Manzano and Lourdes López-Valpuesta, "The Decline of the Traditional Travel Agent Model," *Transportation Research Part E: Logistics and Transportation Review* 46, no. 5 (September 1, 2010): 639–649, https://doi.org/10.1016/j.tre.2009.12.009.

47. Hayles, "Intermediation," 100.

48. Wolfgang Ernst, *Digital Memory and the Archive*, ed. Jussi Parikka, trans. Christopher Jenkin-Jones (Minneapolis: University of Minnesota Press, 2013), 60.

49. Wolfgang Ernst, "Let There Be Irony: Cultural History and Media Archaeology in Parallel Lines," *Art History* 28 (2005): 601.

50. Raymond Williams, *Television: Technology and Cultural Form*, 2nd ed., ed. Ederyn Williams (London: Routledge, 1990).

51. On photography as cultural form, see Peter Buse, "Polaroid into Digital: Technology, Cultural Form, and the Social Practices of Snapshot Photography," *Continuum* 24, no. 2 (2010): 215–230, https://doi.org/10.1080/10304310903363864; Peter Osborne, "Photography in an Expanding Field: Distributive Unity and Dominant Form," in *Where Is the Photograph?*, ed. David Green (Brighton: Photoforum and Photoworks, 2003), 63–70.

52. "Digitization, n.," in *OED Online* (Oxford University Press), accessed April 4, 2019, http://www.oed.com/view/Entry/240886.

53. J. Scott Brennen and Daniel Kreiss, "Digitalization," in *The International Encyclopedia of Communication Theory and Philosophy* (Hoboken: John Wiley & Sons, 2016), 1–11, https://doi.org/10.1002/9781118766804.wbiect111. For examples of "digitalization" used in this sense, see Mercedes Bunz, *The Silent Revolution: How Digitalization Transforms Knowledge, Work, Journalism and Politics without Making Too Much Noise* (Basingstoke: Palgrave Macmillan, 2013), https://doi.org/10.1057/9781137373502; Ingrid Hoelzl and Rémi Marie, *Softimage: Towards a New Theory of the Digital Image* (Bristol: Intellect, 2015).

54. Lisa Gitelman, *Always Already New: Media, History and the Data of Culture* (Cambridge, MA: MIT Press, 2006), 128.

55. Nanna Bonde Thylstrup, *The Politics of Mass Digitization* (Cambridge, MA: MIT Press, 2018), 3. See also Maurizio Borghi, "Knowledge, Information and Values in the Age of Mass Digitisation," in *Value: Sources and Readings on a Key Concept of the Globalized World*, ed. Ivo De Gennaro (Leiden: Brill, 2012), 415–434.

56. My translation from Andreas Budalen, "Skal digitalisere 50 kilometer med kulturarv" ("Digitizing Norway's cultural heritage"), NRK, March 11, 2012, https://www.nrk.no/nordland/digitaliserer-norges-kulturarv-1.8028452.

57. Library and Archives Canada, "How We Serve Canadians: For the Record," May 1, 2012, https://www.bac-lac.gc.ca/eng/news/videos/Pages/for-record.aspx?=undefined&wbdisable=true; Joan M. Schwartz, "'In the Archives, a Thousand Photos That Detail Our Questions': Final Reflections on Photographs and Archives," in *Photo-Objects: On the Materiality of Photographs and Photo Archives* (Berlin: Max-Planck-Gesellschaft zur Förderung der Wissenschaften, 2019), 318, https://mprl-series.mpg.de/studies/12/19/index.html.

58. The term "drafter" is used here as a gender-neutral replacement for "draftsman."

CHAPTER 1

1. Stephen Bann, *Distinguished Images: Prints in the Visual Economy of Nineteenth-Century France* (New Haven, CT: Yale University Press, 2013), 18. See also Pascal Griener, *La république de l'oeil: L'expérience de l'art au siècle des lumières* (Paris: Odile Jacob, 2010), 83.

2. Griener, *La république de l'oeil*, 84.

3. Griener, 65.

4. *An Act for the Encouragement of the Arts of Designing, Engraving, and Etching Historical and Other Prints, by Vesting the Properties Thereof in the Inventors and Engravers, during the Time Therein Mentioned, 1735*, 8 Geo. II, c. 13, 1735, http://www.copyrighthistory.org/cam/tools/request/showRecord.php?id=record_uk_1735; *An Act for Effectually Securing the Property of Prints to Inventers and Engravers, by Enabling Them to Sue for and Recover Penalties in Certain Cases, 1777*, 17 Geo. III, c. 57, 1777, http://www.copyrighthistory.org/cam/tools/request/showRecord?id=record_uk_1777a. A comprehensive overview of sources for the emergence of copyright legislation in a number of countries can be found in the online resource *Primary Sources on Copyright (1450–1900)*, available at: *http://www.copyrighthistory.org* (accessed June 1, 2021).

5. A halftone process emulates the manual "pitting" produced by the engraver's tool by opto-chemical means. It involves projecting a photographic negative through a gridded screen onto a printing plate covered in a photosensitized emulsion, to produce a picture made up of dots of various sizes that, when viewed at the appropriate distance, gives the optical impression of continuous tone. See Sean Cubitt, *The Practice of Light: A Genealogy of Visual Technologies from Prints to Pixels* (Cambridge, MA: MIT Press, 2014), 88–90.

6. Geoffrey Batchen, *Burning with Desire: The Conception of Photography* (Cambridge, MA: MIT Press, 1997), 50.

7. W. J. T. Mitchell, *Picture Theory* (Chicago: University of Chicago Press, 1994), 35.

8. W. J. T. Mitchell, *Image Science: Iconology, Visual Culture and Media Aesthetics* (Chicago: University of Chicago Press, 2015), 19.

9. James A. Secord, "Scrapbook Science: Composite Caricatures in Late Georgian England," in *Figuring It Out: Science, Gender, and Visual Culture*, ed. Ann B. Shteir and Bernard V. Lightman (Hanover, NH: Dartmouth College Press, 2006), 169.

10. For more detail on early nineteenth-century album culture in England, including in the pre-photographic period, see Patrizia Di Bello, *Women's Albums and Photography in Victorian England: Ladies, Mothers and Flirts* (Aldershot: Ashgate, 2007), 29–52.

11. Secord, "Scrapbook Science," 169, 178.

12. Secord, 175. Citing an advert in Thomas Hood, *Comic Annual* (London: Charles Tilt, 1831).

13. Secord, 175 and 186.

14. Di Bello, *Women's Albums and Photography in Victorian England*, 41.

15. Secord, "Scrapbook Science," 174–175.

16. Hans Öjmyr, *Josabeth Sjögrens Stockholm: En unik bildskatt från 1800-talet* (Stockholm: Stockholmia förlag, 2016), 12. This figure is based on calculations using the historical currency converter available at http://historicalstatistics.org/Jamforelsepris.htm (accessed February 17, 2019). See also Rodney Edvinsson and Johan Söderberg, "A Consumer Price Index for Sweden 1290–2008," *Review of Income and Wealth* 57, no. 2 (2011): 270–292.

17. Erika Piola and Jennifer Ambrose, "The First Fifty Years of Commercial Lithography in Philadelphia: An Overview of the Trade, 1828–1878," in *Philadelphia on Stone: Commercial Lithography in Philadelphia, 1828–1878* (University Park: Penn State Press, 2012), 32. The low status of coloring vis-à-vis the actual lithographic printing process is underlined by the fact, reported by Piola and Ambrose, that a formal training college for women printers in 1850s Philadelphia explicitly "forbade students to hand-color lithographs, declaring this a misuse of their education" (ibid., 22).

18. Michelle Henning, *Photography: The Unfettered Image* (London: Routledge, 2018), 54.

19. Tom Gretton, "Signs for Labour-Value in Printed Pictures after the Photomechanical Revolution: Mainstream Changes and Extreme Cases around 1900," *Oxford Art Journal* 28, no. 3 (October 1, 2005): 371, https://doi.org/10.1093/oxartj/kci033.

20. The Engravers' Act was still in force after 1862 and appears to have been used in disputes between printers and photographers, according to McCauley, "Merely Mechanical," 71.

21. Ronan Deazley, "Commentary on the Engravers' Act (1735)," in *Primary Sources on Copyright (1450–1900)*, 2008, www.copyrighthistory.org.

22. Indeed, as Rose notes, the 1735 Engravers' Act is frequently called "Hogarth's Act." It seems clear that Hogarth, who was interested in protecting his income from the engravings made by himself or his own workshop of images that were his own design, used his position as an operator in the print trade to assert, by proxy as it were, his position as what we could now call a content provider for the same trade. See Mark Rose, "Technology and Copyright in 1735: The Engraver's Act," *The Information Society* 21, no. 1 (January 1, 2005): 64, https://doi.org/10.1080/019722405 90895928.

23. Ronan Deazley, "Breaking the Mould? The Radical Nature of the Fine Arts Copyright Bill 1862," in *Privilege and Property: Essays on the History of Copyright*, ed. Ronan Deazley, Martin Kretschmer, and Lionel Bently (Cambridge: Open Book Publishers, 2010), 296–297.

24. Rose, "Technology and Copyright in 1735," 65. See also Lionel Bently, "Art and the Making of Modern Copyright Law," in *Dear Images: Art, Copyright and Culture*, ed. Daniel McClean and Karsten Schubert (London: Ridinghouse, 2002), 350 note llxxviii.

25. Roberton Blaine, *On the Laws of Artistic Copyright* (London: John Murray, 1853), 26; Deazley, "Breaking the Mould?," 297.

26. Deazley, "Breaking the Mould?," 319.

27. As Tom Gretton has observed, the fidelity with which lithography reproduced its originals also worked against the recognition of skill on the part of the printer: "The more successful the labour, the more easily the value it added could be transferred to the account of the authorial artist," as a lithograph "approximated a facsimile, rather than a transcription" of its original artwork. See Gretton, "Signs for Labour-Value in Printed Pictures," 374.

28. Bently, "Art and the Making of Modern Copyright Law."

29. Michel Foucault, "What Is an Author?" (1969), *Screen* 20 (1979): 20.

30. Foucault, 20.

31. The system of printing privileges and licenses that preceded what Mark Rose has called "the inauguration of modern copyright law," which took place in 1710 with the enactment of the Statute of Anne (8 Anne, c. 19), was precisely a system of censorship whereby the granters of licenses, such as the Stationers' Company in London, were tasked with upholding moral and legal standards. See Mark Rose, "The Public Sphere and the Emergence of Copyright: Areopagitica, the Stationers' Company, and the Statute of Anne," in *Privilege and Property: Essays on the History*

of Copyright, ed. Ronan Deazley, Martin Kretschmer, and Lionel Bently (Cambridge: Open Book Publishers, 2008), 67.

32. Hilary Evans, Mary Evans, and Andra Nelki, *The Picture Researcher's Handbook: An International Guide to Picture Sources—and How to Use Them* (New York: Scribner, 1974), 15.

33. Gretton, "Signs for Labour-Value in Printed Pictures," 373.

34. Gretton, 374.

35. Estelle Jussim, *Visual Communication and the Graphic Arts: Photographic Technologies in the Nineteenth Century* (New York: Bowker, 1974), 43.

36. Jussim, 44.

37. In this respect, and if readers will forgive a little anachronism, lithography prefigured the attractions of both the "one-step" process of Polaroid photography and the "what you see is what you get" (WYSIWYG) principles of computerized word processing. Neither of these terms was of course accurate an description of the technical operations involved, but rather invented as marketing slogans to convey the simplicity and directness experienced by users. Inside the Polaroid camera, as Peter Buse reports, mechanism and chemistry performed several hundred steps beyond the ken of its operator. On "one-step photography," see Peter Buse, *The Camera Does the Rest: How Polaroid Changed Photography* (Chicago: University of Chicago Press, 2016), 10–12. On WYSIWYG, see Matthew Kirschenbaum, *Track Changes: A Literary History of Word Processing* (Cambridge, MA: Belknap Press, 2016), 3.

38. Jay David Bolter and Richard Grusin, *Remediation: Understanding New Media* (Cambridge, MA: MIT Press, 1999), 21.

39. Apart from one archive visit to the Mary Evans Picture Library, when I was able to consult the original copy (*sic!*) of the print held in its files, I have mainly been looking at this lithograph through an digitized online surrogate, switching between the modes of "immediacy" (looking past the screen to focus on the image) and "hypermediacy" (making use of sizing tools in the MIA web gallery application). See Bolter and Grusin, 31.

40. Batchen, *Burning with Desire*, 34.

41. Jussim, *Visual Communication and the Graphic Arts*, 44, 48.

42. Jussim, 50.

43. Steve Edwards, *The Making of English Photography: Allegories* (University Park: Pennsylvania State University Press, 2006), 33; Blaschke, *Banking on Images*, 9–10.

44. William Henry Fox Talbot, "A Brief Historical Sketch of the Invention of the Art," in *Classic Essays in Photography*, ed. Alan Trachtenberg (New Haven, CT: Leete's Island Books, 1980), 28.

45. Edwards, *Making of English Photography*, 43–44.

46. Edwards, 32. See also the account of Talbot's attempt at starting a mass-production business in France in the 1840s in Nancy Keeler, "Inventors and Entrepreneurs," *History of Photography* 26, no. 1 (March 1, 2002): 26–33, https://doi.org/10.1080/03087298.2002.10443250.

47. See, for instance, Elizabeth Anne McCauley, *Industrial Madness: Commercial Photography in Paris, 1848–1871* (New Haven, CT: Yale University Press, 1994); Roland Meyer, "Formatting Faces: Standards of Production, Networks of Circulation, and the Operationalization of the Photographic Portrait," in *Format Matters: Standards, Practices, and Politics in Media Cultures*, ed. Marek Jancovic, Axel Volmar, and Alexandra Schneider (Lüneburg: Meson Press, 2020), 147–166.

48. The classic account of Atget's case is Molly Nesbit, "What Was an Author?," *Yale French Studies*, no. 73 (1987): 229–257. For a similarly detailed discussion of Sarony, see Jane M. Gaines, *Contested Culture: The Image, the Voice, and the Law* (London: BFI, 1992), 42–83.

49. See, for instance, Ronan Deazley, "Struggling with Authority: The Photograph in British Legal History," *History of Photography* 27, no. 3 (September 1, 2003): 236–246, https://doi.org/10.1080/03087298.2003.10441249; Anne McCauley, "'Merely Mechanical': On the Origins of Photographic Copyright in France and Great Britain," *Art History* 31, no. 1 (2008): 57–78; Steve Edwards, "'Beard Patentee': Daguerreotype Property and Authorship," *Oxford Art Journal* 36, no. 3 (December 1, 2013): 369–394, https://doi.org/10.1093/oxartj/kct030.

50. See especially Steve Edwards, "Why Pictures? From Art History to Business History and Back Again," *History of Photography* 44, no. 1 (2020): 3–15, https://doi.org/10.1080/03087298.2020.1827832.

51. Blaschke, *Banking on Images*, 42.

52. The classic example is Baudelaire's concession of photography's uses as a "handmaiden to the arts." See Charles Baudelaire, "The Modern Public and Photography" (1859), in *Classic Essays on Photography*, ed. Alan Trachtenberg (New Haven, CT: Leete's Island Books, 1980), 83–89. On the role of graphic reproduction technologies in the dissemination of art, see especially Bann's discussion of "Reproducing Mona Lisa" in Bann, *Distinguished Images*, 21–46.

53. Stef van Gompel and P. Bernt Hugenholtz, "The Orphan Works Problem: The Copyright Conundrum of Digitizing Large-Scale Audiovisual Archives, and How to Solve It," *Popular Communication* 8, no. 1 (2010): 61–71, https://doi.org/10.1080/15405700903502361.

54. Harriet Bridgeman, "Specialist Commercial: The Cooper-Bridgeman Library," in *Picture Librarianship*, ed. Helen P. Harrison (London: Library Association, 1981), 437–442.

55. Bridgeman, 438.

56. Bridgeman, 438–440.

57. Bridgeman Art Library, Ltd. v. Corel Corp., 25 F.Supp.2d 421 (S.D.N.Y. 1998). This account of the case relies especially on Simon Stokes, "Graves' Case and Copyright in Photographs: Bridgeman v. Corel (USA)," in *Dear Images: Art, Copyright and Culture*, ed. Daniel McClean and Karsten Schubert (London: Ridinghouse, 2002), 109–140, and Carla J. Shapreau, "Art, Internet, and US Copyright Law," in *Dear Images: Art, Copyright and Culture*, ed. Daniel McClean and Karsten Schubert (London: Ridinghouse, 2002), 142–159. See also Nina Lager Vestberg, "Copyright between Commerce and Creativity: Art, Photography, and the Law," *The Art Book* 15, no. 1 (2008): 58–59.

58. Bridgeman, "Specialist Commercial," 439.

59. Geoffrey Crabb, "Copyright in Artistic Works," in *Picture Librarianship*, ed. Helen P. Harrison (London: Library Association, 1981), 196.

60. Stokes, "Graves' Case and Copyright in Photographs," 117.

61. Stokes, 120.

62. Stokes, 117–118.

63. Vestberg, "Copyright between Commerce and Creativity," 58.

64. Judge Kaplan cited in Stokes, "Graves' Case and Copyright in Photographs," 117.

65. Wolfgang Ernst, *Digital Memory and the Archive*, ed. Jussi Parikka, trans. Christopher Jenkin-Jones (Minneapolis: University of Minnesota Press, 2013), 98.

66. Wendy Hui Kyong Chun, *Updating to Remain the Same: Habitual New Media* (Cambridge, MA: MIT Press, 2016), 2.

67. Blaschke, *Banking on Images*, 166.

68. Howard Besser, "Imaging: Fine Arts," *Journal of the American Society for Information Science* 42, no. 8 (1991): 594.

69. Geoffrey Batchen, "Photogenics," in *Each Wild Idea* (Cambridge, MA: MIT Press, 2001), 154; Bill Gates, *The Road Ahead*, rev. ed. (New York: Penguin, 1996), 257.

70. Blaschke, *Banking on Images*, 167.

71. Blaschke, 168.

72. Blaschke, 166.

73. Siva Vaidhyanathan, *The Googlization of Everything (And Why We Should Worry)* (Berkeley: University of California Press, 2011), 183.

74. Anne Friedberg, *The Virtual Window: From Alberti to Microsoft* (Cambridge, MA: MIT Press, 2006), 226.

75. Sherry Turkle, *Alone Together: Why We Expect More from Technology and Less from Each Other* (New York: Basic Books, 2011), 279.

76. Andrew Dewdney and Frank Boyd, "Television, Computers, Technology and Cultural Form," in *The Photographic Image in Digital Culture*, ed. Martin Lister (London: Routledge, 1995), 155.

77. Nanna Bonde Thylstrup and Stina Teilmann, "Thumbnail Images: Uncertainties, Infrastructures and Search Engines," *Digital Creativity* 28, no. 4 (October 2, 2017): 279–296, https://doi.org/10.1080/14626268.2017.1375961.

78. See, for instance, McKenzie Wark, *A Hacker Manifesto* (Cambridge, MA: Harvard University Press, 2009).

79. Wark, 197.

80. Wark, 197.

81. For an astute discussion of the contemporary implications of the idea that information should be free, see Sean Cubitt, "Mass Image, Anthropocene Image, Image Commons," in *Photography Off the Scale: Technologies and Theories of the Mass Image*, ed. Jussi Parikka and Tomáš Dvořák (Edinburgh: Edinburgh University Press, 2021), 36.

82. G. Spratt, *The Connoisseur* (1830), published by G. Madeley, printed by C. Tilt. 22.23 × 15.24 cm. Accession no. P.17,459, Minneapolis Institute of Arts (The Minnich Collection, the Ethel Morrison Van Derlip Fund, 1966), https://collections.artsmia.org/art/77469/the-connoisseur-g-spratt (accessed May 13, 2020).

83. In June 2021, Bridgeman's reproduction fees for *The Connoisseur* ranged from GBP40 for personal use to GBP100 for reproduction in a book or magazine. Depending on the terms agreed between the museum and the platform, MIA should be entitled to at least 60 percent of the sum paid by clients upon download from Bridgeman Images. With over 4,000 items "for rent" in this way, the income from even a small number of transactions per item can make a difference to budgets in a publicly funded institution. Bridgeman Images, "The Connoisseur, 1830," accessed June 9, 2021, https://www.bridgemanimages.com/en/asset/880581/.

84. Bonhams, "Lot 106: SPRATT (GEORGE) The Antiquarian; China; The Conchologist; The Mineralogist; The Itinerant Apothecary; The Circulating Library; The Connoisseur; The Entomologist; The Greengrocer, C. Tilt, 1830 (9)," Bonhams, August 19, 2020, https://www.bonhams.com/auctions/26014/lot/106/?category=list&length=265&page=1.

CHAPTER 2

1. Oliver Wendell Holmes, "The Stereoscope and the Stereograph (1859)," in *Classic Essays on Photography*, ed. Alan Trachtenberg (New Haven, CT: Leete's Island Books, 1980), 81.

2. There are of course exceptions to this rule, however, even picture libraries maintained by public or nonprofit institutions such as museums, national libraries, and universities would often be expected to cover the costs of their services to clients through the charging of fees.

3. Estelle Blaschke, "From the Picture Archive to the Image Bank: Commercializing the Visual through Photography—the Bettmann Archive and Corbis," *Études Photographiques*, no. 24 (November 9, 2009), http://journals.openedition.org/etudes photographiques/3435.

4. My use of "commodity form" is based on Tom Gretton's definition of it as a "material correlate of genre"—a novel may be consumed in the different commodity forms of "*roman-feuilleton*, 'railway fiction,' the paperback," or, for that matter, airport fiction, e-book, audiobook, and other formats. The concept of commodity form thus overlaps with that of the format, with one important distinction: commodities, unlike formats, are primarily intended for consumption. See Tom Gretton, "The Pragmatics of Page Design in Nineteenth-Century General-Interest Weekly Illustrated News Magazines in London and Paris," *Art History* 33, no. 4 (September 2010): 682, https://doi.org/10.1111/j.1467-8365.2010.00766.x.

5. Paul Frosh, *The Image Factory: Consumer Culture, Photography and the Visual Content Industry* (Oxford: Berg, 2003), 35.

6. Frosh, 35. This account has been challenged by Diana Kamin, who has found all the hallmarks of a stock photography business in place by the end of the 1920s, in her case study of the US agency H. Armstrong Roberts. See Diana Kamin, "Picture-Work: On the Circulating Image Collection" (PhD diss., New York University, 2018), 244.

7. For an astute discussion of how the same discourse was articulated in different terms by two custodians of public (i.e., not-for-profit) picture collections in the United States during the same period, see Diana Kamin, "Mid-Century Visions, Programmed Affinities: The Enduring Challenges of Image Classification," *Journal of Visual Culture* 16, no. 3 (2017): 310–336.

8. Lisa Gitelman, *Paper Knowledge: Toward a Media History of Documents* (Durham, NC: Duke University Press, 2014), 56. Examples of relevant studies include Trebor Scholz, ed., *Digital Labor: The Internet as Playground and Factory* (New York: Routledge, 2013); Mar Hicks, *Programmed Inequality: How Britain Discarded Women Technologists and Lost Its Edge in Computing* (Cambridge, MA: MIT Press, 2018); Sarah T. Roberts, *Behind the Screen: Content Moderation in the Shadows of Social Media* (New Haven, CT: Yale University Press, 2019).

9. This purpose is spelled out in the title of Hilary Evans's contribution to a 1981 volume on picture librarianship: Hilary Evans, "Exploitation," in *Picture Librarianship*, ed. Helen P. Harrison (London: Library Association, 1981), 171–191.

10. Andrew Ross, "The Ecology of Images," in *Visual Culture: Images and Interpretations*, ed. Norman Bryson, Michael Ann Holly, and Keith Moxey (Hanover, NH: University Press of New England, 1994), 335.

11. Jenny Tobias, "Re-Use Value," *Cabinet*, no. 22 (2006): 44–47.

12. J. Abbott Miller, "Pictures for Rent: From Stereoscope to Stereotype," in *Design Writing Research: Writing on Graphic Design*, ed. Ellen Lupton and J. Abbott Miller (London: Phaidon, 1999), 121–133.

13. Daniel F. Spulber, "Market Microstructure and Intermediation," *Journal of Economic Perspectives* 10, no. 3 (1996): 135.

14. Spulber, 136.

15. Estelle Blaschke, *Banking on Images: The Bettmann Archive and Corbis* (Leipzig: Spector Books, 2016), 135.

16. Blaschke, "From the Picture Archive to the Image Bank."

17. Blaschke, *Banking on Images*, 114.

18. Blaschke, "From the Picture Archive to the Image Bank"; Blaschke, *Banking on Images*, 120–124.

19. Quoted from Blaschke, *Banking on Images*, 131.

20. Otto L. Bettmann, *Bettmann the Picture Man* (Gainesville: University Press of Florida, 1992), 132.

21. Bettmann, 132, 135.

22. Blaschke, *Banking on Images*, 138. In the first edition of *The Picture Researcher's Handbook*, the *Bettmann Portable Archive* is described under the entry for the Bettmann Archive as "not exactly a catalogue, but a splendid sampler containing 3669 pictures, much entertainment, some wise and lucid thoughts on the picture business . . . , and a book which every researcher should have on the shelf." See Hilary Evans, Mary Evans, and Andra Nelki, *The Picture Researcher's Handbook: An International Guide to Picture Sources—and How to Use Them* (New York: Scribner, 1974), 95.

23. Blaschke, *Banking on Images*, 139.

24. Blaschke, "From the Picture Archive to the Image Bank."

25. Craig Robertson, *The Filing Cabinet: A Vertical History of Information* (Minneapolis: University of Minnesota Press, 2021), 101.

26. C. H. Gibbs-Smith, "The Hulton Picture Post Library," *Journal of Documentation* 6 (1950): 12–24. This journal began in 1945 as the scholarly publication of ASLIB,

the UK Association of Special Libraries and Information Bureaux, and since then it has published research, reviews, and think pieces on documentation, libraries, and information management of all kinds. To give an idea of its thematic coverage, in the five volumes preceding the one in which Gibbs-Smith published his article on picture libraries were articles on topics from fine art libraries and sound recording archives to microfilm and an exciting new image transmission device called the Ultrafax. On the history of ASLIB, which existed between 1924 and 2014, see David Bawden, "ASLIB: A De Facto National Library/Information Organization," *Alexandria* 26, no. 1 (April 1, 2016): 15–27, https://doi.org/10.7227/ALX.0038; Dave Muddiman, "A New History of ASLIB, 1924–1950," *Journal of Documentation* 61, no. 3 (June 1, 2005): 402–428, https://doi.org/10.1108/00220410510598553.

27. "Charles Harvard Gibbs-Smith: Noted Aeronautical Historian," *The Times*, December 7, 1981, sec. Obituaries.

28. Gibbs-Smith, "The Hulton Picture Post Library," 13, 12.

29. Gibbs-Smith, 12, 13, 13–14.

30. See, for instance, Evans, "Exploitation"; Helene E. Roberts, "A Picture Is Worth a Thousand Words: Art Indexing in Electronic Databases," *Journal of the American Society for Information Science and Technology* 52 (2001): 911–916; Kamin, "Mid-Century Visions, Programmed Affinities," 323–324.

31. Gibbs-Smith, "The Hulton Picture Post Library," 19.

32. Julia, interview with author, London, January 31, 2008. Julia was employed at the Hulton Picture Library in the 1970s, when it had been acquired by the BBC.

33. Gibbs-Smith, "The Hulton Picture Post Library," 14, 22.

34. Gibbs-Smith, 14, 15, 21.

35. Gibbs-Smith, 22.

36. Terry Cook and Joan M. Schwartz, "Archives, Records, and Power: From (Postmodern) Theory to (Archival) Performance," *Archival Science* 2, nos. 3–4 (2002): 173.

37. See, for instance, S. Muller, *Manual for the Arrangement and Description of Archives: Drawn up by Direction of the Netherlands Association of Archivists*, trans. Arthur H. Leavitt (New York: H. W. Wilson, 1940); Sir Hilary Jenkinson, *Manual of Archive Administration, Including the Problems of War Archives and Archive Making* (Oxford: Clarendon Press, 1922).

38. Terry Cook, "What Is Past Is Prologue: A History of Archival Ideas since 1898, and the Future Paradigm Shift," *Archivaria*, February 12, 1997, 21. See also Jane Birkin, "Describing the Archive: Preservation of Space, Time and Discontinuity in

Photographic Sequences," *Networking Knowledge: Journal of the MeCCSA Postgraduate Network* 9, no. 5 (July 5, 2016), https://doi.org/10.31165/nk.2016.95.457; Cook and Schwartz, "Archives, Records, and Power," 174.

39. Blaschke, *Banking on Images*, 112–113.

40. Costanza Caraffa, "From 'Photo Libraries' to 'Photo Archives': On the Epistemological Potential of Art-Historical Photo Collections," in *Photo Archives and the Photographic Memory of Art History* (Berlin: Deutscher Kunstverlag, 2011), 24.

41. Lanre Bakare, "Getty Uses Remote Working in Effort to Preserve Photo Archive," *The Guardian*, April 2, 2020, sec. Art and design, https://www.theguardian.com/artanddesign/2020/apr/02/getty-uses-remote-working-effort-preserve-photo-archive.

42. Gibbs-Smith, "The Hulton Picture Post Library," 15.

43. Bert Garai, *The Man from Keystone: Behind the Scenes of a Great Picture Agency, by the Man Who Scooped the World* (London: Frederick Muller, 1965), 23.

44. Garai, 24.

45. Garai, 57; Sarah McDonald, "In the Front Line," *Black & White*, no. 30 (February 2004): 94.

46. Garai, *Man from Keystone*, 16. Emphasis in the original.

47. Garai, 20.

48. For more on this topic, see Nadya Bair, "Never Alone: Photo Editing and Collaboration," in *Getting the Picture: The Visual Culture of the News*, ed. Jason E. Hill and Vanessa R. Schwartz (London: Bloomsbury Academic, 2015), 228–235.

49. The opposition between "fast" and "good" photographs was grounded in material differences between the respective distribution networks of so-called wire services, named for their privileged access to the wires and cables of early telecommunications, and agencies that relied on physical transportation methods by land or air. In the logic of the wire service, the best photograph of an event was the first photograph available of it. Regular agencies and freelance photographers, on the other hand, could not in the same way rely on the immediate "news" value of their images, and therefore tended to produce more in-depth coverage of unfolding events and ongoing situations. This often meant constructing a story in a sequence of aesthetically striking, that is, "good" images, which would ideally have a shelf-life (or rather file-life) of much more than one twenty-four-hour news cycle. See Zeynep Devrim Gürsel, *Image Brokers: Visualizing World News in the Age of Digital Circulation* (Oakland: University of California Press, 2016), 37–38, http://search.ebscohost.com/login.aspx?direct=true&db=nlebk&AN=1196937&site=ehost-live.

50. Gibbs-Smith, "The Hulton Picture Post Library," 22.

51. Bair, "Never Alone," 228.

52. One appreciative reader has been identified as Romana Javitz, head of the Picture Collection at New York Public Library, who according to Diana Kamin "referred . . . often" to Gibbs-Smith's article. See Kamin, "Picture-Work," 62.

53. Gibbs-Smith, "The Hulton Picture Post Library," 12, 15. Emphasis added.

54. Robertson, *The Filing Cabinet*, xiii.

55. Julia, interview.

56. Michelle Henning, *Photography: The Unfettered Image* (London: Routledge, 2018), 54.

57. This was documented in a classic study published in 1904, which undertook to document the impact of women workers in this industry around the turn of the previous century. The study was performed by a group of labor movement activists—for the most part women, although they were led by Ramsay MacDonald, who was to become the first UK Labour Prime Minister. Reading the researchers' reports from interviews and observations across a range of workshops and factories, one is struck by the similarities between the rhetoric about women workers in the early years of the twentieth century and that about robots in the early years of the twenty-first: both are either coming to take jobs or have already taken them. See James Ramsay MacDonald, ed., *Women in the Printing Trades: A Sociological Study* (London: P. S. King & Son, 1904), http://www.gutenberg.org/ebooks/42275?msg=welcome_stranger.

58. Henning, *Photography: The Unfettered Image*, 54. Citing Sadie Plant, *Zeros + Ones: Digital Women + the New Technoculture* (London: Fourth Estate, 1997), 121. A compelling example from the field of literature is the children's author Astrid Lindgren (1907–2002), who famously composed her manuscripts in the Melin system shorthand acquired through her training as a secretary. See Jens Andersen, *Astrid Lindgren: The Woman behind Pippi Longstocking*, trans. Caroline Waight (New Haven, CT: Yale University Press, 2018).

59. Friedrich A. Kittler, *Discourse Networks 1800/1900*, trans. Michael Metteer and Chris Cullens (Stanford, CA: Stanford University Press, 1990), 352.

60. Matthew Kirschenbaum, *Track Changes: A Literary History of Word Processing* (Cambridge, MA: Belknap Press, 2016), 143–144.

61. Ruth Matthews, ed., *Who's Who in Photography* (London: Focal Press, 1951).

62. Helen Faye, "About the Picture Division," in Helen Faye, ed., *Picture Sources: An Introductory List* (New York: Special Libraries Association, 1959), vi, http://hdl.handle.net/2027/mdp.39015015193850.

63. Faye, v.

64. "Preface," in Faye, vi.

65. Faye, 20.

66. The back of the print was revealed to me by staff at the Hulton Archive only because I had made a research visit in which I expressed my scholarly interest in original captions and other analog metadata, and when I first sought to license this photograph for publication they kindly provided me with a scan of the verso as an additional service. My thanks to Sarah McDonald and Caroline Theakstone, who in this way demonstrated the abiding value of picture librarians as skilled and knowledgeable intermediaries.

67. For a longer discussion of provenance information gathered on the backs of photographs, including some originating from Keystone's Paris office, see Nina Lager Vestberg, "Archival Value: On Photography, Materiality and Indexicality," *Photographies* 1 (2008): 49–65; Nina Lager Vestberg, "Flytande fotografier—originalitet och upphovsrätt i det digitala arkivet," in *I bildarkivet. Om fotografi och digitaliseringens effekter*, ed. Anna Dahlgren and Pelle Snickars (Stockholm: Kungl. biblioteket, 2009).

68. Joanna Sassoon, "Photographic Materiality in the Age of Digital Reproduction," in *Photographs, Objects, Histories*, ed. Elizabeth Edwards and Janice Hart (London: Routledge, 2004), 186–202. See also Jasmine Burns, "The Aura of Materiality: Digital Surrogacy and the Preservation of Photographic Archives," *Art Documentation: Journal of the Art Libraries Society of North America* 36, no. 1 (April 14, 2017): 1–8, https://doi.org/10.1086/691368.

69. Miller, "Pictures for Rent," 122.

70. Luke Dodd, *The Lost Art of the Picture Library* (London: The Guardian and the Observer, 2008). See also Nina Lager Vestberg, "From the Filing Cabinet to the Internet: Digitising Photographic Libraries," in *Fotografie als Instrument und Medium der Kunstgeschichte*, ed. Costanza Caraffa (Berlin: Deutscher Kunstverlag, 2009), 129–144; Nina Lager Vestberg, "The Photographic Image in Digital Archives," in *The Photographic Image in Digital Culture*, 2nd ed., ed. Martin Lister (London: Routledge, 2013), 113–130.

71. Vestberg, "The Photographic Image in Digital Archives," 116.

72. Robertson, *The Filing Cabinet*, 25.

73. Robertson, *The Filing Cabinet*; Hicks, *Programmed Inequality*; Lilly Irani, "The Cultural Work of Microwork," *New Media & Society* 17, no. 5 (2015): 720–739, https://doi.org/10.1177/1461444813511926; Roberts, *Behind the Screen*.

74. Yanni Alexander Loukissas, *All Data Are Local: Thinking Critically in a Data-Driven Society* (Cambridge, MA: MIT Press, 2019), 67.

CHAPTER 3

1. Hilary Evans, Mary Evans, and Andra Nelki, *The Picture Researcher's Handbook. An International Guide to Picture Sources—and How to Use Them* (Newton Abbot: David & Charles, 1975).

2. Hilary Evans, Mary Evans, and Andra Nelki, *The Picture Researcher's Handbook: An International Guide to Picture Sources—and How to Use Them* (New York: Scribner, 1974), 3. I have been unable to establish why the US edition is dated 1974, when by all accounts the UK edition was the original one.

3. Jill Turner, "Love and Knowledge Builds Huge Collection," *Library Association Record* 78, no. 8 (1976): 362. This referred to the well-known series of eating and travel guides instigated in the United Kingdom in the late 1950s by Hungarian émigré Egon Ronay (1915–2010).

4. Peter Bazalgette, *Egon Ronay: The Man Who Taught Britain How to Eat* (London: Newbaz, 2011).

5. Evans et al., *The Picture Researcher's Handbook* (1975); Evans et al., *The Picture Researcher's Handbook* (1974); Hilary Evans, Mary Evans, and Andra Nelki, *The Picture Researcher's Handbook: An International Guide to Picture Sources, and How to Use Them* (Melbourne: Wren, 1975).

6. Harold Evans, *Pictures on a Page: Photojournalism, Graphics and Picture Editing* (London: Pimlico, 1997), 324. This widely read book on picture editing and photojournalism was first published in 1978. The mention of the handbook was most likely owing to the picture researcher Doris Bryen, who was credited with having given "assistance" to the section on "How to Find a Picture."

7. Evans et al., *The Picture Researcher's Handbook* (1974), 21.

8. "Research, n. 1," in *OED Online* (Oxford University Press), accessed May 21, 2020, https://www.oed.com/view/Entry/163432.

9. Marquard Smith, "Theses on the Philosophy of History: The Work of Research in the Age of Digital Searchability and Distributability," *Journal of Visual Culture* 12, no. 3 (December 1, 2013): 376, https://doi.org/10.1177/1470412913507505.

10. Smith, 376–377. Emphasis removed. The second part of this quote paraphrases the eleventh thesis from Karl Marx, "Theses on Feuerbach" (1845 [1888]), Marx/Engels Internet Archive, 2005, https://www.marxists.org/archive/marx/works/1845/theses/theses.htm.

11. Celeste Olalquiaga, "Dead Stock: The Researcher as Collector of Failed Goods," in *What Is Research in the Visual Arts? Obsession, Archive, Encounter*, ed. Michael Ann Holly and Marquard Smith (Williamstown, MA: Sterling and Francine Clark Art Institute, 2008), 43.

12. Michael Thompson, *Rubbish Theory: The Creation and Destruction of Value* (Oxford: Oxford University Press, 1979).

13. See Estelle Jussim, "The Research Uses of Visual Information," *Library Trends* 25, no. 4 (1977): 764; Laura McCann, "The Whole Story: News Agency Photographs in Newspaper Photo Morgue Collections," *The American Archivist* 80, no. 1 (2017): 163–188, https://doi.org/10.17723/0360-9081.80.1.163.

14. J. Abbott Miller, "Pictures for Rent: From Stereoscope to Stereotype," in *Design Writing Research: Writing on Graphic Design*, ed. Ellen Lupton and J. Abbott Miller (London: Phaidon, 1999), 121.

15. This account of the Mary Evans Picture Library draws on an interview with Tom Gillmor, Head of Content, at the picture library's premises in London in January 2019, as well as biographical details given on the MEPL website: "Mary Evans," Mary Evans Picture Library, 2019, https://www.maryevans.com/about.php?pageName=about5; "Hilary Evans," Mary Evans Picture Library, 2019, https://www.maryevans.com/about.php?pageName=about6.

16. Hilary Evans, "Exploitation," in *Picture Librarianship*, ed. Helen P. Harrison (London: Library Association, 1981), 171.

17. "Our History," Mary Evans Picture Library, 2014, https://www.maryevans.com/about.php?pageName=about3.

18. "Our History."

19. Hilary Evans, *Practical Picture Research: A Guide to Current Practice, Procedure, Techniques and Resources* (London: Blueprint, 1992), 112–113. This principle had been strengthened in the provisions of the Copyright Act 1988, when photographers were granted the same authorial status as artists, and the expiry date became linked to the year of the author's death, regardless of production or publication dates.

20. Anna Dahlgren, *Travelling Images: Looking across the Borderlands of Art, Media and Photography* (Manchester: Manchester University Press, 2018).

21. Thompson, *Rubbish Theory*, 8–9.

22. Thompson, 7. For a discussion of computer obsolescence in part relation to Thompson's rubbish theory, see Jonathan Sterne, "Out with the Trash: On the Future of New Media," in *Residual Media*, ed. Charles R. Acland (Minneapolis: University of Minnesota Press, 2007), 16–31.

23. Thompson, *Rubbish Theory*, 26.

24. Mary Evans Picture Library, *Fifty: 50 Pictures for Our 50th Birthday* (London: Mary Evans Picture Library, 2014), n.p.

25. Thompson, *Rubbish Theory*, 26.

26. Olalquiaga, "Dead Stock," 43.

27. Walter Benjamin, "Unpacking My Library," in *Illuminations*, ed. Hannah Arendt, trans. Harry Zohn (London: Pimlico, 1999), 63.

28. Benjamin, 65–66.

29. Pierre Bourdieu, *La distinction. Critique sociale du jugement* (Paris: Éditions de Minuit, 1979); Pierre Bourdieu, *Distinction: A Social Critique of the Judgement of Taste*, trans. Richard Nice (Cambridge, MA: Harvard University Press, 1984).

30. Thompson, *Rubbish Theory*, 46.

31. Mary Evans Picture Library, *Fifty*, n.p.

32. Thompson, *Rubbish Theory*, 27.

33. Thompson, 27.

34. Evans, "Exploitation," 190.

35. Around 1990 the picture library moved into its current premises at 59 Tranquil Vale, also in Blackheath, which is another conservation-grade building, a former parish hall built in the 1920s on a bombsite from World War I.

36. From this point on I will refer to specific editions of *Picture Researcher's Handbook* using numbered acronyms (e.g., *PRH1* for the first edition, *PRH5* for the fifth, etc.) while "the handbook" will be used when referring to the book on a general basis.

37. Evans et al., *The Picture Researcher's Handbook* (1974), 4.

38. Evans et al., 21.

39. The eight stages were specified as "Preparation," "Primary research," "Ordering material," "Visiting sources," "Receiving pictures," "Selection day," "Returning preliminary rejects," and "Returning used material" (*PRH1*, 22–24).

40. *PRH1*, 22.

41. *PRH1*, 22, 82.

42. *PRH1*, 4, original emphasis.

43. *PRH1*, 4, 32.

44. *PRH1*, 23.

45. *PRH1*, 24.

46. *PRH1*, 21.

47. *PRH1*, 21.

48. *PRH1*, 36.

49. Evans, "Exploitation," 171.

50. Benjamin, "Unpacking My Library," 68.

51. Wolfgang Ernst, *Digital Memory and the Archive*, ed. Jussi Parikka, trans. Christopher Jenkin-Jones (Minneapolis: University of Minnesota Press, 2013), 100.

52. *PRH1*, 83, 87, 112.

53. Yanni Alexander Loukissas, *All Data Are Local: Thinking Critically in a Data-Driven Society* (Cambridge, MA: MIT Press, 2019), 3.

54. Nina Lager Vestberg, "Index/Finger: Medium and Materiality in the Archives," in *The Archive as Project/Archiwum Jako Projekt* (Warszawa: Fundacja Archeologia Fotografii, 2011), 168.

55. Olalquiaga, "Dead Stock," 39.

56. Benjamin, "Unpacking My Library," 68.

57. Alan Bennett, "Baffled at a Bookcase," *London Review of Books*, July 28, 2011, 6, https://www.lrb.co.uk/the-paper/v33/n15/alan-bennett/baffled-at-a-bookcase.

58. Ernst, *Digital Memory and the Archive*, 60.

59. Jussi Parikka, "Archival Media Theory: An Introduction to Wolfgang Ernst's Media Archaeology," in Wolfgang Ernst, *Digital Memory and the Archive* (Minneapolis: University of Minnesota Press, 2013), 12–14.

60. Ernst, *Digital Memory and the Archive*, 68.

61. Parikka, "Archival Media Theory," 12.

62. Smith, "Theses on the Philosophy of History," 382.

63. Bill Gates, *The Road Ahead*, rev. ed. (New York: Penguin, 1996), 144.

64. Hilary Evans, *Picture Librarianship* (London: Clive Bingley, 1980), 13.

65. The sections on how to do picture research would be separated out from the directory and expanded into a separate volume, published first as *The Art of Picture Research* in 1979, and then slightly revised as *Practical Picture Research* in 1992.

Chapter 4

1. Hilary Evans and Mary Evans, *Picture Researcher's Handbook: An International Guide to Picture Sources and How to Use Them*, 5th ed. (London: Blueprint, 1992), n.p.

2. Evans and Evans, n.p.

3. Hilary Evans and Mary Evans, *Picture Researcher's Handbook: An International Guide to Picture Sources and How to Use Them*, 6th ed. (London: Routledge, 1996), n.p.

4. Hilary Evans and Mary Evans, *Picture Researcher's Handbook: An International Guide to Picture Sources and How to Use Them*, 7th ed. (London: Pira International, 2001), vi.

5. Hilary Evans, Mary Evans, and Andra Nelki, *The Picture Researcher's Handbook: An International Guide to Picture Sources—and How to Use Them* (New York: Scribner, 1974), 22–24.

6. Evans and Evans noted the adoption of "computer cataloguing" by a number of picture libraries in the third edition of the handbook; see Hilary Evans and Mary Evans, *Picture Researcher's Handbook: An International Guide to Picture Sources—and How to Use Them*, 3rd ed. (Wokingham: Van Nostrand Reinhold, 1986), viii. As for online access, historical statistics from the International Telecommunications Union (ITU) show that 11 percent of inhabitants in "developed countries" were "internet users" in 1997, and in total only 2 percent of the world's total population had internet access. By the year 2000 these numbers had risen to 31 percent in developed countries, 2 percent in developing countries, and 7 percent in the world as a whole. See ITU, "ICT Statistics," July 15, 2008, http://www.itu.int/ITU-D/ict/statistics/ict/.

7. Evans and Evans, *Picture Researcher's Handbook* (1986), viii; Evans and Evans, *Picture Researcher's Handbook* (1992), n.p.

8. Jonathan Coopersmith, *Faxed: The Rise and Fall of the Fax Machine* (Baltimore, MD: Johns Hopkins University Press, 2015), 145.

9. Coopersmith, 146.

10. Coopersmith, 145–146.

11. Coopersmith, 162–163.

12. Coopersmith, 145–181.

13. Lisa Gitelman, *Paper Knowledge: Toward a Media History of Documents* (Durham, NC: Duke University Press, 2014), 84.

14. Gitelman, 110.

15. Peter Buse, "Polaroid into Digital: Technology, Cultural Form, and the Social Practices of Snapshot Photography," *Continuum* 24, no. 2 (2010): 215–230, https://doi.org/10.1080/10304310903363864.

16. Evans and Evans, *Picture Researcher's Handbook* (1996), n.p.

17. Evans and Evans, n.p.

18. W. J. Mitchell, *The Reconfigured Eye: Visual Truth in the Post-Photographic Era* (Cambridge, MA: MIT Press, 1992).

19. Fred Ritchin, *In Our Own Image: The Coming Revolution in Photography: How Computer Technology Is Changing Our View of the World* (New York: Aperture, 1990), 5. See also Fred Ritchin, "The End of Photography as We Have Known It," in *PhotoVideo:*

Photography in the Age of the Computer, ed. Paul Wombell (London: Rivers Oram Press, 1991), 8–15; Fred Ritchin, *After Photography* (New York: Norton, 2009).

20. Evans and Evans, *Picture Researcher's Handbook* (1996), n.p.

21. Rick, interview with author, London, January 16, 2008.

22. Craig Robertson, *The Filing Cabinet: A Vertical History of Information* (Minneapolis: University of Minnesota Press, 2021), 176.

23. P. G. B. Enser and C. G. McGregor, "Analysis of Visual Information Retrieval Queries," British Library R & D Report (London: British Library, 1993).

24. Enser and McGregor, 25.

25. Peter G. B. Enser, "Pictorial Information Retrieval," *Journal of Documentation* 51, no. 2 (1995): 150.

26. Warren Sack, *The Software Arts* (Cambridge, MA: MIT Press, 2019), 67.

27. Sack, 69.

28. Linda H. Armitage and Peter G. B. Enser, "Analysis of User Need in Image Archives," *Journal of Information Science* 23, no. 4 (August 1, 1997): 287, https://doi.org/10.1177/016555159702300403.

29. Peter Enser, "Visual Image Retrieval: Seeking the Alliance of Concept-Based and Content-Based Paradigms," *Journal of Information Science* 26, no. 4 (August 1, 2000): 206, https://doi.org/10.1177/016555150002600401.

30. The discussion of Poliakoff's drama builds on two earlier publications on this work. The description of plot and characters is largely drawn from Nina Lager Vestberg, "Index/Finger: Medium and Materiality in the Archives," in *The Archive as Project/Archiwum Jako Projekt* (Warszawa: Fundacja Archeologia Fotografii, 2011), 160–176. See also Nina Lager Vestberg, "Archival Value: On Photography, Materiality and Indexicality," *Photographies* 1 (2008): 49–65.

31. Robin Nelson, *State of Play: Contemporary "High-End" TV Drama* (Manchester: Manchester University Press, 2007), 44.

32. Robin Nelson, *Stephen Poliakoff on Stage and Screen* (London: Methuen Drama, 2011), 23.

33. "Shooting the Past (1999)," Stephen Poliakoff, accessed July 3, 2021, http://www.stephenpoliakoff.com/shooting-the-past-1999.

34. Review in the *Sunday Times*, quoted on the back of DVD cover: Stephen Poliakoff, *Shooting the Past* (BBC Worldwide, 2003).

35. Amy Holdsworth, "'Slow Television' and Stephen Poliakoff's Shooting the Past," *Journal of British Cinema & Television* 3, no. 1 (May 2006): 128, https://doi.org

/10.3366/JBCTV.2006.3.1.128. See also Vestberg, "Archival Value"; Christopher Hogg, "Re-Evaluating the Archive in Stephen Poliakoff's Shooting the Past," *Journal of British Cinema & Television* 6, no. 3 (November 2009): 437–451, https://doi.org/10.3366/E1743452109001125; Nelson, *State of Play*, 35–44; Nelson, *Stephen Poliakoff on Stage and Screen*, 23–30.

36. Sarah McDonald, conversation with the author, the Hulton Archive, London, November 7, 2007.

37. Poliakoff, *Shooting the Past* (2003).

38. Stephen Poliakoff, *Shooting the Past: A Screenplay* (London: Methuen, 1998), 4.

39. Nelson, *State of Play*, 27.

40. Poliakoff, *Shooting the Past* (1998), 118.

41. Poliakoff, 22.

42. Poliakoff, 26.

43. Poliakoff, 41.

44. Poliakoff, 82.

45. Michael Thompson, *Rubbish Theory: The Creation and Destruction of Value* (Oxford: Oxford University Press, 1979), 27.

46. Poliakoff, *Shooting the Past* (1998), 62.

47. Poliakoff, 62–63.

48. Poliakoff, 103.

49. Poliakoff, 135–136.

50. In the real-life picture industry of the late 1990s, meanwhile, an investment banker in the United Kingdom (Mark Getty) had recently purchased the Hulton Deutsch Collection in order secure an inexhaustible supply of historical pictures for his online visual content platform, while a software magnate in the United States (Bill Gates) had acquired the Bettmann Archive with the intention of digitizing its entire collection.

51. Poliakoff, *Shooting the Past* (2003). Quote attributed to *Sunday Times* on DVD cover.

52. Enser, "Visual Image Retrieval," 200.

53. Evans and Evans, *Picture Researcher's Handbook* (2001), vi.

54. A. S. Tope and P. G. B. Enser, "Design and Implementation Factors in Electronic Image Retrieval Systems," Library and Information Commission Research Report (London: Resource: The Council for Museums, Libraries and Archives, 2000), 69.

55. Tope and Enser, 64.

56. On the history of computer graphic display, see Anne Friedberg, *The Virtual Window: From Alberti to Microsoft* (Cambridge, MA: MIT Press, 2006), 219–239; Jacob Gaboury, "The Random-Access Image: Memory and the History of the Computer Screen," *Grey Room* 70 (Winter 2018): 24–53, https://doi.org/10.1162/GREY_a_00233.

57. Until this time, according to Enser, computer science researchers had been working on problems of image retrieval from the perspective of "computer, rather than human vision" in isolation from "the practitioner community" of picture researchers and librarians for whom computer-assisted visual search methods would theoretically be most relevant. See Enser, "Visual Image Retrieval," 199–200.

CHAPTER 5

1. Hilary Evans and Mary Evans, *Picture Researcher's Handbook: An International Guide to Picture Sources and How to Use Them*, 7th ed. (London: Pira International, 2001), vii.

2. Evans and Evans, vi.

3. Julia, interview with author, London, January 31, 2008.

4. Marie-Louise, interview with author, London, January 22, 2008.

5. Hilary Evans and Mary Evans, *Picture Researcher's Handbook: An International Guide to Picture Sources and How to Use Them*, 8th ed. (Leatherhead: Pira International, 2006), vi.

6. Evans and Evans, vi.

7. Nick Srnicek, *Platform Capitalism* (Cambridge: Polity, 2017), 42.

8. Estelle Blaschke, *Banking on Images: The Bettmann Archive and Corbis* (Leipzig: Spector Books, 2016), 168. See also Paul Frosh, *The Image Factory: Consumer Culture, Photography and the Visual Content Industry* (Oxford: Berg, 2003), 193–195.

9. In 2016 Bill Gates sold Corbis to the Visual China Group, which immediately entrusted Getty Images with the worldwide management of the platform outside China. Soon after the Corbis platform was discontinued, and its contents have been merged alongside with Getty's numerous other brands on the same platform. See "Corbis Sold to Visual China Group—Absorbs into Getty Images," *Photo Archive News* (blog), January 22, 2016, https://photoarchivenews.com/news/corbis-sold-to-visual-china-group/.

10. Evans and Evans, *Picture Researcher's Handbook* (2001), viii.

11. Evans and Evans, viii.

12. "Blood and Oil," *The Economist*, March 4, 2000, 97. All quotes to follow in this paragraph and the next are from this source.

13. Corbis Images acquired a similar range of picture sources over the same period, including the historical Bettmann Archive, as discussed in chapter 2, as well as two stock photo agencies, the French photojournalist agency Sygma, and the electronic licensing rights to a host of private and public picture collections. See Blaschke, *Banking on Images*, 168.

14. Hilary Evans and Mary Evans, *Picture Researcher's Handbook: An International Guide to Picture Sources and How to Use Them*, 6th ed. (London: Routledge, 1996), n.p.

15. Paul Frosh, "Beyond the Image Bank: Digital Commercial Photography," in *The Photographic Image in Digital Culture*, 2nd ed., ed. Martin Lister (London: Routledge, 2013), 135.

16. For more on the significance of keywords on the Getty Images platform, see Doireann Wallace, "Words as Keys to the Image Bank," in *Revisualizing Visual Culture*, ed. Chris Bailey and Hazel Gardiner (Farnham: Ashgate, 2010), 83–96; Nina Lager Vestberg, "The Photographic Image in Digital Archives," in *The Photographic Image in Digital Culture*, 2nd ed., ed. Martin Lister (London: Routledge, 2013), 113–130.

17. A. S. Tope and P. G. B. Enser, "Design and Implementation Factors in Electronic Image Retrieval Systems," Library and Information Commission Research Report (London: Resource: The Council for Museums, Libraries and Archives, 2000).

18. Tope and Enser, 66.

19. Tom Gillmor, Head of Content at Mary Evans Picture Library, conversation with author, London, January 17, 2019.

20. This confidence was testified by a whole subsection of the introduction to *PRH7*, where Evans and Evans rhetorically asked, "will the digitized image entirely replace the transparency?" before offering a range of possible reasons why it might not. See Evans and Evans, *Picture Researcher's Handbook* (2001), vi.

21. Evans and Evans, vii. Further quotes in this paragraph are from the same source.

22. This usage appears strikingly at odds with the terminology of artificial "intelligence" and "smart" devices that would become ubiquitous in the second decade of the twenty-first century.

23. Evans and Evans, *Picture Researcher's Handbook* (2006), vi.

24. Mary Evans Picture Library, "Mary Evans Picture Library . . . Closer to History," 2004, 3.

25. Mary Evans Picture Library, 48.

26. Lisa Gitelman, *Paper Knowledge: Toward a Media History of Documents* (Durham, NC: Duke University Press, 2014), 117.

27. Evans and Evans, *Picture Researcher's Handbook* (2006), vi.

28. Rick, interview with author, London, January 16, 2008.

29. Rick, interview.

30. Marie-Louise, interview.

31. Julia, interview.

32. Julia, interview.

33. Julia, interview.

34. Rick, interview.

35. Adam, interview with author, London, November 27, 2007.

36. Marie-Louise, interview.

37. Julia, interview.

38. Information on (now disbanded) Keystone classification category from Sarah McDonald, research visit to the Hulton Archive, London, November 7, 2007.

39. Terry Cook and Joan M. Schwartz, "Archives, Records, and Power: From (Post-modern) Theory to (Archival) Performance," *Archival Science* 2, nos. 3–4 (2002): 171–185.

40. Julia, interview.

41. Susi, interview with author, Oxford, February 1, 2008.

42. Peter Buse, *The Camera Does the Rest: How Polaroid Changed Photography* (Chicago: University of Chicago Press, 2016), 9–10.

43. Evans and Evans, *Picture Researcher's Handbook* (2001), vi.

44. As Hilary Evans once noted, any picture researcher should consider "working with pictures . . . a reward in itself." See Hilary Evans, *Practical Picture Research: A Guide to Current Practice, Procedure, Techniques and Resources* (London: Blueprint, 1992), 7.

45. Apparently, several other members of the Getty family also invested in the company, and *The Economist* duly noted that these "have done better since Getty Images floated in 1998 than they would have if they had left their money in oil," comparing the share prices of Getty Images with those of Texaco between 1998 and 2000.

46. As Cheryce Kramer has shown, the decisive difference, in Getty Images' case, was to combine investment and deployment of digital technologies with the advanced

intermediation techniques of the financial sector, manifested among other things in "tiered and complicated royalty arrangements" that could be likened to "carefully calculated instruments of risk management in an arena of financial investment." See Cheryce Kramer, "Digital Beasts as Visual Esperanto: Getty Images and the Colonization of Sight," in *Thinking with Animals: New Perspectives on Anthropomorphism*, ed. Lorraine Daston and Gregg Mitman (New York: Columbia University Press, 2005), 141.

47. Susi, interview.

48. Indeed, far from being replaced by a machine, Susi went on to set up her own business online as a combined picture researcher, footage researcher, shoot producer, and user-generated-content specialist.

49. The platformization of the music industry through both social media and streaming services, and its impact on the record company as a business model, is of course another parallel that could be drawn here.

CHAPTER 6

1. Florian Cramer, "What Is 'Post-Digital'?," in *Postdigital Aesthetics: Art, Computation and Design*, ed. David M. Berry and Michael Dieter (Basingstoke: Palgrave Macmillan, 2015), 24.

2. "Blood and Oil," *The Economist*, March 4, 2000.

3. Beate Löffler and Tino Mager, "Minor Politics, Major Consequences: Epistemic Challenges of Metadata and the Contribution of Image Recognition," *Digital Culture and Society* 6, no. 2 (2020): 225, https://doi.org/10.14361/dcs-2020-0211.

4. Jane Birkin, "Institutional Metadata and the Problem of Context," *Digital Culture and Society* 6, no. 2 (2020): 23, https://doi.org/10.14361/dcs-2020-203.

5. Nanna Bonde Thylstrup, *The Politics of Mass Digitization* (Cambridge, MA: MIT Press, 2018), 3.

6. Lara Putnam, "The Transnational and the Text-Searchable: Digitized Sources and the Shadows They Cast," *American Historical Review* 121, no. 2 (April 2016): 379, https://doi.org/10.1093/ahr/121.2.377.

7. According to computer game theorist Espen Aarseth, for instance, "we became postdigital" sometime in the early 2000s, or at least before 2006, when he declared to an audience of fellow researchers in digital culture that "we can all go home now" because "cyberculture . . . has been subsumed by mainstream culture." See Espen Aarseth, "How We Became Postdigital: From Cyberstudies to Game Studies," in *Critical Cyberculture Studies*, ed. David Silver and Adrienne Massanari (New York: New York University Press, 2006), 37. See also Cramer, "What Is 'Post-Digital'?"

8. Putnam, "The Transnational and the Text-Searchable," 379.

9. Putnam, 378.

10. Putnam, 378–379.

11. Siva Vaidhyanathan, *The Googlization of Everything (And Why We Should Worry)* (Berkeley: University of California Press, 2011), 152.

12. Thylstrup, *The Politics of Mass Digitization*, 42.

13. Emma Rothschild, "The Future of History," in *Going Digital: Evolutionary and Revolutionary Aspects of Digitization*, ed. Karl Grandin (Stockholm: Center for History of Science, 2011), 289.

14. Hilary Evans, Mary Evans, and Andra Nelki, *The Picture Researcher's Handbook: An International Guide to Picture Sources—and How to Use Them* (New York: Scribner, 1974), 21.

15. André Malraux, *The Voices of Silence*, trans. Stuart Gilbert (London: Secker and Warburg, 1954), 13–128; Peter Geimer, "The Art of Resurrection: Malraux's *Musée Imaginaire*," in *Fotografie als Instrument und Medium der Kunstgeschichte*, ed. Costanza Caraffa (Berlin: Deutscher Kunstverlag, 2009), 77–89.

16. The concept of the long tail was launched by the editor of online bible *Wired* in 2004 to describe how e-commerce enabled businesses to reach more diverse audiences and thus make money from a wider selection of its products than just a few big sellers. In stock photography it formed the basis of an entire new business model, microstock, which enabled photo amateurs to sell their pictures at very low prices through online platforms. The original microstock platform, iStockphoto, was acquired by Getty Images in 2006 for USD50 million. See Chris Anderson, *The Long Tail: Why the Future of Business Is Selling Less of More*, rev. ed. (New York: Hachette Books, 2008); Matthew Stibbe, "All Contributions Welcome," *Director* 60, no. 4 (November 2006): 76–81.

17. Putnam, "The Transnational and the Text-Searchable," 395.

18. Löffler and Mager, "Minor Politics, Major Consequences," 225.

19. On the iconicity of the "Times Square kiss," see Robert Hariman and John Louis Lucaites, *No Caption Needed: Iconic Photographs, Public Culture, and Liberal Democracy* (Chicago: University of Chicago Press, 2007), 67–86. On the problematic aspects of the conditions under which this photograph was produced and specifically the lack of consent from the depicted woman, see Brooke L. Blower, "V-J Day, 1945, Times Square," in *The Familiar Made Strange: American Icons and Artifacts after the Transnational Turn*, ed. Brooke L. Blower and Mark Philip Bradley (Ithaca: Cornell University Press, 2015), 70–87.

20. Elizabeth Edwards and Janice Hart, "Introduction," in *Photographs, Objects, Histories: On the Materiality of Images*, ed. Elizabeth Edwards and Janice Hart (London: Routledge, 2004), 12.

21. J. Abbott Miller, "Pictures for Rent: From Stereoscope to Stereotype," in *Design Writing Research: Writing on Graphic Design*, ed. Ellen Lupton and J. Abbott Miller (London: Phaidon, 1999), 122.

22. Annebella Pollen, "Photography's Mise en Abyme: Metapictures of Scale in Repurposed Slide Libraries," in *Photography Off the Scale: Technologies and Theories of the Mass Image*, ed. Tomas Dvorak and Jussi Parikka (Edinburgh: Edinburgh University Press, 2021), 133.

23. See, for instance, the reproduction history of the *Mona Lisa* in Stephen Bann, *Distinguished Images: Prints in the Visual Economy of Nineteenth-Century France* (New Haven, CT: Yale University Press, 2013), 21–45.

24. Peter Walsh, "The Rise and Fall of the Post-Photographic Museum: Technology and the Transformation of Art," in *Theorizing Digital Cultural Heritage: A Critical Discourse*, ed. Fiona Cameron and Sarah Kenderdine (Cambridge, MA: MIT Press, 2007), 28. See also Donald Preziosi, *Rethinking Art History: Meditations on a Coy Science* (New Haven, CT: Yale University Press, 1989); Robert S. Nelson, "The Slide Lecture, or The Work of Art *History* in the Age of Mechanical Reproduction," *Critical Inquiry* 26 (2000): 414–434; Costanza Caraffa, *Fotografie als Instrument und Medium der Kunstgeschichte* (Berlin: Deutscher Kunstverlag, 2009); Costanza Caraffa, ed., *Photo Archives and the Photographic Memory of Art History* (Berlin: Deutscher Kunstverlag, 2011).

25. Ronald E. Day, *Indexing It All: The Subject in the Age of Documentation, Information, and Data* (Cambridge, MA: MIT Press, 2014), 9.

26. Elizabeth Edwards and Christopher Morton, "Between Art and Information: Towards a Collecting History of Photographs," in *Photographs, Museums, Collections: Between Art and Information*, ed. Elizabeth Edwards and Christopher Morton (London: Bloomsbury Academic, 2015), 3.

27. Edwards and Morton, 6–7.

28. Nelson, "The Slide Lecture," 422.

29. For an introduction to the tapestry in English, see Lasse Hodne, "From Centre to Periphery. The Propagation of the Virgo Virga Motif and the Case of the 12th Century Høylandet Tapestry," *Il capitale culturale. Studies on the Value of Cultural Heritage*, no. 10 (June 14, 2014): 23–41, https://doi.org/10.13138/2039-2362/767.

30. Hodne.

31. Edwards and Morton, "Between Art and Information," 13.

32. This information was shared informally by current-day employees of the University Museum in March 2020.

33. See, for instance, Edwards and Morton, "Between Art and Information," 7; Elizabeth Edwards and Sigrid Lien, "Museums and the Work of Photographs," in *Uncertain Images: Museums and the Work of Photographs*, ed. Elizabeth Edwards and Sigrid Lien (Farnham: Ashgate, 2014), 4–7; Georgina Born, "Public Museums, Museum Photography, and the Limits of Reflexivity," *Journal of Material Culture* 3, no. 2 (1998): 243.

34. For more on digitization projects linked to work-to-welfare schemes in Sweden and Norway, see Kajsa Hartig, "Digital Dilemmas: The Impact of Digital Tools on Photograph Collections," in *Uncertain Images: Museums and the Work of Photographs*, ed. Elizabeth Edwards and Sigrid Lien (Farnham: Ashgate, 2014), 223–241; Ole Marius Hylland, "Even Better Than the Real Thing? Digital Copies and Digital Museums in a Digital Cultural Policy," *Culture Unbound: Journal of Current Cultural Research* 9, no. 1 (September 1, 2017): 62–84, https://doi.org/10.3384/cu.2000.1525.179162.

35. Torkel Johansen et al., "Revita-Prosjektet 2006–2015. Sluttrapport" (Trondheim: NTNU Vitenskapsmuseet, 2017), 9–12, https://www.ntnu.no/documents/10476/1264113666/Komplett_Sluttrapport_REVITA.pdf/44983be5-3e97-4383-8046-806641d471a0.

36. Löffler and Mager, "Minor Politics, Major Consequences," 225. See also Jasmine Burns, "Visual Materials in the Archive: Determining and Maintaining Value in a Postmodern Climate," *VRA Bulletin* 41, no. 1, art. 5 (2015).

37. Löffler and Mager, "Minor Politics, Major Consequences," 225. See also Joanna Sassoon, "Photographic Materiality in the Age of Digital Reproduction," in *Photographs, Objects, Histories*, ed. Elizabeth Edwards and Janice Hart (London: Routledge, 2004), 186–202.

38. Löffler and Mager, "Minor Politics, Major Consequences," 226. For an especially illuminating discussion of mass digitization and digital authorship with reference to Google Books, see Kris Cohen, "Literally, Ourselves," *Critical Inquiry* 46, no. 1 (2019): 167–192.

39. Putnam, "The Transnational and the Text-Searchable," 400.

40. Born, "Public Museums, Museum Photography," 243.

41. Sean Cubitt, *The Practice of Light: A Genealogy of Visual Technologies from Prints to Pixels* (Cambridge, MA: MIT Press, 2014), 269.

42. Hodne, "From Centre to Periphery," 25.

43. Burns, "Visual Materials in the Archive."

44. As legal scholar Antoinette Rouvroy has noted, with regard to data mining and data profiling: "Knowledge is not produced *about* the world anymore, but *from*

the digital world. A kind of knowledge that is not tested-by or testing the world it describes and emanates from: algorithmic reality is formed inside the digital reality without any direct contact with the world it is aimed at representing." See Antoinette Rouvroy, "The End(s) of Critique: Data Behaviourism versus Due Process," in *Privacy, Due Process and the Computational Turn: The Philosophy of Law Meets the Philosophy of Technology*, ed. Mireille Hildebrandt and Katja de Vries (London: Routledge, 2013), 147.

45. Hilary Evans, "Exploitation," in *Picture Librarianship*, ed. Helen P. Harrison (London: Library Association, 1981), 187.

46. Edwards and Morton, "Between Art and Information," 3.

47. Lanre Bakare, "Getty Uses Remote Working in Effort to Preserve Photo Archive," *The Guardian*, April 2, 2020, sec. Art and Design, https://www.theguardian.com/artanddesign/2020/apr/02/getty-uses-remote-working-effort-preserve-photo-archive. Further quotes are from this source.

CONCLUSIONS AND IMPLICATIONS

1. "About Us," Shutterstock, https://www.shutterstock.com/about (accessed February 11, 2022).

2. "Stock Images, Photos, Vectors, Video, and Music," Shutterstock, https://www.shutterstock.com/ (accessed February 11, 2022).

3. "Sell Photos, Footage Clips, Illustrations & Vectors," Shutterstock, http://submit.shutterstock.com/ (accessed February 11, 2022).

4. Nick Srnicek, *Platform Capitalism* (Cambridge: Polity, 2017), 76.

5. As Srnicek quotes Marx: "piece-wage is the form of wages most in harmony with the capitalist mode of production." Karl Marx, *Capital: A Critique of Political Economy*, vol. 1, trans. Ben Fowkes (London: Penguin, 1990), 697–698, quoted in Srnicek, 76.

6. Paul Frosh, "Beyond the Image Bank: Digital Commercial Photography," in *The Photographic Image in Digital Culture*, 2nd ed., ed. Martin Lister (London: Routledge, 2013), 138.

7. Sean Cubitt, *The Practice of Light: A Genealogy of Visual Technologies from Prints to Pixels* (Cambridge, MA: MIT Press, 2014), 269.

8. Beate Löffler and Tino Mager, "Minor Politics, Major Consequences: Epistemic Challenges of Metadata and the Contribution of Image Recognition," *Digital Culture and Society* 6, no. 2 (2020): 226, https://doi.org/10.14361/dcs-2020-0211.

9. Emma Rothschild, "The Future of History," in *Going Digital: Evolutionary and Revolutionary Aspects of Digitization*, ed. Karl Grandin (Stockholm: Center for History of Science, 2011), 282.

10. Estelle Jussim, "The Research Uses of Visual Information," *Library Trends* 25, no. 4 (1977): 764. Jussim (1927–2004) prefigured the digital humanities approach to picture-based research by a couple of decades in this article, presciently advocating for the establishment of large-scale research collections of "visual information" to support emerging forms of inquiry that required "sufficient quantity of information to permit generalizations [and] the verification of hypotheses about the nature of various phenomena" (765). She also envisaged a time when "the artist, designer, and scientist can sit down at computer terminals providing some type of access directly to visual elements" (773).

11. Lara Putnam, "The Transnational and the Text-Searchable: Digitized Sources and the Shadows They Cast," *American Historical Review* 121, no. 2 (April 2016): 377, https://doi.org/10.1093/ahr/121.2.377.

12. Sarah T. Roberts, *Behind the Screen: Content Moderation in the Shadows of Social Media* (New Haven, CT: Yale University Press, 2019), 1, 3.

13. Roberts, 209.

14. Sean Cubitt, "Mass Image, Anthropocene Image, Image Commons," in *Photography Off the Scale: Technologies and Theories of the Mass Image*, ed. Jussi Parikka and Tomáš Dvořák (Edinburgh: Edinburgh University Press, 2021), 37.

Index

Note: page numbers in italics refer to figures.